IEMOTO:
THE HEART OF JAPAN

FRANCIS L. K. HSU

SCHENKMAN PUBLISHING COMPANY

Halsted Press Division
John Wiley & Sons, Inc.
New York - London - Sydney - Toronto

Distributed solely by Halsted Press, a Division
of John Wiley & Sons, Inc., New York

Library of Congress Cataloging in Publication Data

Hsu, Francis L   K   1909-
    Iemoto: the heart of Japan.

    "A Schenkman publication."
    1. Kinship—Japan. 2. Gilds—Japan. 3. Japan—
Civilization. I. Title.
HQ682.H85   301.42'1'0952   74-5352
    ISBN 0-470-41756-0 Paper
        0-470-41755-2 Cloth

CONTENTS

Preface

This book offers a non-economic explanation as to why Japan, in contrast to the rest of the underdeveloped world, especially China, has responded so well to the challenge of the West since the 1860's and has risen so rapidly after her total defeat in World War II.

We begin with the assumption that an extremely important determinant of human behavior, in a probability sense, is the nature of man's relationship with his fellow men, not his geographical situation, his individual dreams and capabilities, or the level of his material welfare. To use a trite expression, "man does not live by bread alone." Beyond acquiring the necessities for existence, man everywhere devotes a great deal of ingenuity and effort to "keeping up with the Joneses." But, the "Joneses" he tries to keep up with are not people unknown to him. Instead, they are found within what sociologists have termed his reference group.

For example, many American Blacks are dissatisfied with their lot in spite of the fact that they enjoy a higher standard of living than Hindu peasants. Why? They do not compare themselves with Hindus and other peoples in far away lands. The chief determinant of their happiness is comparison with American Whites close at hand. In our business world we find tycoons who could not possibly spend the millions they are already sitting on, but who nevertheless drive themselves to an early grave or into the hands of "head shrinkers." Why? They cannot relax while their fellow tycoons are piling up bigger gains. One such millionaire frankly told me that he felt he was keeping score on himself. Our self-reliant teenagers cannot bear to be too different from their schoolmates. One of them put it succinctly when he told his father that he must wear white socks because all the members of his class were doing it. "How can I get others to notice me if I'm not dressed like everyone else?" he moaned.

In other words, a major determinant of human behavior is not merely human relationships in general, but a network of human relationships of which the individual is a part, and which he regards as extremely important.

Except for orphans, the first human network for a majority of mankind is the parent-child triad. The ultimate network of human relationships is the tribal or national boundary. That boundary is usually marked by a distinct language, customs, laws and the like, and requires permission for entry or exit.

Our main concern is with the secondary groupings which occur between the elementary kinship organization of parents and children on the one hand, and the tribal or national boundary on the other. The questions for which we try to find answers proceed along two lines. What kinds of secondary groups seem to be related to what kinds of basic patterns of parent-child ties? To put the question in another way, are there any intrinsic factors in the parent-child configuration which lead its products to seek (or feel most at home with) one kind of secondary group rather than another?

The other kinds of questions we ask have to do with the nature of the characteristic secondary grouping of a society and the characteristic way or ways in which its members relate to each other. How are these two phenomena linked? Once we have determined the characteristic types of secondary groups for a society, what can we tell about the way members of that society relate to each other outside such groups as well as within them? And how do these patterns affect the maintenance and transformation of the society and culture over time?

These are among the important questions that we dealt with in *Clan, Caste and Club* (Hsu 1963). In that book we showed how clan, caste and club are the most important secondary groups in Chinese, Hindu and American societies respectively, and how these characteristic secondary groups are each rooted in a particular type of *dyadic dominance* in kinship. Clan is linked to father-son dominance; caste, to mother-son dominance; and club, to husband-wife dominance. We were able to show how these three peoples' relationships to their fellow human beings within the confines of their respective secondary groups were also characteristic of the ways they related to outsiders. In a simplified sense, the Chinese tends to relate to his friends in kinship terms, the American tends to relate to his parents as though they were business partners, while the Hindu tends to see all human interaction in terms of status differences. There is a traceable linkage among kinship, secondary grouping, and behavioral characteristics in each of these three societies and cultures.

Unlike the Chinese, Hindus and Americans, who are products of three very dissimilar kinship systems, the Japanese and the Chinese share the same father-son dominated kinship system. But unigeniture (one son inheritance) and mother-son subdominance (see Chapter 8) are correlated with certain behavioral characteristics which differentiate the Japanese from the Chinese. The Japanese *ie* (household) is different from the Chinese *chia* (home). Persons unrelated by kinship or marriage can become members of the Japanese *ie* in a manner that is unheard of in the Chinese *chia*.

The differences between the two societies become even more pronounced when we compare the Japanese *dōzoku* and the Chinese *tsu*. The Chinese *tsu* is truly a clan, an extended patrilineal kinship group with its members claiming a common ancestor. The *dōzoku*, by contrast, is a kind of corporation, consisting of a *honke* (main *ie*) and several *bunke* (branch *ie*). The *bunke* are absolutely subordinate to the *honke*, yet some *bunke* or their members may have no consanguinal or affinal relationship with *honke* members. On the other hand, even though a *bunke* is related to its *honke* by kinship ties, the *bunke* or any of its members will cease to be part of the *dōzoku* if they move away.

The most distinctive secondary grouping in Japanese society is the *iemoto*, which has no counterpart in China, or elsewhere. The Japanese usually write the term *iemoto* with two Chinese characters: *chia* (meaning household or family in both languages) and *yuan* (meaning origin or root). The combined effect of "family root" is indicative of the nature of this important and unique secondary grouping. In essence it is an organization consisting of a master of some art of skill; i.e. pottery making, flower arranging, calligraphy, judo, songs, etc., and his disciples. The group is called an *iemoto* and the master is the *Iemoto* of his *iemoto*. In its most exaggerated form it can be a vast pyramidical organization with a million or more members. On top of the pyramid is the grand *Iemoto* or his heir, and the immediate disciples. This is the head *iemoto*. Filling in the pyramid are sets of disciples', each forming a branch *iemoto* centering on one master and his disciples, followed by sets of third generation disciples and their separate disciples, each forming a third generation *iemoto*, and so on.

We regard the *iemoto* as the most important and characteristic form of secondary groupings in Japan for several reasons. Firstly, the *iemoto* is most prevalent in urban Japan, and today over 70 percent of Japan's population dwells in cities. Secondly, unlike the *dōzoku*, the *iemoto* is not tied to land; therefore, it can expand enormously in size, and it can be based on an increasing variety of objectives, fitting the increasing complexity of modern society and culture. Thirdly, and this is a crucial point, the *iemoto*, large or small, is not merely an organization. It represents a way of life, a structure in which Japanese men and women see themselves and the world around them organized, a key to problem solution, and a map for dealing with internal dissension and external pressures. The *iemoto* tells us something about how the Japanese relate to each other and to the non-Japanese world at large. The *iemoto* pattern prevails even in secondary groups not called by that name, whether they are simple work shops or giant factories, government offices dispensing welfare checks or modern universities instructing students in the lastest theories and techniques, age-old temples with quaint rituals or militant new religions accused by some of totalitarian tendencies. The *iemoto* pattern of interpersonal relations is, we feel, the foundation to Japan's success before, and especially after, World War II. Hence the title of this analysis is *Iemoto: The Heart of Japan*.

Throughout this inquiry we have contrasted developments in Japan with comparable situations in the United States and China. But the China we speak of in these pages is obviously the China before the Communist Revolution of 1949.

The challenge of the West in the 19th and 20th centuries led to a spectacularly new chapter in the history of both Japanese and Chinese culture. The introduction of Chinese culture into Japan from the 5th to the 12th centuries was, of course, of great importance to the early development of Japan, but the Chinese did not physically invade

Japan. It was the Japanese who voluntarily and zealously brought Chinese culture to their homeland. This was not the situation in the middle of the 19th century when the independence of both of these Asian nations was threatened. The alternatives before both peoples were clear: either strengthen themselves for national defense or accept the fate of Western domination.

This book asserts that Japan responded so well and so rapidly to the challenge of the West because her most important secondary grouping, sometimes in the form of the *dōzoku*, but more often in the form of the *iemoto*, and the *iemoto* pattern of interpersonal relations, enabled her to adapt herself to the requirements of modern industrialization and nationalism. In fact, the *iemoto* and the *iemoto* pattern facilitated the growth and maintenance of the industrial system with an ease unmatched by Western societies. The transition from traditional Japan to modern Japan did not involve fundamental social changes, requiring great psychocultural reorientation on the part of a majority of the people.

The situation in China was quite different. Her most important secondary grouping was the *tsu*, and the most characteristic pattern by which her people related to each other was the kinship pattern. The *tsu* and the kinship pattern of interpersonal relations were simply dysfunctional with regard to modern industrialization and nationalism. Hence the transition from traditional China to modern China involved changes in social structure and psychocultural reorientation that are too complicated to be dealt with adequately in a book focused on Japan. How China has responded to the challenge, both of the West and of Japan, first through the Nationalist Revolution and then through the Communist Revolution, will be the subject of another book to follow, provisionally entitled *Life in New China*.

Francis L. K. Hsu
Evanston, Illinois

Acknowledgements

The year in Japan (1964-1965) was made possible by grants from the Carnegie Corporation administered by the College of Arts and Sciences of Northwestern University under the late Dean Simeon E. Leland, and from the Wenner-Gren Foundation for Anthropological Research in New York. Secretarial and research assistance toward completion of this book was provided by the Council of Intersocietal Studies at Northwestern University and Biomedical Sciences Support Grant FR 7028-05 from the National Institutes of Health. A preliminary and shorter version of this book entitled "Japanese Kinship and *Iemoto*" was translated into Japanese by Professors Esyun Hamaguchi and Keichi Sakuda and published as part of the Japanese translation of my book *Clan, Caste and Club*. The resulting Japanese volume is entitled *Hikaku Bunmei Shakai Ron* (The Sociology of Comparative Cultures. Tokyo, Baifukan, 1971.) The number of people who have helped to make this book possible is large. I am indebted to so many friends and fellow scholars either for their help in the field or for their constructive criticisms that it is impossible to indicate each one by name here. However, in particular, I wish to thank the Honorable John L. Stegmaier, John R. Barnett, Taki Kondo, Keizo Isono, Akiko Hirai, Tetsuo Tanisaki, Hitoshi Suenaga, Hero Okuyama, Thomas P. Rohlen, Professors Teigo Yoshida, Keichi Sakuda, Takao Kawashima, Norman Sun, Hiroshi Mannari, Jun Haga and Masaaki Kato. Professor Esyun Hamaguchi has a special relationship with my work that went into this book. He and I held many face to face discussions in Japan and in Honolulu while he and I were both Senior Specialists at the East-West Center. He also went over the final manuscript of this book and offered various valuable suggestions. Mrs. Marjorie Benton helped me to decide on the title of the book. Frank Pasquale proof-read the galleys and prepared the indexes. Finally my wife, Vera, helped me much in gathering relevant information in the field. She gave me, as always, all sorts of support and encouragement.

Francis L. K. Hsu

Japanese periods of history
(after the introduction of Chinese culture)

Asuka (552-646 A.D.)
Nara (646-794)
Heian (794-1185)
Kamakura (1185-1336)
Muromachi (1336-1568)   (Also called "Ashikaga")
Momoyama (1568-1603)
Edo or Tokugawa (1603-1868)
Meiji Restoration (1868)
Meiji (1868-1912)
Taisho (1912-26)
Showa (1926-present)

1 •

The Economic Miracle of Japan

Japan is a country of sparse resources. Only 15 to 17 percent of her land surface is arable and she needs to import nearly all of her industrial minerals and raw materials. But the Japanese people have risen from the nadir of total defeat after World War II to effect the remarkable feat of rapidly transforming themselves into one of the leading industrial nations of the world.

The Physical Setting

Japan consists of four main islands, which are mostly mountainous. Magnificent scenic beauty prevails everywhere. But aside from the physical beauty, we also find a country with extremes in climate, and a population density of 4,200 persons per square mile of arable land—the highest such density in the world.

The climate of Japan is more varied than that of the United States in spite of the fact that her north to south span is shorter. Part of the reason for this is her mountainous topography. Hokkaidō, the northernmost island (where the 1972 Winter Olympics were held) has a climate similar to that of Moscow. It has short, cool summers and long, frigid winters. Shikoku and especially Kyūshū, the two south-

3

ern islands, enjoy a far milder climate, not unlike that of South Carolina and Georgia. Honshū, which means "foundation land" and is the largest of the four islands, has a variety of climates. *Snow Country,* a novel by the Japanese Nobel Prize winner, Yasunari Kawabata, depicting the romance between a married business man and a geisha, takes place in the cold, snowy, north-central part of Honshū. On the other hand, the southwestern section of Honshū shares the warmth and the long summer growing season of Shikoku and Kyūshū.

The mountains of Japan are not very high by world standards. Even Mount Fuji, the most famous and most sacred mountain in the country, rises less than 13,000 feet. But mountains are so numerous that on a clear day one is never out of sight of them anywhere in Japan. Many of these mountains, like Mount Fuji, rise precipitously, and add to the dramatic beauty of the land. Typhoons regularly hit Japan and the danger of earthquakes is always imminent.

The Love of Nature

The Japanese have developed an unusual love of nature and a preoccupation with their natural surroundings. Nearly all Japanese surnames, and even some first names, in contrast to Chinese or American names, have to do with element of geography and climate. Takashima means "tall island"; Kawabata means "corner of the river"; Yoshida means "blessed field." Other examples are : Shirakawa (white river), Hirai (flat well), Moriguchi (mouth of forest), Yugawa (hot river), Ueno (upper plain), and Nakamura (middle village).

The Japanese attribute human and supernatural qualities to their natural surroundings. The typhoon which destroyed the Mongol invaders in the 13th century was called *kamikaze* (divine wind). Mount Fuji is a deity. The altar of the Kamo shrine in Kyoto stands before a mountain which is the god enshrined. In these matters the Japanese approach is not dissimilar from that of the Chinese. But the Japanese carry this attitude towards nature further. All over Japan there are mountains "married" to each other. In the bay of Ise where the most sacred of all Shinto shrines is located, two rocks jutting out of the sea are "married" to each other. The two rocks, one taller than the other, are linked together with knotted ropes.

No other people in the world have developed the appreciation and handling of flowers and plants into such a high art as the Japanese. Each of the four largest associations devoted to particular traditions of flower arrangement has more than a million members. Japanese devotion to the growth and development of particular plant styles has sometimes seemed to be a perversion to Western eyes. Since the art of *bonsai* requires elaborate and repeated thinning of the roots to dwarf the trees, one Western writer wryly notes that the Japanese should have a society for the prevention of cruelty to plants. The Japanese love travel and sports involving nature. Viewing the cherry blossom is a national pastime. Although skiing is a very recent Western introduction, the *Asahi Shinbun (Morning Sun Daily News)* estimates that there are at least 7 million regular devotees of the sport in Japan, compared with about half that number in the United States.

Traditional Frugality and Resourcefulness

Short of land and natural resources, except for lumber, some poor coal, and a great potential for hydro-electric power, the Japanese have traditionally made extraordinary responses to their geographical limitations. The farmers practice intensive cultivation. The fields are immaculate gardens, and all available footage of land is used, including both sides of railroad tracks and roads. Double cropping and even triple cropping are practiced wherever climate permits.

Most Japanese live very frugally. In contrast to the Chinese, even well-to-do Japanese indulge far less in conspicuous domestic consumption. They have little furniture in their homes. They can make complete (and very tasty) meals out of rice and a little salted fish and pickled vegetables or sea weed.

Besides constantly flattening parts of mountains and filling in the sea to create more land, the Japanese have made extensive use of the water which surrounds their island country. In this matter they contrasted sharply with the Chinese long before the arrival of the West. The main protein source for the Japanese diet has traditionally been fish, in the form of *sashimi* (raw fish) or *sushi* usually made of fish and bamboo shoots, wrapped with rice and sea weed. The Japanese eat five or six different kinds of sea weed and every variety of shellfish. But the sea is a major life line of Japan in another way: she is the source of wealth from abroad. In pre-modern times the sea offered

Japan two important kinds of activity: piracy and trade. The advent of modernization eliminated sea piracy. Instead, the 20th century Japanese concentrated on becoming the greatest sea power in Asia, if not in the world. Before World War II, Japan used her sea power for military domination of other Asian nations, to ensure the flow of raw materials home. After the war she became the biggest ship builder in the world, and trade by sea is the foundation of her spectacular economic recovery and success in the postwar period.

The Revolution in Food Supply

One of the most dramatic economic advances in post-war Japan has been the revolution in food supply. In the years immediately following Japan's surrender in 1945, hunger was common. The average family spent three-fourths of its budget on food and clothing. Yet the average intake of food per person per day was about 1,500 calories, considerably below the daily requirement for good health. United States aid through Occupation authorities probably helped avert mass death by starvation. The total United States aid to Japan came to about four billion American dollars, two-thirds of it for non-military purposes. But this aid was terminated in the early 1960's after which the Japanese forged ahead on their own.

A notable revolution since the 60's has been the change in consumption patterns of the Japanese. Whereas the Japanese diet used to consist mainly of fish, sea weeds, and rice, it now includes beef, pork, mutton, milk, fruit, and vegetables. The average intake per person per day is currently 2,214 calories, only half of which consists of carbohydrates.

American-style supermarkets are seen much more often these days, and Western-style restaurants, which were first introduced in the early days of the Meiji Restoration, have become common. Today, every major hotel in the large cities features three types of restaurants: Western, Chinese, and Japanese.

Japanese food production and marketing methods on land and sea have changed tremendously in the postwar period. Japanese farms are still tiny by American standards, but the traditional intensive cultivation is now augmented by mechanization. Small tractors and mechanical pumps are to be found everywhere, even in the remote Akita and Aomori prefectures near Hokkaidō. The use of chemical fertilizers and insecticides is widespread.

By 1970 Japan had a rice surplus of some 5 million tons. Increased consumption of non-carbohydrates, leading to a 13 percent reduction of rice consumption in the decade 1960-70, is one reason for this surplus. Another is the increased yield per acre due to improved agricultural practices and technology. The Japanese government now gives price supports and has resorted to the American pattern of persuading some farmers to reduce the production of rice or to plant something else.

Japan's postwar advances in fishing are truly spectacular. Even as early as the 1920's Japan was responsible for more than 50 percent of the world's fish products. But during the last decade, this industry has reached new heights. The Japanese whaling industry is thoroughly modern. Japanese fishing vessels range far and wide. When Japan entered the king crab business, her vessels often came into dispute with American vessels operating from Alaska. Japan is now the greatest fishing nation in the world.

The Industrial Revolution

Even before World War II, Japan's industrial advances were envied by Asia and regarded as a constant source of threat by the more developed nations of the West. Her foreign trade rose from a little less than seven and one-half million (U.S.) dollars in 1870 to about 945 million (U.S.) dollars in 1920. Japan had no railroads at all in 1868, when Emperor Meiji assumed power; by 1940 the entire country was covered by one of the world's most efficient rail networks, with a total mileage of about 27 thousand miles. By 1935 Japan had become the leading textile exporter in the world. As Americans know, to their sorrow, the planes, submarines, and other military equipment which decimated the American Pacific Fleet at Pearl Harbor in 1941 were all manufactured in Japan.

The war devastated Japan thoroughly. Tokyo's population shrank by more than half, Osaka's by nearly two-thirds. Nearly 50 percent of the houses in urban areas were burned to the ground by American air raids. To make matters worse, some 6 million Japanese soldiers and civilians were expatriated from Korea, China, and other overseas colonies and occupied territories. Most Japanese, especially city dwellers, were ill-fed and ill-clothed; inflation was rampant and the black market prospered.

Japan was already well on her way to recovery in 1957 when I first visited her. Except in Hiroshima and Nagasaki, where the atom bombs had fallen, signs of the war's devastation were hard to find. Japan's urban population rose from some 50 percent of the total population in 1940, to 80 percent 1970. The decade of 1960-70 saw Japan emerge as a leading world producer of every kind of manufactured goods from toys to automobiles, and from electronics to iron and steel.

Of particular note are the qualitative advances of Japan's industries since World War II. In the 1930's Japanese goods flooded Chinese and other Asian markets. But those goods then had a well-earned notoriety for being cheap and shoddy, deceptive in their superficial attractiveness. *Tung Yang Huo* ("Eastern Ocean Goods," meaning Japanese goods) were identical in Chinese minds with merchandise which did not last. Few Chinese would consider buying Japanese cameras, gramophones, sewing machines, or bicycles.

Since then the Japanese have developed some of the best yet most economical cameras, as well as other fine scientific instruments comparable to and often surpassing in quality, famous German or American brands. Japanese names such as Sony and Nikon today rank among the most respected commercial names such as Zeiss-Ikon and Kodak. Most large Japanese concerns engage in research and development as actively and aggressively as their American and European counterparts. The 1969 World's Fair at Osaka, the first in Asia, was a splendid economic and political triumph for Japan.

Japan's per capita income rose from U.S. $520 in 1962, to U.S. $1,122 in 1968, to an estimated U.S. $1,800 in 1970. These figures are in sharp contrast to the estimated per capita income of U.S. $300 or less for every other Asian nation. Japan's economic growth rate for the last years has been an annual 7 percent or more, higher than that of any nation in the West. Japan's Gross National Product is now second only to that of the United States in the non-Communist world. In 1970 Japan had a foreign exchange surplus of 7 billion (U.S.) dollars, but now Japan has formally revalued the yen vis-à-vis the American dollar.

In less than two decades after World War II, Japan left the ranks of the "have-not nations" to become one of the most affluent countries in the world. There are American and Western economists who fearfully forecast that if the present trend continues, and they have little reason to think it will not, Japan will soon become the leading economic power in the world.

In Search of Explanation

How have the Japanese done it? How have they overcome their geographic limitations not only to erase malnutrition and famine but also to industrialize? What were the conditions which enabled the Japanese to rise so rapidly from the ashes of total defeat? How has Japan managed to solve the problems of a nation wholly dependent on trade with other nations? What lessons does Japan offer to developing countries? Does Japan's experience offer any guidelines to industrially advanced societies in meeting the problems of their own industrial futures?

One facile explanation for the Japanese economic miracle comes to mind. This is Japan's zeal for and success in imitating. Many American visitors have been impressed by how Americanized the Japanese have become. In 1957 I landed at Yokohama for my first visit to Japan. My family and I were returning to the United States by way of Japan after eighteen months in India. Traveling in the commuter train which took me to Tokyo, I felt as though I had already arrived in the United States. The clothes worn by the men, the cosmetics and other fineries worn by the women, the speed with which people moved, the neons, the streets congested with automobiles; these and other sights were at once familiar to me even though I was at that time totally unfamiliar with Japan and the Japanese language. Certainly the entire scene offered an incredible contrast to what I knew in India, even though many more Indians than Japanese speak English.

Later, in 1964-65, during a more extended sojourn in Japan, I was amazed over and over again at how zealously the Japanese adopted Western and especially American ways just as they had followed the Chinese example earlier. Popularity of Western music, both classical and modern, is widespread. Well-to-do Japanese homes invariably have a living room furnished with Western style furniture. The fastest trains in the world run on the Tōkaidō line between Tokyo and Osaka. Industrial pollution in Tokyo and Osaka is reaching alarming proportions. I have seen more of the latest American and European fashions in one hour in Tokyo than in several days in New York or Chicago. The prevalence of English terms in the Japanese language is striking.

Haikingu (hiking), *pikuniku* (picnic), *suto* (strike), *noirōze* (neurosis), *howaitokarā* (white collar), *dansu hōru* (dance hall) — these are but a few examples of the thousands of English words in daily use. Before World War II, a literate Chinese who wanted to learn to read Japanese would be greatly aided by his knowledge of Chinese characters, for about 70 percent of Japanese nouns are of Chinese origin and written in Chinese characters. But now that advantage is increasingly diminishing as the Japanese incorporate more and more English words into their language through phonetic transliterations.

However, the ability to imitate is not by any means a satisfactory explanation of Japan's character and strengths. For one thing, if imitation alone were so important and if Japan can imitate so well, why could not other underdeveloped nations follow her example? Besides, many of the industrial and commercial conglomerates in Japan today were already great financial houses in pre-Meiji days. Mitsui, Sumitomo, and Yasuda were the giants among them; there was nothing like them even in 19th century China.

Another explanation for Japan's rapid economic development, especially as it contrasts to what happened in China, relies heavily on socio-psychological theories of American origin. A systematic presentation of this line of argument is that set forth by Robert Bellah in his *Tokugawa Religion* (Glencoe, Ill.: The Free Press, 1957). According to Bellah, "China was characterized by the primacy of integrative values where Japan was characterized by primacy of political or goal-attainment values. . . . A society characterized by the primacy of integrative values is more concerned with system maintenance than with, for example, goal attainment or adaptation; more with solidarity than with power or wealth." On the other hand, in Japan "the central value system which was found to be present in the Tokugawa Period remained dominant in the modern period, in perhaps an even more intense and rationalized form. The adaptation of that central value system which had been worked out as the status ethic of the various classes proved very favorable for handling the new economic responsibilities which fell to each class" (p. 188 and p. 189).

These interesting observations are not, however, commensurate with many facts. If China were merely characterized by the primacy of *integrative* values, the Chinese would not have been described by Dr. Sun Yat-sen as "a tray of loose sand," and they would have shown far more devotion to their emperors in dynastic times than they did, as well as far more patriotic fervor after the advent of Western pressures. Conversely, if Japan were merely characterized by the primacy of *goal-attainment* values in Western terms, the Japanese would have been far more individualistic and far less pliant to authority and group pressure than they are today. Historically, the Chinese seem to have acted far more individualistically than the Japanese, while the Japanese have been far more effectively patriotic than the Chinese.

We shall return to this question in a later chapter. Let it suffice here to state that, in my view, Japan and China did not have fundamentally different values. What distinguishes the Japanese from the Chinese are their respective patterns of human organization, through which similar values manifest themselves in different ways. In this book I propose to demonstrate the nature of the Japanese pattern in contrast to that of China, which has close cultural links with Japan, as well as to that of the United States which has great affinity with Japan in industrial achievements.

2 ●

Some Comparisons

Let us begin by examining some manifestations of the Japanese pattern of human relations.

From Picnic to Violence

In the spring of 1965 a Japanese friend invited me to a picnic planned by members of his department of the city government of Ashiya (near Osaka). Some seventeen people in all, we went in three automobiles to a relatively secluded spot about 20 miles northwest, in the Rokko Mountains.

It was a lovely spot where we finally spread out our blankets and began to nibble tidbits of candies and confectionery, amidst light conversation. Not far away was a tiny lake surrounded on three sides by lovely trees. Some of the more active members of our party formed a circle on the wide grassy bank and started to kick a soccer ball back and forth.

It was early afternoon and not yet time to eat. The conversation was carried on in a mixture of English and Japanese, and when I had some difficulty in understanding what was being talked about, someone would resort to writing Chinese characters on a piece of paper and

I would be able to work it out. This was characteristic of Japanese gatherings in which I took part, especially during the first half of our year in Japan.

After a while I was attracted by the tiny lake shining in the afternoon sun. Instead of sitting facing the rest of our little group, I turned to the lake and the ball players. Tired of sitting with my legs folded, I partially stretched them out in front of me.

At this point something astonishing happened. My Japanese friend pulled my arm firmly and whispered to me, "Please turn around and sit facing the others." Of course I obliged, but I could not help being amazed. Minor though the incident was, it was utterly foreign to all my picnic experiences in China, England, the United States, and various parts of continental Europe. At all those other picnics, as a child or an adult, no one—friend, relative, or teacher —ever corrected me for what I did that sunny afternoon in Japan. Up to that time I was used to sitting and moving more or less as I pleased on similar occasions, and on these occasions, others too behaved as they pleased.

Having already observed Japanese life for several months, I more or less realised the meaning of my friend's corrective gesture. When one is with a group, even temporarily, he should actively participate in the activities of the group and not venture out on his own. But I had not yet learned how very fundamental and widespread this principle of interpersonal relationships is in the Japanese way of life.

Participation in subsequent picnics and other gatherings showed me that the first experience of mine was no isolated incident. Anyone who has visited Japan's tourist attractions, her famous shrines or temples or scenic spots or the well-known Wedded Rocks in Ise Bay, will have noticed troops of children or adults coming and going in neat formation. The "captains" and "sub-captains" each hold square or triangular banners indicating the identity of the group. There is an orderliness in the procession, an exhibition of a "follow-the-leader" spirit that I have not seen elsewhere, certainly not in China before 1949, nor in Taiwan today.

Another Japanese phenomenon that impressed me was the ubiquitous song and dance processions in temples and streets during big festivals such as Obon, the ancestor festival. Young ladies and often little girls are very much a part of the song and dance routine during Obon. Their activities continue from early evening through the small hours of the morning. Processions during many other festivals feature men and mature ladies, four abreast, dressed almost uniformly in blue and white kimonos, joyfully singing, clapping, and dancing in unison through the streets thronged with gay spectators.

However, these are temporary groups. Of even more interest are the recreational activities of those who work in the same department, bureau, or even the same clinic. Americans work in offices, but they play with their own friends who are not necessarily connected with their offices. They may entertain their office mates or bosses at home, but these are family affairs with spouses included. The Chinese separate office and home less than the Americans do, but their way of life is closer to that of the Americans than that of the Japanese.

The Japanese not only have frequent office picnics, but they enjoy office weekends at least twice a year, and often more frequently. These affairs are characterized by two things which would surprise a majority of Americans and Chinese. To begin with, the participants of these affairs are not people of the same status, but all members of the same department, bureau, or even clinic, including managers, senior and junior officers, and clerks. Each of these activities concerns the entire working unit (in the case of clinics, doctors, nurses, and office workers). Secondly, spouses are excluded from these events including long weekends when the entire office force leaves town by train or in one or more hired buses to live it up in some resort.

It would be easy for the Western observer, in view of such facts, to say that for the Japanese the requirements of the group are more important than the predilections of the individual. But such a conclusion is also easily applicable to the Chinese. Both the Chinese and the Japanese emphasize self-denial (not Western altruism) and regard individualism as equivalent to selfishness. Duties and obligations to others take precedence over personal enjoyment and comfort. But the overwhelming solidarity the Japanese shares with his or her working team members, and the fact that solidarity takes precedence over spouse and family, are concepts alien to the Chinese.

It is in this light that Japanese incidents such as the following become understandable, though no less frightening:

Case 1. Thirteen year old Kazuyo Yamamoto was a member of her school basketball team. Just before the Tokyo high school basketball championship game she came down with the flu and had to miss a week's basketball training. Without warning four of her classmates stormed into her house, grabbed her by the hair, and gave her a terrible beating. After she managed to escape to a neighboring hospital, eleven classmates showed up on the following evening on the pretext of apologizing to her. Instead they forcibly took her to the front of a temple where they gave her a worse beating than before. She suffered bruised ribs, speech defects, fits of paralysis, and possible brain damage.

Case 2. Eighteen year old Ryosaku Anjo, a member of the karate club of the University of Tokyo, repeatedly asked to be allowed to quit. Finding his fellow members adamantly opposed to his request, he asked his father to intercede on his behalf. After his father made a special trip from the provinces to the school for the purpose, the club members apparently agreed. They gave him a farewell dinner where they beat and kicked him to death.[1]

Such incidents, though there might be other sadistic factors involved, exemplify the importance of the group over the individual. We can see from all the examples enumerated above, the extreme to which group requirements and goals predominate over the individual in Japan; this situation must seem strange even to the Chinese and certainly bizarre to Americans.

Two Legends

Now let us look at a very different set of data and see if it can tell us anything about the Japanese pattern of human relations. I shall recount two legends on a similar theme, one popular in China and the other in Japan. Here my assumption is that legends, especially highly popular ones, along with art and fiction, mirror something of the desires, moral judgments, anxieties, fears, and hopes on the part of the people who create them.

An old Chinese legend, popular in drama and opera, is *The Story of the White Snake.* This is about a snake who attained immortality and became a goddess in heaven. Feeling the urge for worldly affairs, she came down in human form to the world of man with her maid, the Black Snake. While the two snake goddesses were enjoying the scenery of the beautiful West Lake in South China, a sudden downpour forced them to take temporary cover under a tree, where young Master Hsu also happened to have sought refuge. Hsu, orphaned since childhood, was an employee of a dispensary and was on his way to pay homage to his mother's tomb on a mountain not far away. White Snake and Master Hsu fell in love with each other. At the request of White Snake, Black Snake served as the matchmaker and the two were married. The happy couple earned their livelihood by running a small dispensary. Soon White Snake was pregnant.

Abbot Fa Hai, head of an important Buddhist temple nearby, decided that it was unpropitious for the world that a snake-turned-goddess live in his area as the wife of a man. So he visited Master Hsu in the dispensary and advised him to get rid of his snake-wife. Seeing that Master Hsu refused to believe that his wife was a snake, the abbot asked him to test his wife and see for himself. The test consisted of slipping some special medicine into her wine on the day of the Dragon Boat festival.

Master Hsu, though skeptical, did as he was advised and, sure enough, his wife reverted into her original snake form under his very eyes. The shock killed Master Hsu. When White Snake recovered from the effect of the medicine and assumed the form of a human being again, she decided to obtain special remedies which only angels in far away mountains could bestow. In spite of her pregnancy she travelled great distances and fought many obstacles and eventually received the necessary remedies which brought Master Hsu back from the dead. Furthermore, White Snake and her maid magically turned a white satin belt into an illusory white snake and convinced Master Hsu that what he saw was another snake, not his dear wife. The two then resumed their harmonious marital life together.

The abbot refused to give up. He told Master Hsu the truth about White Snake's search for supernatural remedies on his behalf. Hsu was shaken and began to waver. Seizing this opportunity the abbot persuaded Hsu to take refuge from White Snake in his temple.

White Snake and her maid Black Snake intuitively realized that the abbot must be responsible for Hsu's absence. They mobilized all sorts of sea spirits and gods to fight the abbot and his forces in front of his temple overlooking the Yangtze River. Handicapped by her pregnancy, White Snake and her forces retired to another locality in defeat. During the battle Master Hsu attempted to sneak out of the temple to join his wife, but was arrested by the abbot's forces. However, seeing that Hsu still cared for worldly romance the abbot allowed him to join his wife again for one more month.

Black Snake, the maid, wanted to kill Master Hsu for having strayed so far, but White Snake asked her to desist since Hsu was her husband. So marital harmony was once more restored and soon White Snake gave birth to a son. Now the abbot came forward with a giant jar to "arrest" the two snakes. At the end of another war, in which each side was helped by different spirits, Black Snake escaped but the power of White Snake was broken. The abbot magically sealed White Snake under a pagoda in West Lake and his curse was that White Snake could only secure her release if the lake water dried up or the pagoda fell down.

Black Snake spent the next 100 years accumulating divine merit. She became an increasingly powerful goddess, and finally she led a group of other deities to rescue White Snake by toppling the pagoda.

This, in bare outline, is the much beloved *Story of the White Snake.*Upon this basic theme of a man married unknowingly to a snake-spirit the Chinese have constructed several variations. In one of these the pregnancy and subsequent birth of the son is omitted. Another has the son grow up to be a brilliant young scholar who attains the highest degree in the Imperial Examinations, and promptly rescues his mother from imprisonment. A third version merely regards the abbot's interference and White Snake's imprisonment under the pagoda as an inevitable period of purification or penitence, at the completion of which Buddha himself personally comes forward to receive her back to heaven. Still another version explains that Master Hsu was a monk of high spiritual merits in his previous incarnation; his life as Master Hsu was only a temporary, predestined interlude, at the end of which he became a god in heaven.

The central themes of this Chinese story are quite obvious. Man meets woman. They fall in love and give themselves to each other. Outside interference disrupts the union. Man is helpless and wavers but woman perserveres, overcomes obstacles and saves his life.

The Japanese legend of Dōjyōji (Dōjyō temple) featuring the lovers Anchin and Kiyohime bears some resemblance to the Chinese story just outlined. Once upon a time, under the reign of Emperor Daigo, there was a priest named Anchin at Shirakawa in Oshu (Tōhoku) district. Being devoted to the gods of Three Kumano shrine in Kishū, he used to go there on a pilgrimage every year. En route he regularly lodged at the home of a village master. The latter had a beautiful daughter Kiyohime, whom Anchin had known since her childhood. He used to joke with her that he would marry her when she grew up.

One year he stayed at her home again during his pilgrimage. Having always taken his words of jest seriously, Kiyohime, now 13 years old, decided it was time for her to be united with him. She joined him in his bed and asked him to take her away with him. He was astonished and reluctant to assume that responsibility, and explained to her that the trip would be too arduous for her. Instead, he continued, he would fetch her on his way back from the pilgrimage. And they consummated their union as man and wife that night.

Anchin left the next morning, after exchanging love poems with Kiyohime. But the poor girl waited in vain for his return, and finally she went out in search of him. She learned from other pilgrims that he was taking another road to by-pass her home, and she immediately set out in hot pursuit. Her hair became so dishevelled and she bore such a terrible expression on her face that other travelers were greatly astonished to see such a person racing by.

Kiyohime caught sight of his back near the village of Ueno and called out to him. Looking back, Anchin responded without stopping that he did not know her and that she must have mistaken him for someone else. As she drew near him he began to run, throwing away all his belongings one by one to lighten his burden and praying to the gods of the Three Kumano shrine for mercy. It seems the gods responded to his prayers because Kiyohime felt dizzy and had to pause for breath. This gave Anchin the opportunity he needed to outdistance the girl.

After crossing a river on a ferry boat, Anchin told the boatman that he was being pursued by an evil woman. When Kiyohime arrived at the river bank, her head already turned into that of a serpent because of her hatred for Anchin, the ferry man refused her a ride. She plunged herself into the river, and as she did so she was transformed into a huge serpent. She crossed the river easily.

Meanwhile Anchin reached the Dōjyō temple and he appealed to its priests for help. They took down the huge temple bell and hid him under it. They also took up arms. But as Kiyohime raced toward the temple in the form of a fire spewing giant serpent, all the priests became frightened and fled. After searching for Anchin in vain the giant serpent noticed the bell on the ground. She wound herself around it, then blew fire all over it while flapping her tail. The bell became red hot. Finally the giant serpent left and dove into a nearby river. When the priests returned and turned the bell over they found only Anchin's charred remains.

To this basic story of love and hate the Japanese have added other embellishments. One version of it entitled *Dōjyōji Tokuhon (Dōjyō Temple Reader)* has a happy ending. Shortly after Anchin's death the chief priest had a dream in which Anchin and Kiyohime appeared as a pair of serpents. They appealed to him to recite a certain *sūtra*[2] on their behalf. The old priest did as he was requested and later the two again came to him in a dream to thank him for his kindness. They had now become a pair of heavenly angels in human form. There are at least three Nō plays, two puppet shows, and four Kabuki dramas based on sections of the Anchin-Kiyohime theme. Dōjyōji, the temple where Anchin met his tragic end according to the legend, is today a prosperous temple in Wakayama prefecture which houses the tombs of Anchin and Kiyohime and also a special tower for the bell. It holds a yearly festival honoring the bell.

Legends and Ways of Life

The Japanese theme bears many similarities to and also differs from its Chinese counterpart. Although I have no clear historical evidence that the two legends have a common origin, there is a strong argument for suggesting their Chinese ancestry in view of the long and sustained cultural diffusion from China to Japan. But whether or not they share a common ancestry, the similarities and differences between the two legends can perhaps explain the similarities and differences between the Chinese and Japanese ways of life.[3]

Being polytheistic, both the Chinese and the Japanese have many gods and do not share the Western absolutism in differentiating between the world of the spirits with that of man. This is why in both tales the transformation from a human being to a spirit and vice versa is not immutable. Both peoples regard intervention by a third party in romance, as in other interpersonal undertakings, as quite usual. That is why the priest figures prominently in both tales. In both tales the female is stronger than the male in spite of the external, traditional inequality between the sexes in the two cultures. The woman in both cases must bear the burden for the defense of the union. And finally, both the Chinese and the Japanese legends emphasize the importance of the individual's proper place among his fellow human beings, and lead to a socially sanctified conclusion which is essential to give it a proper social context. Individual desires and actions are not enough; the interpersonal nexus is far more important. These are some of the psycho-cultural similarities revealed in the two tales.

But the differences revealed in the legends are no less striking.

Whereas Master Hsu was the innocent husband with good intentions, who took as his wife a snake goddess turned woman, Anchin cohabited with and promised marriage to an innocent girl who never suspected his contrary motives. Could this contrast indicate a feeling of greater possibility of marital infidelity among the Japanese? In the Chinese legend, White Snake went to all sorts of trouble to defend her husband, including reviving him from death, in spite of his weakness in having listened to the meddlesome abbot, while Kiyohime put her man to death in spite of the protective actions of the monks. Could this suggest the greater power of Japanese women over their men (or a stronger fear of women on the part of Japanese males)?

The observation is reinforced by other contrasts between the two stories. Anchin's worldly existence ended in a pile of charred bones but Master Hsu suffered no comparable fate. Furthermore, the Chinese female began as a snake but turned into a thoroughly good wife, while the Japanese female began as a loving girl but turned into a vicious killer snake.[4]

The contrast is intensified when we consider the relative importance of sex as a factor in the two stories. In the Chinese case the man and wife are evidently satisfied in their love life and they even have a son. Sex is neither a problem nor dangerous. The romantic rupture comes only when an outsider, the abbot, interferes. Even after the revelation of his wife's un-worldly identity Master Hsu still wished to cleave to her. On the other hand the central theme of the Japanese story is clearly the direct link between sexual involvement and death. The male's attempt to escape is followed by the female's hot pursuit, leading straight to their double death. All this, in addition to the fact that the Japanese story makes veiled but unmistakable references to sexual activity between the lovers (including the use of the artistic expression *kakekotoba* and the exchange of erotic *waka*), while the Chinese story does not.

Finally, as will become clear in the following chapters, although the Japanese received Buddhism through the Chinese cultural filter, the role of Buddhist temples, clergy, and theology in Japan is quite different from the role of Buddhism in China. For one thing, monks in China remain outside regular society while they are a far more integral part of Japanese daily life. In fact, it would be a strange Chinese home which welcomed monks as visitors at times other than a funeral or a wedding. On the former occasion, monks are hired to recite *sūtras.* On the latter, they come to beg for alms. Is it any wonder that in the Chinese story the abbot is the central cause of the marital disruption while in the Japanese legend the monks are the protectors of a man in danger but have nothing to do with the break-up of the romance?

The messages contained in the two legends and in the picnic manners, as well as in the violent samples of group solidarity, seem disparate on the surface. In reality they tell us something basic about the larger tapestry of Japanese culture. In the design of this tapestry, solidarity of the group is paramount. The group in question is not the kinship group into which the individual is born or married as in China, but an extra-kinship one. Yet the extremely binding nature of this group differentiates it from the free association or club in the West. Instead, the members of this extra-kinship group relate to one another as though linked by kinship.

Besides solidarity in the extra-kinship group, another element in Japanese culture is the Japanese type of man-woman relationship. American and Western European societies approach this problem by preoccupation with sex, through medieval repression, or modern-day proliferation. When sex is repressed, guilt is used as the chief weapon to exact compliance; when it proliferates, freedom of the individual becomes the chief justification. The Chinese approach the man-woman problem by assigning it to specific but restricted areas in society. Sex is not denied and never a sin where it is legitimate, but is absent in most other areas where absence is its proper role.

The Japanese approach to the man-woman problem is basically similar to that of the Chinese. But while the Japanese assign sex to specific times and places, the number of such places is so large that sex or sex-linked activities are far more in evidence in Japanese than in Chinese culture. Although Japanese wives and mothers appear at first sight to be more subservient to their husbands and sons than their Chinese sisters,[5] they are in fact more overpowering.

These two themes, namely, the predominance of the group over the individual, and the greater play of the sexes in Japan, are the most important points of reference in the Japanese pattern of human relations, especially in comparison to the Chinese example.

All human relations begin with some kind of family, an arena in which every individual is begotten by his parents and reared by them for five, ten, or more years. This arena is important not only because it comes first in the life of every individual, but also because it occurs (1) when the individual is totally helpless, (2) when he experiences a faster rate of growth of his mental powers than at any later time, and (3) when he acquires the foundation for his feelings about himself and his relations to the rest of the world.

The importance of the family in the larger social organization is recognized by all social reformers, leaders of new religious movements, and protagonists of political revolutions. The larger society cannot function well in the long run if the basic social germ cell, the family, fails to produce in the individual patterns of behavior and feeling that are commensurate with its goals.

The kinship system is, therefore, the first key to the larger society. For this reason we shall compare kinship in Japan with the Chinese and American kinship systems.

[1] There are some variations in the reports, especially in Case 2. One account said Ryosaku Anjo did not die at the restaurant but died shortly afterwards in a hospital. Both cases were reported in the *Seattle Post Intelligencer*, Sunday, November 29, 1970.

[2] Holy text.

[3] Some of the elements embodied in these tales are, of course, not peculiar to the two peoples. A man and a woman chance to meet; their romantic attachment is disrupted by obstacles. These themes are common to many stories in many parts of the world. Even the important role played by the priests in the two romances and the identification of the female with the serpent are not particularly Asian.

[4] The more active role of Japanese females in man-woman relationships is reflelcted in the union of the god Izanagi and his sister Izanami found in *Kojiki* and *Nihongi*. After building a house with a great central pillar, Izanagi sid to Izanami, "Let me and thee go round the heavenly august pillar, and having met at the other side, let us become united in wedlock." After she agreed he told her, "Do thou go round from the left, and I will go round from the right." When they had gone round, Izanami spoke first and said, "How delightful! I have met a lovely youth." Izanagi was displeased and said, "I am a man and by right should have spoken first. How is it that on the contrary thou, a woman, shouldst have been the first to speak? This was unlucky. Let us go round again." Upon this the two deities went back, and having met anew, this time the male deity (Izanagi) spoke first, and said, "How delightful! I have met a lovely maiden." (translation by Aston 1924:13)

[5] Westernized Chinese men often say that an individual's ideal life should have three components: to live in an American house, to eat Chinese food, and to marry a Japanese wife.

Japanese and Chinese Kinship Systems

In general, the Japanese and Chinese kinship systems resemble each other far more closely than either resembles the American system. An American reader will have no difficulty in determining how thoroughly different the two Far Eastern systems are from the patterns with which he is familiar.

Basic Similarities

Central to the Japanese kinship system is the concept of filial piety which the Japanese borrowed from China. The Chinese primer of filial piety, *Hsiao Ching*, or *Filial Piety Classic*, has become part of the Japanese literary heritage. *The Twenty Four Examples of Filial Piety* is a Chinese exposition of the tenets of filial piety through concrete examples, allegedly taken from history. The Japanese have not only adopted this book but also have their own book entitled *Fu Sō Kō Shi Den* or *Biographies of Filial Sons of Japan*. Instead of a mere twenty-four examples, the latter contains seventy-one stories. It also provides the reader with the exact locations and times as to when and where these filial sons lived.

Japanese rulers, like their Chinese counterparts, conferred special gifts or honors on citizens who exhibited exemplary conduct according to the tenets of filial piety. The Shogun[1] Ieshige (1745-1760 A.D.) for example, was recorded as having awarded "much gold" to a filial son named Heizō. "Heizō was a native of Mutsu Uta Gun. He was faithful in serving his parents since childhood. His wife also served her parents-in-law well. His parents were fond of *odori* (dancing with songs), so on every Chūgen (*Bon* festival) he invited the villagers to dance in front of their house for the parents' pleasure. He and his wife both participated in the song and dance. After the parents' passing, he had two small statues of them carved and would take leave of them when departing from the house and would report to them upon his return. During the summer heat he would fan the statues, and hang a mosquito net over them just as when they were living. So the Shogun publicly honored him." (Kondo 1877, vol. 5:5).

Japanese rules of propriety are similar to Chinese rules in insisting upon a separation between the sexes and in considering women inferior to men. They stress the concept of hierarchy among members of a kinship group. Seniority in generation and in age gives an individual adequate reason for a superior position over others who are in a lower generation and younger in age. The Japanese or Chinese father is not afraid to express or to use his authority. The father does not have to search his soul or consult counselors as to how he may become a friend to his children. He does not have to defer to his wife in disciplining his children.

Marriage has traditionally been arranged by the parents, so that a man does not have to be self-supporting in order to get married. In fact, the Japanese father's authority was in the past so great that he had the "prerogative" to sell his daughters as *geisha* (entertainers) and prostitutes. Embree noted in 1939 that "a recent law says a girl's consent must be obtained, but in practice this is a mere formality" and that "a girl is in no position to refuse her consent" (Embree 1939:81).

After marriage the son and his wife and their children ideally live under the same roof as his parents. As among the Chinese, servants are often relatives. Even if they are not relatives, they are often treated as members of the family. Embree noted that usually the wages for such servants were not paid to the individuals themselves but to their parents. Often these servants would eat with the family and work side by side with them in the fields. Occasionally a daughter in the household, having worked with a man servant in the fields for some months and having become intimate with him, became pregnant and a marriage might result (Embree 1939:80).

Like the Chinese, the Japanese believed in and practiced joint responsibility among family members before the law. Prior to the

Meiji era, innocent family members and relatives were often punished according to the Chinese system of *renza* (criminal responsibility by relationship). One of the Kabuki plays of the Tokugawa period (1603-1868) featured a robber hero who uttered verbal protests against inhumane punishments while being boiled to death with his little son in his arms (Abe 1963:325). The head of a household could shut a criminal or a mentally ill member in a locked room with impunity even though he had no legal right to do so. Village ostracism or banishment was common and effective against offenders and the custom still exists today (Hirano 1963:291).

The Japanese practice ancestor worship; each household usually has a shrine to honor the dead relatives. Individual ancestors are represented by tablets with written characters denoting the particulars about their lives. Offerings are made at frequent intervals. Major offerings are made on the *Bon* festival which occurs in the middle of the seventh month according to the lunar calendar. The Chinese visit the graves of the ancestors and pay homage to them in the spring, on the occasion of Ching Ming which is the Chinese version of Easter. The Japanese observe the same custom twice a year, on the days of the Vernal Equinox and the Autumnal Equinox.

The Japanese have developed a sort of lineage system. In some parts of Japan there is a kind of lineage organization which unites many related families. Beardsley, Hall, and Ward report for Niiike in western Honshū that there are five lineages each called *kabu* or *kabu-uchi* (Beardsley, Hall and Ward 1959:262-275). Some Japanese lineages even have genealogical books, featuring many generations and give details of the achievements of the illustrious ancestors.

As in the Chinese kinship system, divorce had traditionally been a male prerogative, with the parents of the husband often having much more to say about the matter than the husband himself. A majority of the people practice monogamy but polygyny is allowed if there are no male heirs, or for the satisfaction of male desire or to bolster male status. For example, emperors (and *shogun*) before the Meiji Restoration in 1868 had sizeable harems, and influential or affluent men kept *geisha* or other girls as concubines. Even Emperor Meiji had several concubines. These were social customs that wives were in no position to prevent.

Differences between Chinese and Japanese Systems

So far we have dealt with similarities in the Chinese and Japanese systems. However, differences between them are considerable. The following diagram will help us understand the differences between the Chinese, Japanese, and United States kinship systems.

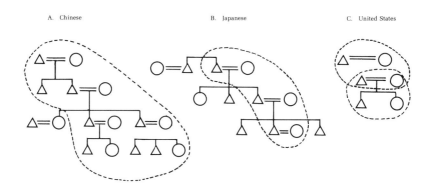

DIAGRAM 1:   Differences between Systems

Of the three, the United States system is the simplest. It says to the individual that as soon as he reaches the age of maturity, he should stand on his own, with his own family. His effective kinship organization is, therefore, a spouse and their unmarried children. The Chinese system is nearly the opposite of this. It says to the individual that whatever his age level, he is tied to his forebears and his descendants yet unborn, as well as to all collateral relatives in the patrilineal line. His effective kinship organization is, therefore, far larger than the American one. The Japanese system on the other hand, neither lets the individual loose when he reaches the age of maturity nor does it tie him down for eternity.

At the heart of the Chinese-Japanese differences is the rule of unigeniture under which one son, often the eldest, inherits the house, the property and the family shrine for ancestors, sometimes with some economic provision for the other sons.[2] Closely related to this feature is the markedly hierarchical relationship between the heir (most likely the eldest son) and his brothers (most likely the younger sons). In fact where the brothers of the heir receive some part of the patrimony (or maintain some economic link with it such as when they serve as tenants working the heir's land) they are not only subordinate to him, but also dependent upon him. There are some differences between northern Japan (the northern part of Honshū) and south-western Japan (the western part of Honshū, Shikoku and Kyūshū) in the relationship between the heir and his brothers which will be dealt with briefly later. For the moment, however, we shall presume this pattern to be true for all of Japan.

The Japanese pattern stands in striking contrast to that in China where the principle of equal division among brothers,[3] and the lack of binding hierarchical ties among them, has prevailed for the last two thousand years. But what happened in Japan is also different in three ways from the situation of, say, England and the early United States of America where primogeniture was the rule. Primogeniture in England and colonial America meant that the heir was determined by custom, but in Japanese unigeniture the heir was usually selected by the father, even when primogeniture was favored by the law. In English and early American custom the younger sons had no legitimate share in the patrimony, but in the Japanese situation the other sons were usually entitled to an unspecified portion of it. Finally, while younger sons in England and colonial America were free to leave their elder brother and seek their own fame and fortune elsewhere, Japanese younger sons were subordinate to the heir; they had to serve in his army, or pay him a part of the returns from the land, and otherwise submit to his orders.

Separation vs. Big Family Ideal

We shall leave the Japanese-Western differences for later consideration and examine, for the moment, some implications of the Japanese-Chinese differences. Firstly, the Japanese do not share the Chinese ideal of a Big Family. The non-inheriting sons, usually the younger ones, according to custom, leave the ancestral household usually before and most certainly after marriage. This makes for the well-known Japanese distinction of *honke* versus *bunke*. The former is the household that the heir has inherited while the latter are the separate households established by the other sons. Even though much closer relationships exist between the *honke* and *bunke*[4] than among separate households established by brothers in the United States, the establishment of separate households by several brothers is the Japanese rule, and not, as in China, an eventuality to be avoided unless the various wives really cannot get along. In other words, living together was desirable and honorable for the Chinese married brothers just as separation was the ideal for the Japanese.

So important is the ideal of separation that even aged parents, after the father has relinquished his position as head of the household, often live separately from the new head of the household. The parents may move into a separate wing of the house or a separate house to the side of or behind the main house. The custom is commonly known as *inkyo*. The house into which parents will retire is called *inkyo-va* or *hanare*.[5] Although this custom is not invariable, the concept of *inkyo* is known in all parts of Japan. Even in cities like Tokyo and Kyoto and suburbs like Okamoto and Ashiya near Kobe or horticultural villages near Ikeda, *hanare* can be found. When the aged parent or parents are too old or too infirm to live alone the eldest son's household may take them back. In such a case the *hanare* part of the house may be rented out to a tenant who is a widow or widower. The last arrangement is especially likely to occur in the city or suburb where housing is at a premium. But all throughout Kansai, mid-central Honshū, I have found many *hanare* inhabited by an aged parent or parents.

This customary sanction for separation of married younger brothers from the heir and of retired aged parents from the ancestral household may be related to another interesting contrast between Japan and China. In China the big family ideal operated more strongly among the well-to-do and the socially ambitious than among the poor. Therefore large households of the kind depicted in the Chinese novel *The Dream of the Red Chamber* (translated by Wang: 1929 & 1958) were more likely to be found in cities and towns than in rural areas, and the size of the households was, in general, larger in cities and towns than in villages and hamlets. The situation in Japan seems to have been reversed. There was, of course, no chance for developing the Chinese type of huge households, but Beardsley, Hall and Ward have found that present-day Niiike, a very rural hamlet, has the lowest percentage of small households; the farmers of Inari and Harakozai,

who live among shopkeepers, have a large proportion of such households. The shopkeeper households include the greatest percentage of
the nuclear family type (Beardsley, Hall and Ward, 1959:228). However, in spite of such differences between rural and near-urban situations, the large households of the Chinese kind are not to be found in
Japan anywhere. Kojima reports the existence in 1682 A.D., of large
households consisting of "twenty, thirty and twelve family members
respectively, each of which included collateral kin with their elementary families." But seven years later "these households separated into
smaller units." For example, "the household of twenty members
appears as four separate households in the registration" on the later
date (Kojima 1948:116-18 and Nakane 1967a:66).

Lineal Versus Horizontal Linkage in Names

Chinese family names are usually very old in origin. Most of them
have been in use for the last 2000 years. When brothers separated they
always kept the same family name no matter how far they moved
away from the ancestral home and village. A majority of the Japanese
had no family names before the Tokugawa period. It was impossible
to relate two brothers from the records.

The pattern of traditional Japanese first names is also relevant.
For the Chinese, not only all members of the clan shared the same last
name, but brothers and all patrilateral parallel cousins (who are
members of the same clan according to Chinese rule) shared an
element in common in their given names. For example, if the given
name for that generation consisted of two words, say L.K., then all of
the brothers and cousins would be L.R., L.O., etc., or W.K., O.K., etc.
Thus a person's name would in one glance enable others to ascertain
his generational position in his clan. By the same token his generational position with reference to those above or below him was usually also ascertainable by the existence in most clans of some jingle or
phrase, which consisted of characters shared by successive generations of brothers and patrilateral cousins. For example, in the Hsu
clan, the jingle at the time of my birth was as follows:

> Ching, Yun, Chi, Kwang, T'ien;
> Chia, Ch'uan, Teh, P'ei, Hsien.

Brothers and patrilateral male cousins of my father all shared the same character "Chi," so my given name, and those of my brothers and patrilateral male cousins, all shared the character "Kwang" (which accounts for the "K" in my initials), while males in the generation after me all shared the character "T'ien." This jingle then, took care of several generations of males of the Hsu clan above me and several generations of males in it yet unborn.

The Chinese manner of naming thus exemplifies the quality of continuity and inclusiveness within the patrilineal extended kin group. It is inclusive because all males who are members of the kin group and their spouses are bound together by the surname and all males of the kin group belonging to the same generation are identified by the common element in their personal names. It is continuous because members of a clan keep their common surname forever and the different generations of males are linked by pre-determined and serialized common elements in their personal names.

The Japanese naming practice is less continuous but far more exclusive. We have already noted that a majority of Japanese had no family or clan names before the Tokugawa period. Since then, while an inclusive surname has become the rule, Japanese first names have exhibited no inclusiveness within the kin group. Instead, the Japanese have often assigned one character in common to all males who have succeeded in a given lineage, especially in the *samurai* class. Thus one descent line (probably the main one) of the Lord Ikeda (a *daimyō*, or feudal lord whose domain was in the western part of Honshū) shared the character "Yoshi" so that the first person in the line was "Yoshi Yuki," his eldest son and successor was "Yoshi Nari," his eldest grandson and successor was "Yoshi Taka," etc. But the next descent line began with the name "Tada Tsugu," which was followed by "Tada Shige," his son, "Tada Sada," his grandson, etc.[6] This practice was not limited to feudal lords but was also extended to those of much lesser rank.[7] Both among the descendants of the feudal lords and among commoners this pattern was sometimes interrupted so that the descent line may read:
AB —— AC —— XY —— AE —— , etc.

The Chinese pattern exhibits pure patrilineal continuity and inclusiveness. All those who fit the criteria of the kinship organization are included. For those who fit these criteria the kinship principle operates to unite the past with the present, and the present with the future. It generates a centripetal tendency which encourages persons who are related to remain in the same locality if possible, to return to the group if separated, to think about the kinship group and to react to the wider world in its terms when away from it, and also to maintain a relationship with those who once lived and were members of it.

The Japanese pattern is at once simpler and more complicated. It is more exclusive because it cuts off lateral relatives and lateral ancestors so that the Japanese patrilineal line becomes more narrowly defined than the Chinese one. The simplicity of the Japanese situation is that, for the individual, the household (*ie*) consisting of those who actually live under the same roof is the most important group. Members of the *bunke* have to look up to those of the *honke*, but that is clearly and by design an *external* relationship, and the two units are distinctly separate from each other. Hence, as we shall see in the next sections, children who died in infancy, and unrelated guests who resided and died in the households, tend to figure importantly on the Japanese household ancestral altars; for individuals unrelated by kinship or by marriage may be much closer to the people with whom they reside in the same household than kinsmen who live elsewhere.

Lateral relatives cut off from the main line have to find some place to go. This means that they must join or create groups in which they can establish their lives. However, in the villages the non-inheriting brothers are often not really free to leave and seek their fortunes elsewhere. Instead they are subordinate to the heir and often have to work for him.

The right of one brother to inherit everything and the separation of retired parents from the main house make for exclusiveness. The lack of a common surname between fathers and sons as well as among brothers and their descendants (before the Tokugawa period) signifies discontinuity. These characteristics are also found in the best known grouping lying immediately outside the household, the *dōzoku*. But the picture is actually not so simple, for the *dōzoku* is also distinguished by other features.

[1] Military dictator.

[2] Available evidence indicates that up to about 700 A.D. primogeniture characterized the Japanese rule of inheritance. About that time a new law was promulgated, in imitation of Chinese laws, providing for equal division among the sons in case the father left no will (Aoki 1965:155). Among the *samurai* (warrior) class some sort of division of inheritance among the sons (*bunkatsu sōzoku*) continued throughout the Kamakura (1185-1336) period but the division was not necessarily *equal*. One son (sometimes not the eldest) was appointed heir, usually by the father, and the other sons were duty-bound to serve in the heir's army if ordered to do so; they did not even enjoy full ownership of their portions of the divided property. They were more or less "tenants" of the heir (Sato 1965:186). In the ensuing Namboku-cho period and thereafter, unigeniture became more and more widely practiced (Sato 1965:192). Under the Tokugawa, primogeniture was prescribed by law for all classes, so that the father was obliged to follow it regardless of his own desires. More recent field reports indicate the practice of ultimogeniture in villages of southwestern Japan (southern Kyūshū and elsewhere) where the other sons receive unspecified shares.

Kawashima thinks that the term ultimogeniture is inappropriate here because the practice is generally a result of circumstances rather than of law or custom and is therefore not strictly adhered to. As Kawashima puts it, after the departure of the other sons, "the son who was living with the head of the household at the time of his death succeeds to his position. As boys marry young in farming villages, the youngest son generally is living with the head of the household at the time of his death so that the youngest son becomes the heir. If a son other than the youngest one still is living with the head of the household at the time of the father's death, he becomes an heir and is responsible for his younger brother's living" (Kawashima 1957:71).

Reviewing these and other data I find that though the picture is complicated, the undisputable fact is that some sort of unigeniture seems to have prevailed in most of Japan throughout most of her known history. Since World War II primogeniture has been abolished in Japanese law, but it has not disappeared in practice.

[3] Nakane, based on the studies of S. Oishi on the Tokogawa peasant, mentions that ". . . the customary rule of inheritance normally practiced at this time (about 1713 A.D.) was that of equal division of lands" (Nakane 1967a:64). But I have not seen this alleged custom mentioned in any other publication. Nakane also gives it no place in her entire analysis. One can only conclude that this statement was a mistake or presented a highly aberrant and rare situation.

[4] The *ke* in *bunke* or *honke* is the Chinese pronunciation of *ie*.

[5] In Shikoku such a separate house is called *heya*.

[6] According to an old genealogical book entitled *Genealogical Records of a Group of (related) Villages of Kibi* (dated 1757 A.D.; private copy); this was also the rule followed with few exceptions by the Tokugawa Shogunate throughout the duration of its power.

[7] For example, in Yoshi Ura there are several related lineages which still use the family name Suenaga.

4 •

Clan and *Dōzoku*

The Japanese term *dōzoku* is sometimes translated into English as "clan" or "lineage." It is now generally agreed that this conventional usage is inappropriate (Nakane 1967a:84-5). There are basic differences between the Chinese *tsu* which is truly a clan, and the Japanese *dōzoku* which is not.

The Chinese Tsu

The Chinese clan (*tsu*) includes all males who are descendants of a known male ancestor, and all females who have married into this group. No matter how far they have dispersed geographically, efforts are made to track them down so that they will all be recorded in the same genealogical book of the clan and their dead will all be brought to the same clan temple. In fact, as we noted elsewhere (Hsu 1963:62-63), often two or more clans bearing the same surname thought previously to be unrelated were found later to be linked by a common ancestor. Sometimes this link was established only after stretching the facts. The Chinese describe the linking up of *tsu* as *lien-tsung* and the resulting larger group may theoretically be called *tsung*. Although the latter term may be regarded as being more all-inclusive since it refers to two or more newly associated *tsu*, in fact this distinction is not so important. For our purposes, this larger entity will be referred to as *tsu*, since there tends to be no permanent distinction between a coordinated *tsu* and a normal *tsu*, the members of which were known to be descendants of a certain ancestor in the first place.

Within the total Chinese clan system, the often not so clear distinction between *fang* (branch) and the more definite *wu fu* lineage have also been previously discussed (Hsu 1963:63-65), and need not detain us here. At this time, there are two important points to remember. Firstly, membership and even solidarity of the clan and its subdivisions are not dependent upon the factors of residence or locality. Relationship through birth and marriage along the patrilineal line is the primary criterion for membership in a clan. Adoption is practiced but its incidence is very low and generally confined to persons already related, such as brother's sons or father's brothers' sons. The other point that concerns us here is that, although intra-clan dividing lines exist, the Chinese clan tends to be highly centripetal, so that there are usually continuous and repeated efforts on the part of clan members to locate lost branches in distant places and to reestablish forgotten relationships.

The Japanese Dōzoku

The outstanding fact is that dōzoku membership, in contrast to *tsu* membership, is not confined to those related through kinship or even by marriage. However, Nakane's definition that the Japanese *dōzoku* is a "set of households which recognize their relationship in terms of *honke* and *bunke* and which, on the basis of this relationship, have developed a corporate function as a group" (Nakane 1967a:90-91) does not carry us very far. This definition is safe enough. But it is safe because of its vagueness, for it does not specify more than the fact that the *dōzoku* is a corporate group composed of households which stand in a *honke-bunke* relationship to each other.

Inheritance

The *dōzoku* embodies many more features than the *tsu* does and the roots of the *dōzoku* are found in the Japanese *ie* or household. The latter, too, is very different from its Chinese counterpart *chia* although the English translation of both terms is household. To be sure, the Chinese *chia* may contain servants who sometimes use kinship terms in relation to their employers and the employer's family members. But the terms are never those for members of the nuclear family such as "father," "mother," "son," and "daughter" (as in the Japanese ie), but those for more remote kinsmen such as "uncle," "great uncle," or "niece," and "grandnephew."[1]

In much of Shantung Province and among the Shantung immigrants in Manchuria some tenants addressed their landlords using kinship terms. However, in no case could these tenants and servants and their families participate in any of the ancestral rites and become part of the clan genealogy or temple. They certainly never expected to receive any part of the family inheritance. I cannot be absolutely certain that, in the whole of China, there might not have been one case in which a servant received some small portion of his employer's land, but I do not recall seeing or hearing about any such incidents in the places where I did field work or in the area where I was born and went to school, and in the many provinces through which I have travelled. The possibility of servants inheriting their master's property was not prevalent in China. Had such a case ever occurred it would have certainly been mentioned in the District Histories as an event of note.

Adoption

These features of the Chinese chia are very different from those of the Japanese ie. But now we must go further and examine the Chinese-Japanese differences in adoption. A Chinese would prefer to adopt his brother's son in case he had no heir; his second preference would be a matrilocal marriage for one of his daughters through which the son-in-law would assume his family name. Only in rare circumstances would he and his wife adopt an unrelated person from the outside. In adopting a relation the Chinese would in no case violate the generation principle. In matrilocal marriages the new son-in-law would usually come from a poor family. Such an arrangement was not looked upon with favor especially by the son-in-law and his own family.

The Japanese situation is quite different. A Chinese observer would be surprised to note that a Japanese might adopt his younger brother as his son if the latter were sufficiently younger in age. Embree reports for Suye Mura the example of a 35 year-old head of a household adopting his 15 year-old brother as a son (Embree 1939:83). Such a solution would be inconceivable and intolerable to the Chinese. It would be regarded as a violation of the basic tenets of the kinship system, a criminal offense in fact. In other words, for the Chinese individual his place in the kinship hierarchy has traditionally been of primary importance and unchangeable. Even relatives by marriage were subject to the same regulations, and marriage with a father's brother's widow was considered incestuous by the Chinese (although it was permitted in Japan).

The next contrast is that the adoption of a son-in-law or *mukoyōshi* is much more common in Japan than in China. In fact, this kind of adoption has rarely occurred in China, but it seems to have been more frequent in southwestern China, such as in Yunnan Province. Furthermore, Japanese sons of well known and affluent families may become *mukoyōshi*. Many famous brothers have married in this manner. The prime minister until June, 1972, Mr. Sato, is a *mukoyōshi*. Mr. Kishi, sometime prime minister before Sato, is his brother. One of the Japanese Nobel Prize winners, Mr. Yukawa, is separated by adoption from his brother, Mr. Ogawa, a professor of Chinese at the University of Kyoto. The scholar of Japanese folklore, Mr. Yanagida, who began his career as a government official, was a *mukoyōshi*. His original family name was Matsuoka. The well-known Japanese linguist, Shinmura, was a *mukoyōshi*. His brother, a well-known astronomer, carried the original family name, Sekiguchi. I know of no adopted Chinese who has risen to similar prominence.

Finally, the incorporation of unrelated persons by way of *mukoyōshi* or legalized adoption or ritual adoption into the kinship organization is much more common in Japan than in China. For example, while servants and tenant farmers often used kinship terms as a matter of courtesy in addressing their employers and landlords in parts of north China, and participated in their superiors' social activities to some extent, during weddings, funerals and New Years' celebrations, they never held any *definite* kinship position in any but their own true kinship organizations. In south and central China kinship terms were rarely used by servants. Chinese servants and tenant farmers have never had any ritual obligation to the ancestral spirits of their superiors and they certainly would never have assumed the latters' clan names.

What the Chinese avoid in employer-employee relationships are precisely the common patterns of linkage between Japanese servants and tenant farmers on the one hand and their employers and land-lords on the other (Ariga 1939 and Nagai 1953). Some Japanese scholars maintain that "ritual" or "fictitious" relatives in Japan are not to be confused or equated with either legally "adopted" or blood relatives (Nagai 1953:5). But the undeniable fact is that there is in Japan a closeness of relationship among those who live and work in the same household unknown in China. For one thing, blood relatives who live in separate households are less close to one another than "ritual" relatives who live together. Blood relatives who reside in distant localities tend to sever their relationships altogether. The closeness of those who reside in the same household is also indicated by the assumption on the part of some servants of the master's sur-name, the burying of the dead of true and ritual kin members in the same graveyard, and the worship of the master's ancestral spirits; this has been the case in the Saito dōzoku of Ishigami buraku (village) near the northern end of Honshū (Ariga 1939 and Nagai 1953:18 and 53). These facts transform the ie into a sort of corporation (albeit a kinship corporation) distinct from any Chinese kinship group; the vertical orientation of the traditional Japanese manner of giving first names, as contrasted to the horizontal and vertical emphases of the Chinese, which we noted before, only highlight the same differences.

Five Distinguishing Features

There are, then, it seems to me, five features which distinguish the dōzoku, of which the first and the most basic is the fact that it is a corporation consisting of a parent corporation (honke), with a head, and a number of branch corporations (bunke), each with a head. The membership of a dōzoku is not made up of individuals but of superior and subordinate groups.

By contrast, a Chinese person's membership in his clan is strictly an affiliation based on his individual place in the total hierarchy of the clan: he is an older brother to his younger siblings, an older patrilineal first cousin to all of his father's brothers' children younger than himself, a patrilineal nephew to all of his father's brothers, but a patrilineal grandson only to his father's parents. This individual affiliation extends broadly, according to where the kinship relation-ships can be traced, in the same locality or in far off areas.

Secondly, Chinese *tsu* membership is more specific in criterion but less restrictive territorially than Japanese membership in the *dōzoku*. A Chinese individual cannot join another *tsu* except through matrilocal marriage, a method not held in social approbation, or through a rare legal adoption. There is little room for maneuvering. Kinship is the *tsu*'s principal recruiting mechanism, and the use of this mechanism is practically limited to those who are genuinely related. When a Chinese moves from one locality to another he simply has to ascertain his actual place with reference to his distant kinsmen in his own true kinship hierarchy and reactivate ties that may be dormant, but will never have been completely eradicated.

His Japanese counterpart will find no comparable route by which he can enter into kinship relationships with men and women in other localities even though they may be his true relatives. Because of the custom of frequent incorporation of unrelated persons, the basis for entry into the *ie* and the *dōzoku* is broader than that of mere kinship. But at the same time it is more restrictive territorially. An individual's membership in an *ie* or a *dōzoku* requires residential propinquity, namely his actual presence (and in the case of the *dōzoku*, the actual presence of his *ie*) in the local area, and active economic, ritual, and social relationships (*bunke* are tenants of the *honke,* have been given a certain amount of property by the *honke* or are otherwise economically dependent upon the *honke*). There are only rare exceptions to these rules.

The remaining three features of the *dōzoku* are (1) hierarchy (the *bunke* are clearly subordinate to their *honke* in a ritual, social and economic sense); (2) a particular definition of kinship relationships and the importance of pseudo-kinship relationships; and (3) the notion of obligation in perpetuity.

These five characteristics influence or mutually support each other. They are not of equal importance. Once this is understood, some of the academic confusion about the *dōzoku* may be cleared up. One such confusion concerns the question of kinship relationships in the *dōzoku*. There is no doubt that the core families in most (if not all) *dōzoku* are likely to be related through kinship. The basic ties may be through a son or a daughter, or an adopted child, but they are unmistakably of kinship character in conception and substance. (For an example of this fact see the recent report of Keith Brown on the rural hamlet of Nakayashiki, Iwate Prefecture, 1966:1146-1147.)

However, true kin will not be members of the same *dōzoku* if they live in different localities and if they have no economic relationship with one another. On the contrary, ritual kin who are in fact also servants, tenants, etc., though they have to validate their statuses in the *dōzoku* by work, are its members and fully participate in, and reap the benefits of, its economic, social, and ritual activities.

In spite of such facts, scholars of Japan either stress the rules of descent and succession according to Japanese kinship, considering the economic or other factors as modifying agents or as primary agents which determine the kinship rules. Thus Befu observes that Japanese inheritance practices undergo *many exceptions to the ideal of male primogeniture dictated by practical exigencies* and that the personal kindred is bilateral even in communities with the supposedly patrilineal descent groups (Befu 1962 and 1963; italics mine). More recently, Brown has concluded that "in complex societies there are more *possibilities* for a wide range of phenomenal structures emanating from the same or similar (kinship) ideologies because *there is a greater variation in the social, cultural and ecological environments*" (Brown 1966:1147; italics mine). Nakane used the same argument, though from a different point of view. She observes that "above all, the arrangements involved in this *dōzoku* situation are *the outcome of internal as well as external economic and political factors*," and "the absence or existence of *dōzoku* is closely *related to the given economic conditions*" (Nakane 1967a:86-89; italics mine).

The fallacy of such arguments becomes clear when we examine the Chinese situation. A majority of Chinese farmers used to divide their holdings generation after generation according to the Chinese inheritance rule of equal division among the sons. Most Chinese farms became so fragmented they were smaller than the optimum size (of seven acres) from the point of view of economic efficiency. The Chinese kept dividing against their best economic interests because, to them, the kinship rule of equal inheritance was of supreme importance (Hsu 1943). Then, too, the Chinese have rarely allowed exigencies to influence their custom of patrilineal descent. It certainly cannot be said that China, so vast in size, did not possess "variation in the social, cultural, and ecological environments." Why have descent, inheritance, and succession practices not exhibited any comparable degree of variation in China, even though the Chinese must also have experienced similar "practical exigencies"? If comparable "practical exigencies" lead one people to deviate from their ideal more than another, is it not plausible to suggest that the particular ideal is less important for the former than for the latter?

Our inevitable inference is that, while the Chinese consider their basic kinship arrangements to be primary, the Japanese obviously hold other factors to be of equal or greater importance. In the same light we must scrutinize Nakane's view that "economic conditions" or "political factors" are decisive in the picture. For example, with all her detailed data on land tenure and agricultural practices, Nakane has not shown how the economic factor has led to, or even supports, the custom of *inkyo*. In fact, Nakane herself states that "in some cases the strained household economy may not allow an *inkyo* house to be built until a few years after the successor has married" (Nakane 1967a:12). It is interesting that faced with this kind of fact, Nakane shifts her ground and observes that *inkyo* "is a normal arrangement, and one to which *positive moral value is attached....*" (Nakane 1967a:12; italics mine).[2]

What seems to be of primary importance to the Japanese situation is neither patrilineal or bilateral descent nor even the economic factor, but rather the indefinite continuation of each *ie* as a corporation and each *dōzoku* as an organization of corporations.

The basic mechanism for insuring indefinite continuation of the *ie* as a corporation is unigeniture. Hence, we find the frequent occurrence of *mukoyōshi* and of other forms of adoption of unrelated individuals as heirs when a biological heir is incompetent or absent. Economic or other factors may take over *after* the major premise of unigenitural continuation of the *ie* as a corporation has been satisfied. For example, in any corporation the need for retirement in old age and for one person to serve as executive head is an obvious necessity. Hence, we observe an adherence to the custom of *inkyo* even when it is economically not advantageous.

The basic mechanism for insuring indefinite continuation of the *dōzoku* as a corporation consists of the binding hierarchical relationship between the *honke* and the *bunke* and the notion that they are tied to each other by mutual indebtedness in perpetuity because this debt can never be completely repaid (Nagai 1953:18 & 56). In fact, if the present members of the *bunke* did not do favors for the present members of the *honke*, or vice versa, then the past actions of the father or even the grandfather of the present head of the *honke* or *bunke* would be invoked as reason for this perpetual mutual indebtedness (Nagai 1953:54-5). Hierarchy may be sufficient for binding together *honke* and *bunke*, which are formed by older and younger brothers respectively, but the concept of perpetual indebtedness is more useful for securing the continued cooperation among those not related by blood.

From this point of view, the peculiar kinship terms used in the *dōzoku* makes sense. Previously we noted that some unrelated *bunke* assume the privilege of the *honke's* surname. But a much more general custom in Ishigami, for instance, is the following: the head of the *honke* and his wife are "father" and "mother," the heads of the *bunke* and their wives are respectively "uncles" and "aunts" while the sons of the *honke*, regardless of their age, are addressed by the sons of the *bunke* as "older brothers" exactly as the latter are addressed by the former by their personal names since they are "younger brothers." Although this picture is based on data from Ishigami, I expect future field work to discover similar patterns in other areas.

This usage of kinship terms is a permanent one: all succeeding generations of heads of *honke* and their spouses will be "fathers" and "mothers" and their sons and daughters will be "older brothers" and "older sisters" to all succeeding generations of members of the *bunke* (Ariga 1939 and Nagai 1953:51-53). This can be held to be a form of kinship terminology, but it is of a peculiar kind. It once again clarifies the fact that *dōzoku* membership is not an individual matter, but that the *dōzoku* is a corporation in which the units of membership are subordinate corporations. There is autonomy in each of the member corporations and these are linked together by an expanded web of kinship or pseudo-kinship in which each corporation as a whole is assigned a kinship position and keeps that position through an indefinite number of generations. This expanded web of kinship or pseudo-kinship makes it possible for *bunke's bunke* to be assigned the place of a grand *bunke* (as in grandchild; *mago-bunke* in Ishigami; Nagai 1953:8), followed by members of even lower ranks such as *bekkekaku-nago* (tenant who is treated like *bekke bunke*); *bunke-nago* (tenant who is head of *bunke*); *yashiki-nago* (tenant who rents a house-site); and *sakugo* (a tenant who began as a child cultivator; Nagai 1953:32). "Insofar as terminology is concerned, from the standpoint of the members of the ritual kin households, the head of the main household and those of other true kin branch households all are 'parents' [sic]" (Nagai 1953:52).

We see then that kinship certainly has some importance in the *dōzoku*, but its prominence is greatly modified in consonance with other requirements of the *dōzoku*. Reviewing the evidence thus far, we can say that the Japanese *dōzoku* is a corporation consisting of a strong hierarchy of member-corporations which must reside near each other and be linked to each other by kinship or pseudo-kinship ties.

Previously we noted the higher frequency of adoption in the Japanese *ie* as compared with the Chinese *chia*. Although we do not yet have adequate data, I suspect that the proportion of kin members in the *tsu* is higher than in the *dōzoku*. I believe that future research will bear me out.

What we have in the Japanese *ie* and especially in the *dōzoku* is a degree of *voluntary* association of human beings not found in the Chinese *chia* and *tsu*. Human beings cannot choose their parents, children, uncles, or aunts. But they certainly have greater room for maneuvering when they can adopt adults to whom they are not related into their *ie* and *dōzoku*. In other words, they enjoy more liberalized criteria for recruitment.

This greater maneuverability would seem to find further intensification in a custom reported for Gorohei-Shinden village in Nagano Prefecture in S. Oishi. This custom seems to have been prevalent throughout the Tokugawa period (Nakane 1967a:61-73). In this village there were two classes of people: *Honbyakushō* or titled farmers and *kakaebyakushō* or non-titled farmers. *Honbyakushō* were full members of the village. They controlled important decisions affecting the welfare of all and they alone were eligible to be village officials and to vote for such positions. The *kakaebyakushō* lacked these rights and were their dependents. Some *kakaebyakushō* were branched from main households, but more often kinship ties between them could not be established though quite a few *kakaebyakushō* and the *honbyakushō* to which they were attached belonged to the same temple. Though the *kabu* of *honbyakushō* was attached to the *ie* and handed down to the heir, it could also be purchased so that a *honbyakushō* might become a *kakaebyakushō* and vice versa.

The use of the word *kabu* here is interesting. It means "stump," as the stump of a tree, and signifies the foundation rights of a *honbyakushō*. The modern Japanese term for shares in a corporation is also *kabu*. The corresponding Chinese term for shares in a corporation is *ku*. But there was nothing in a Chinese village that was comparable to the Japanese *honbyakushō-kakaebyakushō* pattern, nor could a household sell its basis of power or prestige.

The sale of *kabu* by a *honbyakushō* was a special development which did not apply to the *dōzoku* in general. For the *honke* in a *dōzoku* could never sell its position in the form of *kabu* to any *bunke*. Nor do we have any information that a particular *kakaebya-kushō* and the *honbyakushō* to which it was attached could exchange their respective places by purchase. But the transferability of the *honbyakushō's kabu* is a significant fact which will be of interest later when we examine Japan's response to the challenge of the West.

At the same time we must not fail to note that, in spite of the greater maneuverability in recruitment in the Japanese system, the strongly hierachical nature of its organizational relationships, both within and between organizations, is intensified when we move from the *ie* to the *dōzoku*. For although membership in either group may begin voluntarily, by adoption devices, the ties as well as the duties and obligations are permanent. The *honke* and its *bunke* cannot alter their relative positions, nor can they change places, exactly as the superior-subordinate relationship between a Chinese father and his sons is irreversible in life and in death. In other words, the Japanese, though they have broadened the basis for recruitment into the *ie* and the *dōzoku*, have nevertheless adhered strongly to the permanency so characteristic of the Chinese kinship system.

---

[1] In a famous Chinese novel, *Chin Ping Mei* (better known to Western readers in its English translation as *The Golden Lotus*) the chief male character, Hsi Men-ch'ing, is addressed regularly by some of his concubines and mistresses as "father." He addresses them individually as "child," especially during the sex act. Some of his boy attendants, especially those who serve from time to time as his passive homosexual partners, address him in the same way. But this is obviously a special kind of usage, and it never extends to other servants.

[2] As for political factors, it is true that all strong governments, all dictatorships, and all utopia creators have tried to reorganize social groups. But Nakane has not revealed how the "arrangements in this *dōzoku* situation" are specifically related to the facts of Japanese political life.

5 ●
The Relationship with Ancestors

Some of my fellow scholars have objected to my use of the term "relationship" in dealing with the subject of ancestors. They asked, "How is it possible to have a relationship with dead people?"

I cannot accept this objection because I think it springs from the Western cultural pattern in which the living are seen as absolutely separate from the dead. To the Chinese, a human relationship, especially a kinship relationship, is one whose ties are not severed by death, but only modified. An infant does not know right from wrong. Thus a Chinese father's relationship with his infant son or daughter is different from that which exists when the latter has reached adolescence or is married. In the Chinese scheme of things, the changes in the parent-child relationship from infancy to adolescence to marriage are in each instance a modification but not a severance. They are not basically different from the modification which takes place at the death of a parent.

The Household Shrine

The Japanese share this same basic feeling of continuity with their ancestors. Their ideas of ancestor worship are not unlike those of the Chinese. But their practice of ancestor worship is quite different.

To begin with, there are two kinds of Japanese household shrines: *kamidana* (shrines for Shintō spirits) and *butsudan* (altars for Bud-

47

dhist deities). These contrast with the prevalent Chinese ones: the altar for the Kitchen God and his wife, and the altar for ancestors. The Kitchen God and his wife are found in all households (C. K. Yang 1961:28); but their function is that of house supervisors for the Supreme Ruler of Heaven. Toward the end of each lunar year they are believed to ascend to heaven to make their annual report on what they have observed. The Japanese *kamidana* on the other hand, usually houses the Supreme Sun Goddess Amaterasu. Sometimes other gods and goddesses are added to the *kamidana* (such as Inari, the fox spirit), by members of the family who have visited their public shrines and brought back their images or representations *(ofuda)*. The Chinese Supreme Ruler of Heaven and the Kitchen God and his wife are administrators quite unrelated to the family where they are worshipped, but Amaterasu is the mythical founder of Japan and ancestress of all the Japanese, including the reigning emperor who is traditionally believed to be her direct descendant.

A much greater contrast between Japan and China is found in their concepts of the ancestral altar. To begin with, while the Chinese ancestral altar in all parts of the country except the southwest, is for ancestors only, the Japanese *butsudan* houses both an image (or occasionally images) of a Buddhist deity and tablets *(ihai)* representing the ancestors. Secondly, while only those males who were married and their wives would qualify for a Chinese ancestral altar, many boys and girls who died in infancy or as children are represented in Japanese *butsudan*. Thirdly, while the Chinese ancestral altar is a place for patrilineally related ancestors and their spouses, the Japanese *butsudan* often houses the wife's parents (even without matrilocal marriage), maternal uncles, and even friends. The most frequently offered reason for the inclusion of the latter classes of persons is that they lived and died in the household. The pattern of inclusion is highly irregular: in some *butsudan*, one ancestor several generations removed is included while those nearer to the living are not; in others, many near ancestors are included but anyone more remote than a few generations back is excluded.

Consequently while the Chinese I know and have worked with had no confusion about who were represented in their own ancestral altars, even heads of Japanese households often fail to identify all the persons represented by the tablets. Some Japanese men and women have responded to my query as to who are honored in the *butsudan* in the negative: "We don't know."

Before I went to Japan, Robert Smith of Cornell University told me that in one *butsudan* he found tablets representing dead persons unrelated and *unknown* to members of the household. After a typhoon which destroyed many homes, members of this household had found some tablets on the beach. Since such tablets must contain, according to Japanese belief, the spirits of the dead, they felt that it was "pitiable that they should be uncared for" and they took the tablets home. I have since confirmed this kind of report in two separate households in Kure and in Ashiya, on the southwestern portion of Honshū. The Chinese, while sharing the same idea as to the association of such tablets with the spirits of the dead, would not take care of them in this way at all. Some Chinese who are bent on accumulating otherworldly merit might collect such stray tablets and burn them in a Buddhist temple, in the same way that they might provide coffins for the bodies of unknown dead, but they would never take any signs or symbols of these non-kin to their own homes. On the other hand, since the Japanese include their infant dead in the *butsudan*, they are more likely than the Chinese to recall the total number of children born in several generations, a fact that may help census takers and population researchers.

Funerals and Graveyards

Among the Chinese, dead parents are buried in exclusive or clan graveyards. The different tombs in a clan graveyard are arranged according to generation and age, befitting the rules of kinship propriety. The Chinese have traditionally referred to their tombs as their *yin tsai* (other-worldly residence), to be distinguished from their *yang tsai* (worldly residence). Thus it was believed that death only changed the conditions of one's existence but not one's kinship relationships. Tombs of ancestors of the Wang clan would remain in a separate group from those of the Li clan. Furthermore, for the well-to-do, the funeral for a dead parent would not take place a few days after death. Instead the corpse, in a sealed coffin, would be kept in the family home for a period of multiples of seven days (7, 21, 35, etc.). Thus a funeral for the parent of an affluent or highly placed Chinese was by custom a protracted affair. This was supposed to indicate a desire on the part of the living to delay the departure of the dead.

In most of Japan, cremation of the dead is the customary procedure and the funeral takes place within a few days of death.[1] Instead of
being interred in family or clan graveyards, the dead in the cities are
buried in the graveyards of the Buddhist temples of which their
families are members. In villages they are likely to be buried in
common village graveyards.[2] All Japanese families were once and
most of them now are *danka* (member families) of local Buddhist
temples of particular sects, such as the Tendai, Jōdo, Jōdo Shinshū,
and other sects. The chief priest of each temple is known to the family
as its family priest. Thus the Okuyama family of Ashiya is a *danka* of
the Shinshū temple in Ashiya and the Takahashi family is a *danka* of a
Zen temple in Akita.

This kind of definite affiliation with a particular temple was
unknown among the Chinese, although it is similar to the situation
found among Western Christians. However, the Christian parallel
cannot be drawn too closely. For one thing, this Japanese affiliation
with a temple is for the family as a whole, and there is no need for
individual conversion or confirmation. In fact, an individual member
cannot alter his family's affiliation. For another, this affiliation is not
simply with the local temple of the sect but also with the *honzan*
("root mountain" or head temple of the sect). A Christian parallel may
be found only in the Church of England or in the Catholic Church,
with some modifications.

When the body is cremated all of the ashes except for the Adam's
apple, which is usually in a charred form, are buried in the graveyard
of the family temple.[3] This concludes the funeral. The Adam's apple,
designated for this purpose as *nodobotoke* (or throat Buddha) is separated from the rest of the ashes and kept in a jar.[4] It is then placed in
the *butsudan* for a certain number of days after which it is brought to
the *honzan* of the particular sect to which the family belongs. At the
honzan temple it will receive the benefit of the priests' scripture
recitation and rest forever among *nodobotokes* of hundreds of other
unrelated dead. The number of days the *nodobotoke* is kept in the
family altar varies. I know of one family in which the *nodobotoke* of
the mother-in-law was kept at home for over a year. The daughter-in-
law, the mistress of the house, told me that she should have brought it
to their *honzan* sooner, but she had loved her mother-in-law so much
and felt so lonely that she did not want to part with it earlier. Some
families make the day of the dispatching of *nodobotoke* to the *honzan*

an occasion of elaborate ritual, while other familes are less ceremonial about it.

Contrasting Patterns of Ancestor Worship

This Japanese pattern of disposal of the dead is paralleled in the other areas connected with ancestral rites. Japanese dead are given a Buddhist name by the officiating family priest. Henceforward it is this name and not the dead person's original name, that will usually appear on the tablet in the *butsudan*, and invariably on the tombstone. When the *butsudan* becomes overcrowded the older ancestral tablets are taken to the family temple. The priest will "remove" the soul from each tablet with a special prayer and then place it in the group of ancestral tablets of each particular family, either in the back of the main Buddha statue or beside it. In many local temples the hall behind the main Buddha statue houses hundreds of ancestral tablets from diverse households.

During the Kamakura Period, the warriors (*bushi* or *samurai*) had their own clan temples. But as the manor system which was their economic support became disorganized, the clan temple became the so-called *dannadera*. The *dannadera* served, and was supported by, plural kin groups including farmers who had formerly been excluded from the clan temples of the *bushi* class. This development corresponded with the transformation of the clan deity (*ujigami*) into the local deity of the village (*ubusunagami* or *chinjugami*) although the latter is still called "*ujigami*" (clan diety; Takeda 1957:150-185). Consequently, it can be said that today, except for the temples of a few aristocratic families who have imitated the Chinese extravagance, there are no clan temples in Japan. The nearest thing to a clan temple is the grand shrine for the imperial family at Ise which is dedicated to the goddess Amaterasu. Because the goddess is considered to be the ancestress of all Japanese, this shrine may be regarded as a "clan" temple for all Japanese.

Again, the Chinese customs are quite different. Chinese dead retain the names they had in life. Ancestors beyond the third or fifth generation are honored in clan temples belonging to a particular kinship group. There is no ancestor or ancestress common to all Chinese. In fact, the clan temple or graveyard of each imperial dynasty was the concern of members of that kinship group alone.

The custom of the clan temple belonging exclusively to a particular kinship group was such an immutable feature of Chinese society that certain Emperors were unable to introduce any changes to it. The founder of the Han dynasty (206 B.C. to 211 A.D.) had his ancestral temple erected in every province of the empire. Six of his successors had their own temples erected in all the provinces during their life times. An elaborate emperor cult was certainly in an embryonic stage (Ho 1968:21-22), but this cult did not last long. From the time of the later Han (25-220 A.D.) onwards, no more temples were built for individual emperors, during their lifetimes or after their deaths. Instead, each dynasty had its own ancestral temple in which all deceased rulers, beginning with the founder, were honored after death. The concept of kinship solidarity was so basic to the Chinese worldview that even the august emperors, who had limitless power over their subjects, could not change it (Hsu:1967). No Chinese emperor in recent centuries has ever thought of asking the people to worship the imperial ancestors any more than citizen Wang would dream of asking citizen Li to honor the Wang ancestors.

We have already noted that while Japanese ancestors share the butsudan with the Buddha, Chinese ancestral spirits were housed in family shrines or clan temples, just as Chinese ancestral tombs were located in particular clan graveyards separated from the burying grounds of other clans. If some members of a household were devotees of the Buddha or other deities, they would house these deities in separate, personal altars or shrines. But in Japan members of a bunke who are unrelated to the honke in kinship have been reported to worship the ancestors of the honke (Nagai 1953:16).

As far as the treatment of deceased ancestors is concerned, the greater kinship solidarity among the Chinese expresses itself in two important ways. On the one hand, even the Chinese emperors had to take care of their own ancestors, being unwilling to share the latter with the people or unable to exact their ritual compliance. On the other hand Chinese devotees of particular gods did not care to combine, or see the need for associating their ancestors with their personal deities, nor did they allow these deities to take precedence over the ancestral spirits.

Further Contrasts

These Japanese-Chinese contrasts in ancestor worship find additional support by the way in which a number of Japanese village communities have claimed to be descendants of the boy emperor Antoku, who perished in the famed Battle of Dannoura in 1185 A.D.; this battle resolved the decades-long conflict between the Taira (Heike) and the Minamoto (Genji) clans in favor of the Genji. In 1961, Sofue and a group of nine students from Meiji University studied the Miyako *buraku* located in Niyodo village, Takaoka district, Kōchi Prefecture in Shikoku. They found a community which shared the following belief:

> After the defeat at the Battle of Dannoura, the remaining forces of the Heike took the young Emperor Antoku and fled. They came to settle in this place and called it the "capital." They built residential quarters here to house his majesty. At that time, the most important attendant of the emperor was a 32 year old man named Yamauchi Jinsuke, who was entirely responsible for protecting the young emperor. The entourage lived here from that time onward. The emperor died at 18 years of age. However, Jinsuke did not die until he was 66 years old, after he had energetically developed the entire area. This Jinsuke was the founding father of the present leading family of this buraku, named "P." At first the "P" family retained its lineage name Yamauchi for 13 generations. At the time of the 14th generation, a Yamauchi Kazutoyo became the Lord of Tosa. Because it was impolite for a commoner to have the same surname as a lord, the descendants of Yamauchi changed theirs to the present "P." Since then the "P" family has continued for 32 generations. But if we count from the founder Jinsuke the line has continued for 45 generations. (Sofue 1962:91).

The Miyako *buraku* contains the Antoku shrine, the shrine of Antoku's wet nurse, Jinsuke's tomb, the spot where Antoku's treasure (a sword, a spear, a mirror) were once secretly buried, a shrine where Antoku turned his flute into a bamboo tree,[5] the palace where Emperor Antoku lived, and the residence of Antoku's wet nurse, etc. The emperor's "treasures" are now kept in a room in the "P" household into which no one is admitted (Sofue 1962:93-96).

According to Sofue there are at least six other communities not far from this *buraku* in Shikoku which also claim similar connections to the unfortunate emperor.

In China there were villages which claimed some connection to certain emperors, notably Emperor Kuang Wu (25-57 A.D.), of the later Han dynasty and Emperor Ta'i Tsu (1368-1398 A.D.), founder of the Ming dynasty. The association was usually a nebulous one. For example, in Chao Yang district, Hupei province, there is a Pao En Temple allegedly built by Liu Hsiu (Emperor Kuang Wu's name). Once when Liu Hsiu was a struggling leader fighting for his empire, he was cornered by pursuing enemies. As a last resort he hid in the hollowed inside of the main idol of the nearest temple. When the pursuers arrived they found nothing but an old temple, its entrance covered by spiders' webs. This gave his pursuers the impression that no one could possibly have entered the temple recently, so they left and Liu Hsiu escaped death. After Liu became emperor, he rebuilt the temple and named it Pao En, which means repayment of kindness (to the spiders which spun the webs to save him). According to the local legend mosquitos were never found in this temple (Chu 1967:53).

Other legends found in other parts of China concerning Liu are similar to this one. There was even one village named Huang Ts'un (Imperial Village), located in the modern Chao Yang district of Hupei province which was allegedly Liu Hsiu's birthplace. The town nearby had a Ch'eng Huang temple (temple of the district or prefecture governing god), reputed to be the Head Ch'eng Huang temple of all China. It is also reported that the town's inhabitants were exempt from real estate taxes throughout dynastic times (Chu 1967:54). But even there no member of the village claimed to be the descendant of the emperor or any of his aides.

Contrasting Patterns of Solidarity

Thus while the Chinese link with personal ancestors was so strong that even the emperors had to abandon their attempt to make the people worship the imperial forbears, the Japanese desire for a closer association with noted historical persons was so strong that even a defeated emperor became the object of perpetual communal adoration.

Diagrams 2 and 3 may help us to gain a clearer picture of the respective relationships of the Chinese to his ancestors and the Japanese to his ancestors.

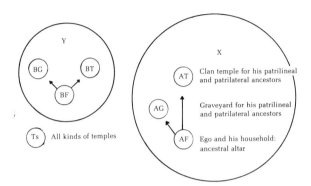

DIAGRAM 2:   Chinese Pattern of Relating the Dead

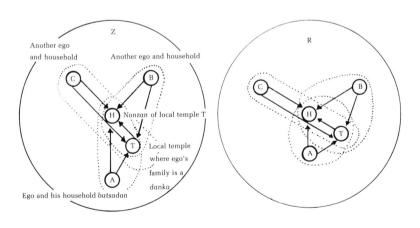

DIAGRAM 3:   Japanese Pattern of Relating the Dead

In the Chinese pattern (Diagram 2), the relationship between Ego and his ancestors in the household ancestral altar (AF), his ancestors buried in the family or clan graveyard (AG), and his ancestors honored in the clan temple (AT) is a straightforward one. Within the big circle (X) are found only those who were born or married into the family. There are other similar circles (such as Y) which are unrelated to each other and to X. Various temples (Ts) which house different gods are considered beneficial and may be visited from time to time. However, those who frequent such temples are not bound by any ties to their departed ancestors to do so.

In the Japanese pattern (Diagram 3) the relationship between Ego and his ancestors in the household *butsudan* (A), his ancestors' local temple of which Ego's family is a *danka* (T), and his ancestors in the *honzan* (H) is more complex. To begin with, the ancestral spirits have already been removed from the original kinship sphere since they are given new Buddhist names. Secondly, ancestral tablets share offerings with the Buddha in the household *butsudan*, and finally, ancestral remains share resting places with many unrelated souls under the protection of a Buddha who is unrelated to any of them in kinship.

Precisely because of this diluted relationship with his own ancestral spirits through wider organizations representing the all embracing supernatural, the Japanese individual and his household have a more specific and automatic non-kinship basis for linking themselves with other individuals and households than their Chinese counterpart (resulting in Z or R in Diagram 3, instead of X or Y in Diagram 2).

In this context, we can understand why the Chinese believed that their ancestors never would do them harm (such as causing illness or misfortune because of neglect), for the tie between the living and the dead was a close and closed one, a mere extension of the relationship that had existed when the family members were still alive. The Japanese, on the other hand, do believe that their ancestors can cause misfortune, sometimes for unexplained reasons (Yoshida 1967), for the tie between the living and the dead is a much looser one.

[1] Traditionally cremation was uncommon in rural areas. But cremation has become increasingly popular even there.

[2] In one year of residence in Japan I found only one Japanese family living in a suburb of Tokyo which even claimed to have a dōzoku graveyard. If the graveyard of Saito dōzoku as reported by Ariga was not unique (Ariga 1939:312; Nagal 1953:53), then there must be similar graveyards belonging to other distinguished and once powerful honke with their satellites of bunke. However, there is little doubt that the pattern described here holds true for a majority of the Japanese people. This aspect of Japanese burial customs is similar to that found in the West before the proliferation of public cemeteries having no connection with churches.

[3] Household members are buried near each other insofar as this is possible. But bodies of honke and bunke members are usually separated.

[4] I think that this custom is based on the Hindu belief that sound expresses Ultimate Reality or Atma, since all finite phenomena in the world have names. The Hindu represents all sound by the syllable sign AUM, which contains the first and last sounds possible. The larynx is the individual's instrument for making all sounds. There is probably an archetypal relation to the Judaeo-Christian idea: "In the beginning there was the word . . . ."

[5] Emperor Antoku "stuck his flute to the ground, drew a circle around it, and ordered it to grow into a bamboo tree within that circle. Even today the bamboo leaves thrive only within the circle, not stretching outside of it. The shrine is dedicated to the 'Bamboo Leaf Great Bright God' " (Sofue 1962:95).

6 ●

Iemoto

Our basic assumption is that human beings must live in association with one another in some form of human grouping. Within that general framework our thesis revolves around the following points: (a) Members of any society begin life in some form of kinship group. (b) They either continue their membership in that group for life or they have to seek entrance to or form some other kinds of secondary groups. (c) The nature of the secondary groups to which they seek entrance or which they form, and their behavior as members of these groups, tend to be strongly influenced, if not determined, by the content of the kinship groups in which they were nurtured.

With this framework in mind I examined in the book *Clan, Caste and Club* (Hsu 1963), the kinship system of Hindu India, in contrast to that of China on the one hand and of the United States on the other. The attributes of the Chinese kinship system, especially continuity and inclusiveness, kept the Chinese individual tied to a basic kinship mooring so that the most characteristic Chinese secondary grouping was *tsu* or clan. The attributes of the United States' kinship system, especially discontinuity and exclusiveness, compel the American individual to break away from his kinship and seek or form extra kinship alliances in the form of free associations or clubs, where he and his fellow members are equal and where voluntary entry and membership are the rule. In Hindu India, the attributes of diffuseness and unilateral dependence are commensurate with caste. Caste is an artificial barrier that suppresses individual initiative and cuts through kinship but makes a larger social order possible. In addition, the conflict between discontinuity and inclusiveness gives the Hindu caste system its apparent dynamism (through constant caste raising claims and activities) but also its fundamental lack of change in the long run (all caste raising efforts solidify and "protestant" groups simply become new castes in the same rigid caste framework).

In each case, the basic ideal institutionalized in the larger culture fortifies the organizational pattern of the society. Mutual dependence propels the Chinese individual to seek public ways of displaying his ties with his kinship group and he is much concerned about maintaining the honor of his ancestors. Individualism goads the American individual to go into business on his own and to build a psychological wall around himself, so that he can exhibit to his fellow men his self-reliance, his personal success and his ability to keep his options open at all times. The ideal of Atma encourages the Hindu to grant special importance to the world of the gods, so that he believes he must observe the caste rules to ensure a better place for himself in the ultimate scheme of all existence.

Thus, the secondary groupings of the societies concerned closely dovetail their respective kinship systems. The Chinese secondary grouping, the clan, is founded on the kinship principle of human organization, since it is a direct extension of the basic unit in which all human beings begin their lives. The American secondary grouping, the club, is built on the contract principle, since effective membership in it requires disengagement from one's kinship affiliation, since its members are equal, and since entry and its continuance are voluntary. Inequalities, if they exist, are seen as temporary and open to change through individual efforts. The Hindu caste begins with the kinship principle, since one is born into his caste or subcaste. But a Hindu's caste affiliation, which is larger than his kinship group, determines his position in society. Furthermore, a Hindu's future, including his life after death, has far more to do with his caste-linked activities than with his kinship-linked activities. The principle of hierarchy runs through the entire Hindu caste system in all its ramifications. In its most extreme form it insists that all hierarchical differences are inborn and changeable only through reincarnation.

Japan's kinship system is, as we have explained in the preceding chapters, fundamentally similar to its Chinese counterpart. In both, the father-son dyad[1] and its continuation is considered primary. Starting with this central focus, both systems accord filial piety and parental authority honored places.

But the Japanese system is also characterized by unigeniture and a markedly hierarchical relationship between the heir and his brothers. These features change the impact of the Japanese kinship system in two ways. First of all, the Japanese non-heir sons have no claim on the ancestral estate and no legal or social or religious grounds for remaining in the ancestral home. If they received anything or if they remain in the ancestral home it is usually at the insistence of the father or the heir. In reality, the heir might tolerate their presence and even find them useful. Previously, we noted how the younger sons among the *samurai* class had to submit to the heir even in Kamakura times. As a matter of fact, research has revealed that in some parts of Japan younger sons were forced by custom to remain in the eldest brother's household as unmarried workers. However, younger sons would no doubt feel the psychological need *much more* than Chinese sons to seek their fame or fortune elsewhere. If we assume, as we must, that non-heirs outnumbered heirs, then a majority of Japanese males would act under this compulsion.

This is why adoption of non-kinship members and *mukōyoshi*, the custom whereby a man goes to live in his wife's household and assumes the family name of her father, are more prevalent in Japan than in China. This is why adoption of younger brothers as sons in violation of generation principle is possible in Japan and never practiced in China. This is why, in Japan but not in China, ancestral spirits can share household altars with the Lord Buddha and the souls of non-patrilineal relatives and of non-relatives can enter the ancestral shrine. This is why Japanese ancestral remains are buried or grouped with those of strangers. This is why the Japanese have *dōzoku* but not the Chinese clan.

The second way in which Chinese and Japanese differ is to be found in their respective attitudes toward authority. In line with and probably as a result of unigeniture, the social distance between the inheriting son and his brothers under the Japanese system became much greater than the corresponding distance between the eldest son and his brothers under the Chinese system. Hierarchy, already important in the Chinese father-son dominated kinship system with its emphasis on authority, became more pronounced in Japan. In China, the hierarchical relationship between a father and his sons was to a certain extent balanced by the greater equality of inheritance and position among brothers. In Japan, the hierarchical relationship between the father and his sons was accentuated by the inequality of inheritance and of position among brothers.

For a majority of Japanese the secondary group away from the households of their origin is primary, in contrast to the Chinese, for whom kinship affiliation is primary (Levy 1953:182-184). However, in contrast to the Western individual's urge for affiliation in non-kinship groupings, the desire of the Japanese for such non-kinship affiliation involves no *rejection* of kinship either as an ideology or in practice. This is because the institutionalized ideal of Japanese culture is mutual dependence but not individualism. What the Japanese does is to carry his kinship structure, and especially its content, into his secondary grouping. Therefore the manifestation of the Japanese need for secondary group affiliation is not found in clubs where members are equal and free to join or depart, but in something uniquely Japanese namely, *iemoto*.

The principle of solidarity on which *iemoto* is built is what may be called kin-tract.[2] By this term I refer to a fixed and unalterable hierarchical arrangement voluntarily entered into among a group of human beings who follow a common code of behavior under a common ideology for a set of common objectives. It contains elements of what Nakane (1967b:31-37) terms *ba*. It is partly based on the kinship model so that, once fixed, the hierarchical relationships tend to be permanent, and partly based on the contract model, since the decision for entering, and occasionally for quitting a particular grouping rests with the individual.

Characteristics of Iemoto

The number and variety of *iemoto* in Japan is large. There are not only the well-known schools of flower arrangement, tea ceremony, judō, painting, and calligraphy, but there are also schools of dancing, Kabuki, Nō drama, archery, horsemanship, singing, cloth-designing, *koto* playing, miniature gardening, cooking, the art of manners, incense burning and, of course, the groups of *samurai* who were not called *iemoto* but who nevertheless were organized on the same principle. The famous case of the 47 Ronin dramatized in song and on stage (*Chusin Gura*) was one such group. The ultra-imperialistic Black Dragon Society, well-known in pre-World War II militaristic Japan, is another example. There are even modern Japanese painters who are known as members of (for example) the "Cezanne School," and mathematicians who band together into a "Wasan" School (or school of mathematics in the Japanese style).

According to Kawashima (1957:322-369) there were more than 64 different *iemoto* in the field of Japanese dancing alone in 1952. Kawashima explained the *iemoto* system in the arts as being characterized by the following four major structural features:[3]

1) *The Master-Disciple Relationship.* Any change in the interpretation of the content of the arts by the disciple is forbidden. Analysis and organization of the basic technique and the style are determined and controlled by the master. The central core of teaching is *haragei* (literally, abdomen technique) through which the disciple learns not by receiving explicit instructions but by unconscious imitation of the master. The instruction is often secretive and frequently given orally so that the position of the master retains its superiority and mystery.

The establishment of the master-disciple relationship is accomplished in two stages. The first stage occurs when the disciple assumes the position of an apprentice but is not yet a member of the pseudo-family relationship under the *iemoto* system. The second stage is reached when the disciple has attained a certain degree of proficiency and becomes accredited. In various schools of dancing there is a test taken between the first and second stages.[4]

Accreditation means that the disciple has been given the prestige of the school with which to operate in Japanese society at large. In the Hanayagi School of dancing, for example, each disciple is given a new personal name as his "personal name in the arts" and the school's name as his "family name in the arts." There is an assumption of "blood relationship" in the arts. Often the disciple's new "personal name in the arts" shares one character in common with the master's "personal name in the arts," in the same way that, as we saw before, the name of an eldest son-heir in the real kinship structure shares one character in common with that of his father. Thus in the Hanayagi School of dancing "Hanayagi Sumi" would be the "direct disciple of Hanayagi Suho," while "Hanayagi Rokumi" is the "direct disciple of Hanayagi Rokuju," etc. The accreditation ceremony involves considerable fanfare during which the disciple receives from his master the school's emblem on a cup and fan and a seal of his full "name in the arts." After the ceremony, the disciple is qualified as a master and this accreditation enables him to earn a living and to enjoy his social position, just like a Ph.D. in the modern scholarly world.

Accreditation involves the following duties and obligations: (a) The master will give his disciple professional protection and advertise him professionally. (b) The disciple must fulfill his duty of faithful service to his master. This is a highly personal relationship. He cannot change masters. "A faithful minister does not serve two emperors." He must faithfully reproduce the style of his master's art. The disciple must offer his master suitable monetary gifts on all important personal or ritual occasions.

The master's obligation to promote the disciple professionally and the disciple's obligation to serve the master faithfully are mutual. This "return value relationship" *(taika kankei)* [5] is a very real relationship and cannot be dissolved. These mutual obligations, like the obligation between fathers and sons, are not quantifiable and there are therefore no limits, though the master will not, of course, make extra-legal demands on the disciples.

2) An Interlinking Hierarchy. The *iemoto* organization is strictly a hierarchical one. Various disciples are interlinked with other disciples through their master, and the masters are linked to each other by way of older masters. In this manner an enormous organization is built up.

Unlike the pyramid of medieval feudalism, which began with the lowest rung of working farmers and built up to the level of the nobility, the establishment of the *iemoto* system begins at the top, with the *"mei jin"* [6] who is the father figure. The function of the *iemoto* system is to expand the "blood relationship" of the head of the school through incorporation of more and more disciples on different levels strictly on the basis of the master-disciple model. The highest *mei jin* has what Max Weber would call "Erbcharisma." The *mei jin* transmits this to the younger generations of masters by what Weber would designate as esotericism.

Each *iemoto* corporate group has a territory which is maintained and expanded through the cooperative efforts of all the members. The Japanese use the term *habatsu* to describe such a group. *Habatsu* means something like "powerful school." (The word *batsu* is the same one applied by the Chinese and Japanese to groups of Chinese militarists during the period between 1912 and 1931 when China was kept in constant turmoil by a number of autonomous militarists. But the Chinese militarists never formed groups comparable to the Japanese *habatsu*.) Members of the *habatsu* must guard the secret of their style from the outside world and never teach an outsider. A subgroup within the school can voluntarily give some of its territory to another subgroup within the school but not to outsiders. Inside the organization, any change in its hierarchical arrangement is forbidden (for example, a master cannot exchange positions with his disciple). The system prevents competition and limits the extent of operation for each master. For example, the bylaws of one of the schools of dancing say, "when an accredited disciple is open for business, other disciples of the school cannot open for business within a radius of 3 *chō* (blocks)."

There are many concrete and interesting examples illustrating how the territorial control of the *iemoto* system works. In 1950, an American ballerina studied under a Japanese dancing master A. Later on this American went to master B of the same school, in the belief that she could freely choose from different masters the artistic techniques that she desired. From the point of view of her Japanese masters, this was both shocking and immoral. So master A talked to master C (a third party) and asked him to help find a solution to this situation, but C could not give any advice. In the meantime, master B had refused to instruct the American ballerina becouse he did not want to disturb "the spirit of harmony" of the school. So master C asked the grand *Iemoto* (who is master of A, B and C) to settle the matter. The grand *Iemoto* asked the ballerina to become a temporary disciple of master C. In doing so the grand *Iemoto* designated C to be his temporary representative whose acceptance of the ballerina would cool the tension which deveoloped. This also preserved "the spirit of harmony" in the *iemoto*. And the matter was settled by the ballerina's eventual return to A. In other words, it was improper for the disciple to change a master herself, but it was perfectly acceptable for her to go to another master if her original master asked her to do this.

Another function of the *habatsu* is mutual aid. When a disciple is having a rehearsal or giving a public performance, it is the duty of other members of the *iemoto* to come and help in the performance, to assist as one of the performers for example, or to contribute to the expense. Members who are situated on levels of the hierarchy higher than the chief performer assist in the performance. Those who are situated on lower levels of the hierarchy sell tickets and offer congratulatory gifts, usually in the form of money.

Finally, within each *habatsu*, each accredited disciple's position is related in a specific way to the other disciples as Diagram 4, according to Kawashima, shows.

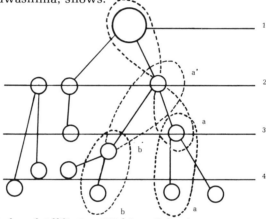

DIAGRAM 4:   Order of Affiliation Within a School

The affiliation is not only generational but also lineal. That is to say, 4a is a disciple of 3a, and 4b is a disciple of 3b, while 3a and 3b are disciples of 2a, etc. The organization is like an army. Each group commander has under him several divisional commanders, each of whom in turn commands several regiment commanders, who in turn have under them several battalion commanders, who then in their turn command several company commanders, have under them several platoon commanders, and each of them in turn command several section leaders. Although there is no master-disciple relationship between the disciples of early generations of masters and present generations of masters, the latter are definitely successors of the early masters' positions. The highest master has a right to command and each member of the heirarchy has a personal rank exactly as in the military with its full generals, lieutenant generals, major generals . . . privates first class, privates second class,[7] etc. This organizational hierarchy is based upon three elements which stand in the following order of importance: (a) "blood relationship", (b) the year of accreditation, and (c) technical achievement. There is a tendency for disciples who have demonstrated exceptional skill to be given higher "face" positions regardless of their age positions.

3) *The Supreme Authority of the Iemoto.* The third structural principle is the supreme authority exercised by the master of the entire school. Such a person is called, in Japanese, the Iemoto[8] (the same word which refers to the system). He has the right to control the style,[9] that is, to preserve the style of his school, to maintain a standard of excellence in an adjustment of territory (some masters in the school may be judged by the Iemoto to have too large a territory and thus the Iemoto can decide that some of his territory be conceded to another master), and the Iemoto has the right to ostracize any member for misbehavior.

The Iemoto receives part of the disciples' income as an accreditation fee and on various other occasions as specified earlier. When the Iemoto builds a new house, he may request offers of money from the disciples. The Iemoto has the right to sell a special uniform and belt displaying the school's emblem to the disciples. The disciples are under *giri* (obligation) to buy it.

The Iemoto has the right to bequeath his position to a blood successor. (The only exception to this rule is found in the Wakayagi School of dancing in which the successor to the Iemoto is elected.) The successor is usually a grown son highly proficient in the art, but even if he is young and lacks the technical qualifications, his position as Iemoto is not jeopardized. When there is no male heir, matrilocal marriage for one of the Iemoto's daughters and succession to the position of Iemoto by the son-in-law is the rule.[10]

The position of the Iemoto involves a vested interest which is called *kabu*. If there is no blood successor the *kabu* may pass to the Iemoto's widow; in the absence of a widow, the right goes to the most powerful supporter of the Iemoto. This *kabu* can be transferred by negotiation to non-blood relatives. When the *kabu* is transferred to someone else because of the absence of an heir, it is up to the new possessor of the *kabu* to assume the duty of worshipping the ancestors of the original owner as well as to take over his genealogy.

4) *The Iemoto System as a Fictional Family System.* The last structural principle is that the *iemoto* is a fictional family system. The
masters consider themselves heads of families in which the various
disciples are children. The Iemoto Ichikawa, of the famous Young
Girl's Kabuki group in Hamamatsu, told a newspaper reporter during
a public performance: "At present I have 17 daughters and I am very
happy. In the coming five or six years, when they all get married, I will
have to give each of them a chest of drawers at least. It is indeed a lot of
trouble."[11]

The *iemoto* system in Japan is not only confined to the arts and
other legitimate professions. Professional gamblers, thugs, day laborers, unskilled laborers, etc., are also organized in the same way. The
disciples receive names from the masters. They talk about "schools."
The individuals in the same school are called "uchi no mono" or
"members of the household." The gangsters even call each other
"miuchi," a term used to denote kinsmen. They also use the term
ichmon no han'ei (the prosperity of one family) just as in the Kabuki
schools. On the anniversaries of the deaths of the *iemoto's* ancestors,
they generally all go to worship at their tombs. Members of the group
are even obliged to wear uniforms with the "school" emblems. They
also are responsible for holding and attending formal meetings just as
in the legitimate *iemoto.*

Such is the nature of the Japanese *iemoto.* What Kawashima says
of the dancing *iemoto* applies equally well to other kinds of *iemoto.*
For example, some of the most famous schools of the art of *ikebana*
(flower-arranging) are the Sōgetsu School based in Tokyo, the Ohara
School, based in Okamoto, and the Ikenobō, based in Kyoto. Each
claims to have over one million members and hundreds of chapters in
Japan and some chapters abroad. The use of the term "chapter" is
modern and the holding of all-school conventions in a big hotel is also
a recent innovation. But the spirit in these schools is traditionally
Japanese. The Ohara School, for example, holds its annual convention with representatives from all the chapters in a big hotel in Osaka.
Mr. Ohara has no son and his eldest daughter, a graduate of Ohio
Wesleyan University, assists her father in his affairs. According to
her, the major function of the convention is to show the chapter
representatives what the artistic trends for the coming year will be. I
asked her how the trends were established. She said, "My father sets
them."[12]

Iemoto-like Organizations

Previously we noted that, although the principles of kinship, hierarchy and contract are characteristic of the clan, caste and club, they are by no means confined to just these spheres. In other words, the Chinese individual is influenced not only by his family and clan, but tends to carry over the essentials of his kinship relationships when he interacts with outsiders. He will be attracted by pseudo-kinship ties. He will respect age and seniority and attribute to them superior judgment and wisdom. The American is a greater joiner of clubs than the Chinese and the Hindu, and he tends to relate to his parents and children or his foreman and subordinates with informality as though they were his equals and as though their interpersonal bonds were voluntary and changeable. The Hindu individual tends to view all relationships as unequal, both in and out of castes.

In this light it becomes clear that, although the preponderant form of social grouping in Japan is the *iemoto* governed by the kintract principle, there are diverse *iemoto*-like groupings which do not bear that name but which nevertheless illustrate the kin-tract principle. There are *iemotos* which are maintained only by one Iemoto (master) and a few disciples. There is the case, for example, of a man in a small village in Okayama prefecture, who in his leisure time, teaches a style of *judō* handed down from his ancestors. He and his pupils are called an *iemoto*. But instead of charging tuition he takes care of all expenses incurred in the *iemoto* activities (Teijo Ito 1968).

We are quite safe in stating that nearly all Japanese secondary groups partake of the essential characteristics of the *iemoto*. For example, the Japanese are far more serious than the Chinese in their religious affiliations. This seriousness is indicated by a variety of features. For one thing, the Japanese hold specific memberships in their temples and shrines while the Chinese merely worship or visit temples wherever they please. For another, the Japanese believers are far more fanatical and sectarian than the Chinese; this fanaticism is based on a personal devotion to the founders of the sects.

We shall discuss religion more extensively in a later chapter. It is only necessary to state here that *iemoto* characteristics are to be found in all aspects of Japanese society, in religion, in business, in schools and universities, in workshops and offices. I realize that by lumping together groups specifically known in Japan as *iemoto* and others not so designated, I am exposing myself to the criticism of improper use of the term *iemoto*. But my procedure is a usual one in science. For years, anthropologists have spoken of family and marriage in different societies. It was only recently that we were forced by our need for greater precision into admitting that the Iroquois family or marriage is not the same as its counterpart among the Eskimo, and that the Chinese family or marriage is not the same as its counterpart among the Trobriand Islanders. However, although we now have terms such as "nuclear family" and "matricentric family," etc., for differentiating the various kinds of basic human groupings (some anthropologists think we ought to dispense with the term "family" altogether), and terms such as "patrilocal marriage" and "neolocal marriage," etc., for differentiating diverse kinds of mating, we still have no terms to help us distinguish marital bonds that are more brittle from those that are less so. These are examples of the movement from the general to the specific in terminology. The terms "money" (are cowrie shells money?) and "father" (when applied to all father's brothers) have experienced the same scrutinization.

On the other hand, there is no paucity of examples of terminological movement in the opposite direction. "Frigidaire," "Victrola," "Kleenex," and "Coke" each began as a trade name respectively for a particular brand of refrigerator, phonograph, cleaning tissue, and soft drink. They have now become the terms commonly used for the goods in general. Similarly, the terms "tabu" and "mana," which came from Polynesia, and "potlatch," which is native to the Kwakiutl and Haida in the northwest United States, have become widely used terms describing general classes of phenomena. There is no scientifically valid reason for not using the Japanese term *iemoto* to designate a certain form of human grouping provided that we clearly delineate its intrinsic characteristics.

Contrast with China

The question may be asked, is the *iemoto* as an organization a relatively recent phenomenon in Japanese history? According to Japanese authorities, most of the *iemoto* in their present form began in the Tokugawa period. If the *iemoto* did not exist earlier than 300 years ago, how can we think of it as the most important form of secondary grouping in Japanese society?

My answer to this question is thus: to begin with, similar relationships must have long predated formally-established iemoto. How else can we explain the widespread occurrence of the former? Secondly, if the roots of the iemoto system were not deep, it would hardly have survived Japan's modernization so well. As a matter of fact, instead of waning, the iemoto as an institution has prospered and proliferated in recent years. However, the third and most important aspect of my answer to this question can be found when we compare the abundance of iemoto groups in Japan with their total absence in China.

In traditional China, the teacher-disciple or master-apprentice relationship was an important one. Confucius reputedly had about 3000 disciples during his lifetime and, of course, he had numerous followers in the literati class in the subsequent two millenia. Other learned masters also had large or small groups of disciples either during their lifetimes or later, although the size of their followings never matched that of Confucius.

There are famous Chinese calligraphers such as Wang Hsi-chih of the Eastern Chin dynasty (A.D. 317-420) and Yen Chen-ch'ing of the T'an dynasty (A.D. 681-907) who had followers in all ages. Calligraphy has traditionally been valued in China as much as painting, and good calligraphic works adorn many Chinese homes alongside paintings. Some Chinese calligraphers are known to practice only the Wang style or the Yen style.

Of course Chinese painters are also sometimes known by their "schools." There were Chinese painters who painted after the famous master Wu Tao-tsu of the Five Dynasties (A.D. 907-960). Even in the twentieth century there are well-known painters who bill themselves as disciples of greater masters. David Kwok, now living in New York, is known to be a disciple of the old master still residing in mainland China, Ch'i Pai-shih. In fact, inscriptions or the signature of his old master expressing approval are to be found on many of David Kwok's well-known earlier works. Mr. Ch'i usually signs himself as "Ninety years old Pai-shih."

However, there were no iemoto-like organizations among the followers of Confucius, the sage, or Wang, the calligrapher, or Wu, the painter. The followers of each of these men could be termed a "school" but these schools do not compare in structure or in complexity with the Japanese *iemoto*. There were never patriarchs or central councils or initiation ceremonies in any Chinese "school."

In traditional China, a Confucian tablet was placed near the main entrance of every schoolroom and the students would pay homage to it when entering and leaving. The teacher-pupil relationship was more important among the literati class than among other sectors of the population, and it was emphasized as one of the five cardinal relationships. But teachers and their pupils did not form any kind of long-lasting organization. The relationship between a teacher and a pupil was individual: Mr. Wang acknowledged Mr. Lee as his teacher, and Mr. Lee might have several hundred pupils scattered in different parts of the country, in different stations of life. Mr. Wang might later have many pupils of his own. But there was no continuing formal relationship between Mr. Lee and his pupils and especially Mr. Lee and his pupils' pupils.

In fields of craftsmanship such as porcelain-making or wood-carving, the relationship was even more casual. The average Chinese craft shop usually had one master and a couple of journeymen and some apprentices who were signed up for a little over three years, the total period of apprenticeship. During most of those three years, the apprentices worked like servants and could only learn the trade on the sly, after they had done all the chores (a condition not unknown among disciples in some Japanese *iemotos*). At the end of the apprenticeship period, the young man might or might not find a job in his master's shop. If he left it the relationship might continue in some fashion but it was not of great and long-lasting importance to the master or his one-time apprentice. One can speak of craftsman "schools" even less than one can speak of "schools" of scholarship or painting in China. Those who were practicing a craft and had completed their apprenticeship were often organized into guilds. There were also merchant guilds, such as those of the cloth dealers or silk traders. But these were all local affairs so that there would be a blacksmiths' guild of, say, Naperville, Illinois, or a rice-sellers' union of Carmel, New York. There were no national or even provincial organizations.

Some craftsmen did practice a kind of craft "ancestor" worship. Thus an altar dedicated to General Chang Fei of the Three Kingdoms (A.D. 221-265) would be found in a butchers' guild, one to Fan Li (also known honorifically as T'ao Chu Kung) in a traders' guild, one to Lu

Pan in a carpenters' guild, one to Hwa Tuo in a guild of the practitioners of Chinese medicine, one to the Emperor Ming Huang of the T'ang
dynasty in an actors' guild as well as backstage in an opera house, and
one to the famous T'ang poet Li Po in a wine-sellers' guild. But the
objects of worship were not in any instance the genetic or adopted
"ancestors" of the present practitioners, nor were they the inventors
of the particular crafts. Some of them did not even have anything to do
with teaching the craft. Chang Fei was a successful general who had
merely worked as a butcher before he commanded armies. His explo-
sive temper was feared by all and was the cause of his eventual
assassination. His exploits were legion and provided popular themes
for Chinese operas and novels. The Emperor Ming Huang is best
known for his romantic attachment to his favorite concubine, Yang
Kuei Fei, for whose amusement he ordered many theatrical perform-
ances in his court, thus encouraging the art. The poet Li Po was
famous for his drinking bouts and eccentric behavior. He is known
popularly in China as an Angel of Wine (chiu hsien). Fan Li was a
millionaire businessman in his own right before he became the prime
minister of Ch'i, one of the warring states in the Spring and Autumn
period (ca. 700-500 B.C.). Only Lu Pan (a contemporary of Confucius)
and Hwa Tuo were true professional practitioners of the crafts that
honor them (carpentry and medicine respectively); they remained
masters of their crafts to the very ends of their careers. But the modern
Chinese practitioners do not claim to have inherited their styles, their
secrets, or even some element of their names.

During certain periods of Chinese history such as the Tsin, Sung,
and Ming dynasties, some scholars assembled to discuss various
national affairs. During the Tsin dynasty (A.D. 265-420), seven scholars who did this were known as the "Seven Sages of the Bamboo
Grove" because their meetings were held in a bamboo grove. But the
subject matter they discussed was described by others as "high and
empty," and they had no disciples. During part of the Sung dynasty
(A.D. 960-1280) scholar-officials were divided according to those
who supported the reformer, Wang An-Shih, and those who were
opposed to him. In the Ming dynasty (A.D. 1368-1644), a group of
scholars was known as the Tung Lin Tang, or Eastern Forest Party.
They were involved in actual government affairs and at one time
suffered from imperial persecution. Such developments were rare,
and each group lasted only a short period of time. There were no later

groups which claimed to be their disciples or successors, and they have no modern representatives. The Confucian dictum on this subject is:

> The superior man is dignified, but does not wrangle.
> He is sociable, but not a partisan.[13]

The two notable organizations that have maintained themselves over time are the *hui kuan* (or Landsmanschaften) and the *pang* (principally gangster associations). The former were always localized (e.g., a Cantonese *hui kuan* in Peking) for the convenience of traveling tradesmen and office seekers away from home (Hsu 1968). The latter were wider in geographical scope and their aims were predatory and sometimes rebellious. The ill-fated Boxer Uprising temporarily linked some gangster organizations with some esoteric religious practitioners as well as some locally organized physical culturists. Like other rebellions in Chinese history, including the Yellow Turban Revolt of the later Han dynasty (A.D. 25-221) and the White Lotus Rebellion of the Ch'ing dynasty (A.D. 1645-1911), these were short-lived. The famous Chinese novel, *All Men Are Brothers* (translated by Buck 1933), is an imaginary romance concerning one hundred and eight persons (two women and 106 men) who came from different walks of life, who got into trouble with the central government or local powers, most of whom did something charitable in the Robin Hood style, and who all ultimately went on to form a single community on Mount Liang. But even in a novel, the group did not last long; they dispersed some time afterwards. There were no later Chinese groups which rose claiming to be their descendants in spirit or in kinship. The fact is that there rarely were clearly defined, sizable, and legitimate secondary groups in China which were non-territorial and which continued over the generations.

The *iemoto* system appeared and prospered in Japan but not in China because the *iemoto* flows from the Japanese pattern of *ie* by way of *dōzoku*; it is not commensurate with the Chinese pattern of family and *tsu*. Table 1 will help us appreciate the links.

Grouping	Attributes	
	Major	Minor
Ie	Continuity Exclusiveness Authority (intensified)	Discontinuity Inclusiveness Volition (germinal)
Dōzoku	Continuity Exclusiveness Authority (more intensified) Volition (important)	Discontinuity Inclusiveness
Iemoto	Continuity Exclusiveness Inclusiveness Authority (even more intensified) Volition (very important)	

TABLE 1:   Component Attributes in Ie, Dōzoku and Iemoto

Three basic attributes (continuity, exclusiveness and authority) are major in all three forms of grouping. In the case of ie the attributes of discontinuity and inclusiveness are less strong than their opposites because the central concern of the ie is its vertical and perpetual succession, while the attribute of volition is present because of the popularity of the customs of mukoyōshi and other forms of adoption of unrelated individuals.

As we go from ie to dōzoku the attribute of authority is intensified because of the father's role in selecting his heir, the unequal position among the brothers, and the power of the heir to choose whether or not to provide for his brothers (and sisters). The attribute of volition assumes major importance in this situation on account of the much greater possibility (and frequency) for unrelated *ie* to become part of the corporation. Finally, the *iemoto* not only gives even greater expression to the attributes of authority and volition, it also more fully embodies the attribute of inclusiveness, since all disciples of a master remain members of his corporation.

Why has the attribute of inclusiveness become so pronounced in the *iemoto*? I think the reason is that the *dōzoku* is primarily characteristic of rural life and is tied to the land and the village, while the *iemoto* is characteristic of urban life, with no comparable limitations. Universally, rural life is more localized than urban life. Part of the reason is undoubtedly economic: those who depend upon agriculture are necessarily less mobile than those who derive their livelihood from commerce, manufacturing or politics. For one thing, a farmer's basic means of production are immobile. For another, a farmer's mobility is limited by his technology in utilizing his landed resources. In any case, his objectives and scope of operation cannot be as far-ranging as those of merchants, handicraftsmen or politicians. Under such circumstances the largely rural *dōzoku* can hardly be inclusive of those who have no role in its basic economic concerns.

The primarily urban *iemoto*, dealing with means and objectives that were capable of much wider organizations even under Japan's pre-modern technology, needed to be more completely inclusive than the *dōzoku*, so that each could expand its sphere of influence and operation.

Superficially our observations here concerning the influence of the economic factor on the greater importance of the attribute of inclusiveness in the *iemoto* would seem to be the same as those of Nakane which we criticized before. This is not the case. The *dōzoku* and, at its foundation, the *ie*, are goal-oriented corporations, each concerned with the results of its activities and with its own indefinite perpetuation. The attributes of continuity, exclusiveness and authority are highly instrumental in achieving these ends. The attribute of volition provides the *dōzoku* with a safety-valve for compensating deficiencies when members related by kinship are either incompetent or absent. But the maintenance of true kinship ties is never its central concern.

Consequently, the size of the group, the rules of descent and succession, and the extent to which unrelated households are incorporated into a system tend to be responsive to economic exigencies: when farming is important (as in the case of the *dōzoku*), inclusiveness is overshadowed by exclusiveness; when the sources of livelihood permit or even require wider circles of affiliation (as in the case of *iemoto*), then inclusiveness becomes as important as exclusiveness.

The obverse of this Japanese pattern is the Chinese case where, as we noted before, even though the optimum size of a farm holding is about 7 acres, most Chinese farms were divided and redivided into smaller plots. In fact, most Chinese, who must have had similar economic needs as their Japanese counterparts, shunned *mukoyōshi* and avoided adoption where possible, but went to enormous trouble to trace and relate to their kinsmen, however scattered apart they were. This was why kinship became the principal stumbling block in preventing China from modern industrialization after a hundred years of contact with the West. In Japan, on the other hand, kinship never prevented modern industrialization, because the Japanese kinship system, though sharing with its Chinese counterpart the attributes of continuity and authority, was also characterized by the attributes of exclusiveness and volition. Exclusiveness necessitated or prompted the separation of brothers who had to seek their destinies elsewhere, and both exclusiveness and volition made the criteria for membership in Japanese primary and especially secondary groupings less rigid and more responsive to changing conditions.

Regional Variation

So far we have treated the kinship system and the culture of Japan with no regard to regional differences. But there is some obvious variation from region to region even in the customs concerning ancestor rites (Maeda 1965) and funerals (Inoguchi 1965). As for kinship, the main difference in structure seems to lie between southwestern Japan, chiefly Shikoku, Kyūshū, and Western Honshū, and northern Japan, chiefly northern Honshū. The difference has by no means been clearly documented, but we have some evidence for it. Yoshida, in a paper on Umani, a rice-growing village in Hata-gun, Kochi Prefecture in southwestern Shikoku, says of the local social structure:

> As in other parts of Japan, the rules of descent, inheritance, and succes-
> sion in Umani are patrilineal and primogenitural, and residence is
> patrilocal, except in cases where a man lacking a male heir adopts a
> husband for his daughter to perpetuate his family line. Social ties of
> kinship, including both patrilineal and affinal kinsmen, are strong in
> Umani compared with other Japanese villages where non-kin associa-
> tions such as occupational and neighborhood groups, are increasing in
> importance. (Yoshida 1967:237).

The first part of this statement places Umani in the same kinship
pattern we have already described. But the second part seems to make
Umani somewhat different. Yoshida also says in the same article:

> These patrilineally organized groups are locally known as *ittō* and
> correspond to what are usually called *dōzoku* by Japanese sociologists,
> but differ from other *dōzoku* groups in Japan which are hierarchically
> organized, for the economic and political control of the "main" family
> over the "branch" families does not exist in Umani. (Yoshida 1967:240).

I questioned Yoshida and found that what he means by the
statement "social ties of kinship including both patrilineal and affinal
kinsmen are seen to be strong in Umani when compared with other
Japanese villages . . ." is that, in contrast to northern Japan, the *bunke*
(branch family) tends to exhibit greater independence from the *honke*
(chief or root family) in Umani. The Umani *bunke* tends to revolve
around its own immediate consanguine and affinal relations. Furthermore, according to Yoshida and others, there is not only greater
equality in the southwest among the various *bunke*, but even occa-
sional instances of ultimogeniture in inheritance (Naito and Yoshida
1965, Gamō 1958, Omachi 1958).

Masao Gamō's work on "Shinzoku" (kinship) generally supports
this distinction between northern Japan and southwestern Japan not
only in *honke-bunke* relationships but also with regard to several
other features. Table 2 gives us a good idea of the differences (Gamō
1958:255).

Generally speaking, the first four areas belong to one group while
the last five belong to another. Among the first four areas the outstanding characteristics are: village exogamy (and therefore usually
shinzoku exogamy), the subordination of the *bunke* to the *honke*, the
household as the basic unit, and patrilineal descent. Rights and obli-

Area (one village in each area)	Descent	Privilege and responsibility	Unit	Bunke	Marriage	Name of the grouping	Type name
Tōhoku	Patrilineal	Over three generations	Household	Subordinate to *honke*	Exogamy	Maki	Maki (a)
Tōhoku	"	"	"	"	"	Edōshi	"
Chūbu	"	Limited to household	"	"	"	Jirui	Jirui (b)
Chūbu	"	"	"	"	"	"	"
Tōkai	"	"	Individual	Independent	Endogamy	Ittō	Ittō (c)
Kinki	Bilateral	"	"	"	"	Shinrui	Haroji (d)
Chūgoku	Patrilineal	"	?	"	?	Kabuchi	Ittō of Jirui (b) or (c)
Shikoku	"	"	Individual	"	Endogamy	Ittō	Ittō (c)
Kyūshū	Bilateral	"	"	"	"	Haroji	Haroji (d)

TABLE 2: Four Types of Shinzoku Groupings

gations in two of these areas extend to more than three generations, while in the other two they are limited to three generations only (usually within the household). The characteristics of the last five areas are generally: village endogamy (and therefore frequent *shinzoku* endogamy), independence of the *bunke* from the *honke*, the individual and not the household as the basic unit,[14] rights and obligations binding three generations only (usually within the household), and patrilineal descent in three of these areas, with bilateral descent in the other two.

Ultimogeniture does not make the kinship system of some parts of southwestern Japan really different from that of the rest of Japan. Both primogeniture and ultimogeniture are forms of unigeniture and express the attribute of exclusiveness and, by extension, a degree of discontinuity. But the greater independence of the *bunke* from the *honke* results in less intensification of authority, while the limited generational relationships and the tendency toward bilateral descent make the attribute of exclusiveness (and also discontinuity) even more obvious in the kinship system in southwestern Japan than in the rest of Japan. In terms of our hypothesis, southwestern Japan, with these differences, should have more *iemoto and* pseudo-*iemoto* but a less aggressive instance of the kin-tract principle of human relationships than in the rest of the country. In other words, there should be more *iemoto*-like secondary groupings but greater independence of spirit among their members and component units in the southwest as compared to the rest of Japan.

This problem is more easily posed than solved. The difficulty is that we have no concrete and comparative figures on the relative prevalence of the *iemoto* system in the two regions. Nor do we possess information on the differences between their respective organizations. However, while we do not possess the kind of facts that will enable us to prove or disprove this part of our thesis, we can offer the following observations in the spirit of a footnote, hoping that future students of Japan will test their validity in field work. In making the following observations I have been aided in no small measure by Teigo Yoshida.

One has the strong impression that more entrepreneurs—both before and after the Meiji Restoration—originated from southwestern Japan than from northern Japan. Omi (later Ōsaka) and Hakata merchants were not only famous but also financially powerful and reputed to be more skillful, creative and imaginative than their counterparts elsewhere. In fact, one of the well known complaints of Edo (Tokyo) merchants was that they could hardly compete with the Osaka merchants *(katenai)*. Merchants from southwestern Japan figured more prominently in Japan's political struggles than those from other areas.

All seven prime ministers under Emperor Meiji were from the southwest, as were many, if not most, of the active and well-known figures of that period.

There is a good deal of evidence to indicate that more naval officers and men came from southwestern Japan than from other areas. Admiral Togo is a well-known example. According to the *Biography of Admiral Kato Hiro Haru*,[15] another admiral originating from the southwest, his naval graduating class of 1891 consisted of 61 men. The breakdown of their local origin shows that 40, or two-thirds, came from southwest Japan: Fukui 3, Hiroshima 1, Ehime 1, Kumamoto 2, Ōita 1, Kōchi 4, Kyoto 2, Saga 6, Okayama 1, Nagasaki 2, Kagoshima 6, Aichi 6, Yamaguchi 3, Tokushima 1, Fukuoka 1 (total 40). (Fukui and Aichi are borderline cases.) The remaining 21 were from nine other prefectures. Prominent among the nine was Tokyo, which supplied nine of these 21 officers. The preponderance of Kagoshima, Aichi, Saga, and Kōchi in this picture is extremely striking.

Southwestern Japan, especially Shikoku, Kyūshū, and the Yamaguchi Prefecture of Honshū, was also a main supplier of Japanese army leadership. The Tokugawa Shogunate, the military dictatorship of Japan before the Meiji Restoration, was never able to subjugate three feudal lords in the southwest: the lord of Chōshū, whose domain was in the extreme western portion of Honshū, the lord of Satsuma, whose domain was in the extreme south of Kyūshū, and the lord of Tosa, whose domain was in southern Shikoku. These three were known as *San Pan* (the Three Lords) and were famous for their independence of mind and action. A reading of Japanese political history of the Tokugawa Period leaves little doubt that the Shogunate at Edo had considerable trouble controlling these feudal lords from the southwest. And even after the Meiji Restoration, there was trouble. Saigō Takamori, founder of the Japanese army, and a great tragic hero in his native prefecture of Kagoshima (formerly under the lord of Satsuma), killed himself when he was surrounded by government forces in a war of rebellion against the new regime under Emperor Meiji.

This link between an increase in the attribute of exclusiveness in the kinship system and greater independence and freedom in behavior characteristics (discontinuity and less intensified authority and dependence) finds some support in the works of a few recent observers. DeVos and Wagatsuma, in an analysis of their TAT responses from women of two Japanese villages, report that Niiike (in Okayama Prefecture), a farming village, has a kinship structure that is more centralized and hierarchical, with the northern Japanese type of *honke-bunke* relationship, whereas Sakushima (in Aichi Prefecture) is a fishing village with a kinship structure of the southwestern type. They find that the women of Sakushima, as contrasted to those of Niiike, are freer in their expression of emotions and place greater emphasis on love in mate selection. These women also exhibit greater aggressiveness—even violent aggression against their husbands—as well as non-submission to mother-in-law dominance (DeVos and Wagatsuma 1961:1225-1226).[16]

Finally, Douglas Haring, who held the view that Tokugawa "sumptuary legislation molded traditional Japanese character," unexpectedly came upon a pocket of Japanese "whose forebears escaped Tokugawa domination and whose customs still preserve traces of pre-Tokugawa Japan." He found this group on the island of Amami Ōshima, located between Kyūshū and Okinawa. According to Haring, the inhabitants of this island had preserved a kind of archaic "cultural base" which still includes "ideas and beliefs long extinct in Japan, but recorded in ancient Japanese documents." He went on to say,

> Amamians meet friendly advances more than halfway. American G.I.s stationed there soon became attached to them. To stress these aspects of Amamian character detracts nothing from the hospitality and friendliness, usually unfeigned, of the people of Japan Proper. In Japan Proper, however, frankness and friendliness without suspicion are new, cultivated with a bit of effort; the Tokugawa mask is not quickly discarded. In Amami there never was any Tokugawa mask. As far as the "planned quality" of Japanese behavior goes, Amamian behavior is less cast in the rigid mold of codes of conduct, more spontaneous and fun-loving. Their rich and durable sense of humor withstands the disasters of storm and famine that sweep their islands. They "kid" each other with the same abandon that American young people manifest;

they even poke fun at Japanese ceremonial suicide, saying, "Why commit suicide? Living is too much fun!" True, they retain the habit of watchful attention to the whims of authority; two hundred and fifty years of slavery taught them to anticipate the wishes of rulers and avoid torture. But their folk songs run the gamut of human emotions, their folk dancing is superb, and the carefree abandon of the southern islanders has not been destroyed by prolonged serfdom.

Ridicule and shame carry weight in Amami but do not pass endurance. The child who blunders in public still is loved and cherished by his family. Never have I seen families whose members openly, unselfconsciously love each other more devotedly. The reverse of this affection appears in sudden rages that may end in murder if a mate is unfaithful or love is rejected. There is none of the impassivity so characteristic of the prewar Japanese. As for politeness, Tokugawa etiquette reached only the small ruling class on Amami. Spontaneous hospitality, consideration of others, and kindness outweigh the equally open tokens of hostility under frustration; genuine emotions are not camouflaged by poker faces. As one Amami gentleman said to me at a party when a geisha danced: "That's a Japanese dance. She looks like a funeral: deadpan. Now wait for an Amami dance; the girls will smile and laugh, and everyone will be happy." So indeed it happened. (Haring 1956:436).

From what we know about the Amami Ōshima kinship structure, we find it indeed approximates the pattern of southwestern Japan. In fact it carries the trend further. It is definitely bilateral; the bunke is independent of the honke; lateral relatives of other lineages are not even called cousins (itoko), but within the three generations, kinship terms for ascending, collateral, and descending relatives of both patrilineal and matrilineal lines are the same; genealogical records are split between honke-bunke lines so that they have no common ancestors, etc. (Gamō 1958:241 and 251-252).[17]

Yoshida and I are of the opinion that what Haring saw among the inhabitants of Amami Ōshima applies not only to other areas such as Koshiki Island (Kogashima Prefecture; Naito and Yoshida 1965:209-227), but also to most of southwestern Japan as well.

[1] The smallest unit in a kinship group. See Chapter 7 for a detailed elaboration of the dominant kinship dyad hypothesis.

[2] I am indebted to Thomas Rohlen for suggesting this term. For a fuller exposition of the meaning of kin-tract principle and its behavioral expressions, see Hamaguchi and Sakuda (1971: 373-377). I am also indebted to Professor Hamaguchi for clarifying certain conceptual details (Hamaguchi 1970).

[3] All of the characteristics described below are either based on Kawashima's book or on my own observations, except where otherwise noted.

[4] After passing the test, the disciple has to pay a large amount of money to the master for the license. This is one of the major sources of the master's income (Nishiyama 1962: 67-68).

[5] Professor Kawashima tells me that the term can be best equated to the German word *Entgelt*.

[6] In all the Japanese *iemoto* and even outside them, the man who has excelled over all others, or, in the case of the "gō" game, has beaten all others, is given the title *mei jin* and *honinbō*. In 1968 and 1971 a Chinese from Taiwan by the name of Lin Hai-Feng was *mei jin* and *honinbō* of "gō" in Japan.

[7] In the U.S. Army there are only "private first class" and "private." The ranking referred to here is Japanese.

[8] The first letter of the term *Iemoto* is capitalized when it refers to the head of the *iemoto*.

[9] But even the *Iemoto* cannot change the traditional form or style of his school. For example, Kanze Motomasa, the *Iemoto* of the Kanze School of Nō drama, once tried to perform "Yuzuru" to the accompaniment of singing in *colloquial language* instead of *literary language*. This was considered too radical and he failed to bring about the reform. (Nō drama is always accompanied by a chorus singing in the classic literary language.) (Nishiyama 1962:9).

[10] Recently (1967) a daughter succeeded to the position of *Iemoto* in the Hanayagi School of dancing.

[11] The connotation of this little speech was that this "father" was very happy. He was actually bragging.

[12] Many modern criticisms have been levelled against the *iemoto* system. See Kawashima 1957:357-369 and Nishiyama Matsu no Suke: "Iemoto ni okeru dentō" ("Tradition in the Iemoto System"), *Ningen no Kagaku (Science of Man)* Vol. 2, No. 11, 1964 (Journal), Tokyo, pp. 12-21.

[13] Translated by Legge 1960:300.

[14] According to Yoshida this cannot be applied in Umani, where the inhabitants conceive of the units of *"rui-uchi"* (equivalent to *shinrui* in standard Japanese, or "kindred") as families rather than as individuals (Yoshida 1967:260).

[15] The biography is in the hands of Dr. Masaaki Kato, the admiral's grandson, Chief of Psychiatry, Japanese National Institute of Mental Health, Tokyo.

[16] Superficially the fact that Niiike is situated in southwestern Japan and Sakushima in central Japan would seem to vitiate the argument here. This is not the case. Our interest is in the link between differences in kinship system and differences in behavior characteristics. The peculiarities in kinship between the two areas in question

may also be related to the fact that Niiike is agricultural and Sakushima depends on fishing. But this is also not the main point.

[17] The area on which Gamō based his statements in Kikai-jima, an island immediately to the east of Amami Ōshima inhabited by the same kind of people.

7 •

Kinship, Society, and Culture

Kinship has been treated in anthropological studies in several ways. The descriptive works simply state what the family or household and the roles look like to the ethnographer. The works by componential analysts attempt to ferret out all the possible meanings of each system through its kinship terms. The mathematically inclined works make fancy models of kinship systems which generally have nothing to do with behavior.

There are many studies which, for want of a better generic term, may be called functionalist, since they try to relate some aspect of kinship to extraneous phenomena. Some works deal with the effect of industrialization or modernization or urbanization on family behavior, household size, or kinship usages. Others deal with the links between specific elements in kinship such as mother-infant sleeping arrangements and institutional provisions such as severe initiation rites.

Finally, there are anthropological studies of the Freudian persuasion which seek clues to personality characteristics or even patterns of society and culture from such early experiences as the quality of maternal care or modes of resolution of the Oedipus Complex.

Insofar as it is aimed at the effect of kinship on society and culture, my approach is broadly functionalist. To the extent that it relates what goes on in the earliest groupings of all human beings with their behavioral characteristics and culture pattern, it is also loosely Freudian. However, I am neither tied to Freudian mechanisms

87

such as repression or projection nor to Freudian concepts such as the Oedipus Complex or the superego, though I do not deny their possible validity in some circumstances and for some purposes. Furthermore, my focus is not directed towards fathoming the depths of the individual psyche but is aimed towards an understanding of interpersonal aspects of human existence. For this purpose I have developed my Dominant Kinship Dyad hypothesis.

The Dominant Dyad Hypothesis

The hypothesis, in skeletal form, is as follows: the attributes of the dominant dyad in a given kinship system tend to determine the attitudes and action patterns which the individual in such a system develops towards other dyads or his roles in them within this system as well as towards his relationships outside of it.

This hypothesis was first outlined in 1961 (Hsu:1961), demonstrated in 1963 (Hsu:1963), and formally published in 1965 (Hsu:1965). It was further scrutinized in a 1966 symposium by seventeen anthropologists and sociologists, and the results of this deliberation were published in 1971 (Hsu:1971).

For a more complete statement of the hypothesis the reader should read "A Hypothesis on Kinship and Culture" (Hsu 1971:3-29). In that publication we explicated the hypothesis in three parts: first, an examination of four basic kinship dyads and their attributes, listed and defined as in Table 3 below; second, the effect of dominant dyads on other kinship dyads in the same kinship system; third, the effect of dominant dyads on non-kin relationships. Since then we have made some further advances in the testing and refining of this hypothesis. Some of these more recent efforts will be reflected in the following chapters.

Dyad, Attributes, Role and Affect

Basic to this hypothesis are eight concepts beginning with dyad and role on the one hand, and attribute and affect on the other hand. Dyad is the socially defined link between two individuals. At least eight dyads are basic in every nuclear family: father-son, mother-son, father-daughter, mother-daughter, husband-wife, brother-brother,

Relationship	Attributes	Definition of Attributes
Husband–Wife	1. Discontinuity	The condition of not being, or the attitude of desiring not to be, in a sequence or connected with others.
	2. Exclusiveness	The act of keeping others out or unwillingness to share with them.
	3. Sexuality	Preoccupation with sex.
	4. Volition	The condition of being able to follow own inclinations, or of desiring to do so.
Father–Son	1. Continuity	The condition of being, or the attitude of desiring to be, an unbroken sequence, or connected with others.
	2. Inclusiveness	The act of incorporating or the attitude of wishing to be incorporated.
	3. Asexuality	The condition of having no connection with sex.
	4. Authority	Personal power that commands and enforces obedience, or the condition of being under such power.
Mother–Son	1. Discontinuity	(Already defined above)
	2. Inclusiveness	(Already defined above)
	3. Dependence	The condition of being or the attitude of wishing to be reliant upon others.
	4. Diffuseness	The tendency to spread out in all directions.
	5. Libidinality	Diffused or potential sexuality
Brother–Brother	1. Discontinuity	(Already defined above)
	2. Inclusiveness	(Already defined above)
	3. Equality	The condition of being or the attitude of wishing to be of the same rank and importance as others.
	4. Rivalry	The act of striving, or the attitude of wishing to strive, for equality with or excellence over others.

TABLE 3: Four Dyads and Their Attributes

sister-sister, and sister-brother.[1] Role refers to the implicit and explicit obligations, duties, expectations, and privileges associated with each dyadic link.

Attribute refers to logical or typical mode of behavior intrinsic to each dyad.[2] The words logical, typical, and intrinsic are crucial to this definition. By them we mean that the attributes of each dyad are what David Schneider describes as "constants" (Schneider 1961:5) because they are universally the potential and inherent properties of that relationship. Affect refers to the feelings and attitudes underlying the behavioral characteristics which inevitably determine the tenacity and intensity of the interaction.

One example which might aid us in understanding the relationship between dyad and attribute is found in the employer-employee dyad. Its intrinsic attributes are functional considerations, calculated obligations and rewards, and specific delineations in duration. A man enters into such a relationship generally because he has work he wants done or he desires wages or their equivalent. The length of time during which the dyad lasts is likely to be understood or made specific in advance. The details vary from society to society, and from employment to employment, but these intrinsic attributes can be found wherever an employer-employee dyad is said to exist. On the other hand, the attributes intrinsic to the employer-employee dyad do not hold at all in the case of a romantic dyad. In fact, the presence of any of them in a romantic dyad will tend to mar or even ruin the love relationship. The intrinsic attributes of each dyad are the basic ingredients and determinants of the interactional patterns between parties composing that dyad.

The relationship between role and affect is far less obscure. Role is the usefulness of one individual to another. Affect describes the way one individual feels about another. "Business is business" expresses a condition in which role alone prevails. "Love conquers all" expresses a condition in which affect alone prevails. "The king is human, he exercises his authority with mercy" expresses a condition in which role and affect overlap.

One or more roles are inherent in every dyad. Every attribute may be expressed with more or less feeling. Role performance will influence the nature and continuance of the dyad, just as the intensity or tenacity of the feeling must bear on its attributes or behavioral characteristics.

The connections among dyad, role, attribute, and affect are schematically represented in Diagram 5.

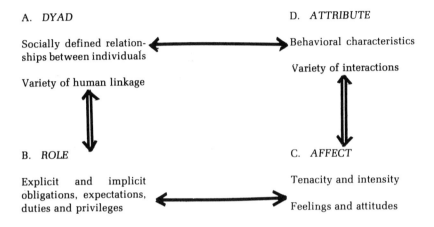

A. *DYAD*

Socially defined relationships between individuals

Variety of human linkage

B. *ROLE*

Explicit and implicit
obligations, expectations,
duties and privileges

D. *ATTRIBUTE*

Behavioral characteristics

Variety of interactions

C. *AFFECT*

Tenacity and intensity

Feelings and attitudes

DIAGRAM 5:   Dyad, Role, Attribute and Affect

Attributes, Origin and Interrelationship

For the purposes of this book we need first to deal with the attributes of father-son and of husband-wife dyads, and then, a little later, of the mother-son dyad. Initially I derived the attribute of discontinuity from the husband-wife dyad because every husband is not a wife and every wife is not a husband (in contrast, e.g. to the father-son dyad through which every father is also a son and every son is also a father). But its attribute of exclusiveness intensifies that discontinuity so that the husband-wife dyad generates more discontinuity than other dyads. Thus, although the mother-son dyad also generates discontinuity by virtue of the fact that every mother is not a son and every son is not a mother, the discontinuity of the husband-wife dyad is stronger than that of the mother-son dyad because the latter is accompanied by inclusiveness as in the father-son dyad but not exclusiveness as in the husband-wife dyad.

The association of the attribute of exclusiveness with the husband-wife dyad is more easily understood. That association comes from the fact that monogamy is characteristic of the vast majority of mankind regardless of culture, whereas polygamy is found only among a minority of members even in societies which tolerate or practice it legally. Exclusiveness is found wherever the roles of the dyad are limited to two performers. For that reason primogeniture, as we shall see later, generates exclusiveness. However, the exclusiveness of the husband-wife dyad is reinforced by sexuality, an attribute which universally is an essential ingredient of that relationship. The core of sexuality, that is, the sexual act, is carried out between two individuals. Besides homosexuality and the use of animals as human substitutes, there are forms of self-eroticism such as masturbation. which can be restricted to one individual alone. There are other forms of sexual practices which can involve more than two individuals. However, there is no question that the one man-one woman union is the universal norm for the sexual act. Consequently the exclusiveness rooted in the husband-wife dyad is stronger than that rooted in any form of inheritance rule alone.

There are convergences between other attributes. Volition is commensurate with both exclusiveness and sexuality. Of all the eight basic dyads in the nuclear family, the husband-wife dyad alone is one which, by virtue of sexuality, involves a kind of need for individual willingness unknown or not required in others. Even in societies where caste or other customary rules preclude individual choice, individual preferences enter into the making, continuation and termination of this dyad. Sometimes the freedom may be exercised by parents or family heads and not the man and woman entering into or forming the dyad. Nevertheless, this dyad involves a kind of freedom of choice which is never naturally true in the other basic dyads in the nuclear family. Furthermore, for the male at least, there is more opportunity for personal choice no matter in what kind of kinship system he lives.

There are other convergences between the attributes of the husband-wife dyad. Discontinuity is more commensurate with exclusiveness than inclusiveness, for discontinuity is a form of exclusiveness in time. We will note in an example of friendship to be discussed below that the shorter the duration of friendship, the less the chances of widening our friendship circle to incorporate others who are not part of the original circle. Thus the more we move from one set of friendships to another in time (discontinuity), the smaller must be the circle of our friendly involvement (exclusiveness).

Sexuality and exclusiveness are necessary for each other because no matter how widely distributed a single individual's sex appeal is, the central fact of sexuality is the sexual act between two persons. This is not the case of the attribute of authority. The latter can be distributed widely among many individuals with the same effect as if it were exercised on a one-to-one basis. Therefore authority but not sexuality is more commensurate with inclusiveness.

Sexuality also falls more in line with discontinuity than with continuity. Sexuality as a physiological phenomenon necessarily waxes and wanes even during the period of an individual's life when his sex drive is strong. As the individual grows older the sexual drive diminishes and recedes. There are known differences between the male and the female in this regard and there are also known individual differences. But there is no question that sexuality recedes and then disappears as age advances. Furthermore, death concludes it. Unlike authority, which can be continued for long periods of time after a man's death, sexuality cannot be exercised in absentia.

We shall now briefly explain the father-son dyad and its attributes. Our basic rationale for deriving the attribute of continuity from the father-son dyad is as follows: Since every father is a son and every son is a father, each father-son dyad is a link in a never ending chain of father-son dyads. In this respect the father-son dyad is dissimilar to the mother-son dyad. The rationale for deriving the attribute of inclusiveness from the father-son dyad is the fact that fathers neither expect to beget only one child nor must they carry out activities with any of the children on a one-to-one basis. Some fathers may prefer one son over others, but that is another matter. For this reason inclusiveness is common to all parent-child dyads: father-son, mother-son, father-daughter and mother-daughter.

The remaining two attributes of the father-son dyad are authority and asexuality. The attribute of authority comes from basic differences in age and experience between fathers and sons. Fathers (and mothers too) are invariably much older and more experienced than sons, at least for the first ten or fifteen years of the sons' lives. During these extended years the fathers' power to impress, direct and coerce far overshadow those of the sons. The link between father-son dyad and asexuality is as obvious as that between the husband-wife dyad and sexuality.

Like the attributes intrinsic to the husband-wife dyad, those intrinsic to the father-son dyad are also mutually commensurate with each other. For example, continuity means a relatively lengthy existence of that relationship in time. With normal birth and marriage, lengthy existence in time means greater chances of involvement of others who were not previously in the picture. Thus two bachelors may develop a friendship. If the friendship lasts more than a few years there are chances of each of them being married to a woman. If their friendship had ended before they were married, there would have been no question of inclusion in their friendship of the two women who came later. But if they continue their friendship after marriage, it is reasonable to expect that the new wives will be involved in the relationship. If their friendship continues still longer, they are likely to beget children who may have some bearing on the friendship of the two older men.

However, the widening of the circle of involvement as this friendship continues is not restricted to birth and marriage. One of the friends may move away, for business or other reasons, to another locality where he will meet new people and make new friends. If he discontinues his friendship with his older friend, then indeed his circle of friendship need not be more inclusive than before. But if he wants to continue the older friendship, then it becomes obvious that the circle is inevitably enlarged. Thus we may generate the following subsidiary hypothesis: the more continuous a relationship between two or more individuals, and the longer it lasts, the more inclusive it will become of other individuals who were not previously part of that relationship. Conversely, any dyad which generates inclusiveness but not continuity is less inclusive than one which generates both. Therefore, the inclusiveness of the mother-son dyad is weaker than that generated by the father-son dyad.

Authority can be exercised generally in one of three ways: firstly, by brutal or economic power on the part of the superior over the subordinates; secondly, through what Max Weber would designate as charisma or what is popularly known in the U.S. as sex (or other personal) appeal of the superior; thirdly, by conviction on the part of the subordinates of the superior's right, duty, or privilege to exercise authority just as they see their right, duty, or privilege being to obey. It is obvious that the first two ways of exercising authority will probably be less permanent than the third. In the first case, resentment is likely to occur among those who are subject to the authority so that they may revolt or attempt to escape from the authority at the first opportunity. In the second case, authority is likely to be disrupted as soon as there is a reduction of charisma on the part of the superior or of his sex appeal through old age or loss of ability. At any rate, death is likely to end his position of authority for good. In the third situation, since the subordinates are taught to respect the superior's authority, this power tends to be longer lasting than in either of the other cases.

The distinctions separating these three ways of exercising authority are relative, but the third is more likely to characterize authority in the father-son dyad. The attribute of continuity encourages the sons to cooperate in support of the father's authority, because they themselves expect to exercise this kind of authority in the same way when it is their turn to do so. In this situation the idea of authority permeates the relationship and is not tied to the brutal power or the special qualities of a single person. Under such circumstances authority does not disappear with the death of the person in authority; it tends to continue after his death in the form of a cult of the dead (in the kinship sphere) or veneration of the past and tradition (in the society generally). Furthermore, on the basis of what we have said concerning the relationship between continuity and inclusiveness, we can infer that the more continuous the worship of the ancestors of a kinship group or the tradition of a society, the more inclusive that authority is likely to be in regard to wider circles of human beings.

Dominant Dyads and Dominant Attributes

The foregoing discussion of the interrelationship among attributes has already made plain that any dyad and its attributes can exercise influence over other dyads and other attributes.[3] We are now ready to go one step further and to deal with the distinction between structure and content, which is the core of our hypothesis. The most important conceptual tools for this distinction are *dominant dyad* and *dominant attribute*. This part of our hypothesis says that, not only do different dyads within a system influence each other, but all of them tend to take shape under the influences of one or two dominant dyads.

No nuclear family would seem to give equal prominence to all its eight basic dyads. What actually occurs is that in each type of nuclear family one (or more) of the dyads takes precedence over the others.

When a dyad is thus elevated above others it tends to modify, magnify, reduce or even eliminate other dyadic relationships in the kinship group. Such a dyad is designated in our hypothesis as the *dominant dyad*[4] while others in the system are *non-dominant dyads*.

If the father-son dyad in the nuclear family is the dominant one, it will increase the social importance of the father-son dyad at the expense of other dyads such as the husband-wife dyad. In such an eventuality the intrinsic attributes of the dominant dyad are designated in our hypothesis as the *dominant attributes* while those of the other dyads in the system are termed *non-dominant attributes*. In each nuclear family the dominant attributes will so influence the non-dominant attributes that the latter will tend to converge in the direction of the dominant attributes. Behavioral expressions of the attributes of the dominant dyad (in the case of father-son, authority, continuity, inclusiveness and asexuality) will greatly overshadow those of the non-dominant dyad (in the case of husband-wife, volition, discontinuity, exclusiveness and sexuality). The parents will have much more to say about the selection of their son's future wife than the son himself (authority over volition). Kinship groups consisting of many generations living under the same roof will tend to be regarded as more socially desirable than a nuclear family consisting of parents and unmarried children (inclusiveness over exclusiveness). A married couple will normally live in the same household with the man's parents and they will hope to beget male children so that they may present his parents with heirs to the family line (continuity over exclusiveness and discontinuity). Finally, outward signs of erotic attraction between spouses will be frowned on (asexuality over sexuality). These are some of the possible consequences of extreme dominance of the father-son dyad.

Conversely, if the husband-wife dyad is dominant, it will alter the parent-child relationship and make it into a temporary arrangement to be replaced or discarded when the child grows into adulthood (discontinuity over continuity). In such a case the kinship group will tend to correspond to the nuclear family at all times because of the exclusion of all consanguineal relatives as soon as a man takes a wife (exclusiveness over inclusiveness). Public signs of conjugal love will be very much in evidence no matter who else is present (sexuality over asexuality). Independence of the children will be encouraged (volition over authority). These are some of the ways in which dominant dyads and dominant attributes can shape the non-dominant dyads and non-dominant attributes.

Structure and Content

The sum of all the attributes converging towards the dominant attributes in the kinship system is designated as its *content*, just as the sum of all the dyads under the influence of one or more dominating dyads is its *structure*.[5] The interrelationships are outlined in Diagram 6.

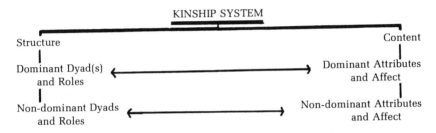

KINSHIP SYSTEM

Structure   Content

Dominant Dyad(s) ←——————————————→ Dominant Attributes
and Roles   and Affect

Non-dominant Dyads ←——————————————→ Non-dominant Attributes
and Roles   and Affect

DIAGRAM 6:   Dyadic and Attribute Dominance

A Food and Vitamins Analogy

At this point it may be asked why I developed the Dominant Kinship Dyad hypothesis and what we hope to accomplish with it. In answer to the first question my answer is that I developed this hypothesis because of our failure thus far to find satisfactory and comprehensive links between varieties of kinship and varieties of society and culture. I am not satisfied with the lack of insight as to why some societies are expansionist while others are inward-looking, why some societies so successfully cope with disasters while others seem unable to take care of themselves, and why some societies exhibit so much internal impetus for change while others move little except under exogenous pressures. In particular, I am unimpressed by those who see social and cultural developments as man's adjustment to ecological demands or changes in economic conditions such as urbanization. Had mankind acted merely in the passive role of an adaptor to nature we would not have been faced with the threats of overpopulation or lethal pollution. Our numbers and our activities would have been automatically limited and curtailed. And if social and cultural changes can only come about via altered economic conditions, we must ask what brought about the economic changes in the first place. I think the causes of economic change, which are part of a larger picture of cultural development, must be sought in man's relationships with his fellow men. And the web of kinship is man's first and most basic interpersonal relationship.

My answer to the second question is aided by an analogy from the field of nutrition. All men know that food has something to do with building our bodies. We need no profound research to determine this. For the general purpose of feeding ourselves and our children, knowing about meat and vegetables or chop suey and bread are more or less sufficient. However, merely differentiating foods in such terms did not enable us to develop the science of nutrition or the art of dietetics. In order to ascertain what food does what to what part of the human body or aspects of its growth, malfunction and health, food analysts have had to go beyond daily use concepts to develop new analytical categories such as those of amino acids and carbohydrates and especially vitamins. Aided by these new categories, nutrition experts are able to pin-point the significance of certain organic compounds. In particular their efforts have led to the radical discovery that the lack of dietary constituents (usually in very small amounts such as 0.0050% to 0.0002% of the diet) can cause disease, in sharp contrast to the more traditional idea that bacteria or some other positive agents are causes of all diseases. Through their efforts modern dieticians have been able with greater confidence to make dietary prescriptions for the sick, for the undernourished, for the growing infant, and for the elderly infirm.

Without fear of being accused of pretentiousness, I shall say that our Dominant Kinship Dyad hypothesis, by looking at kinship systems in terms of structure and content and dominant dyads and dominant attributes instead of in the traditional terms of marriage rules, residential patterns or componential analysis of kinship nomenclature, attempts to move in a similar direction. It promises to do what the theory of vitamins did in linking food constituents with physical health and illness by linking elements of kinship with varieties of social and cultural development.

Our only cautions are these. Firstly, social and cultural affairs are more complex than biological matters. They are made more complex by the student's emotional involvement in them and by our inability to subject them to laboratory conditions. Secondly, in less than ten years since I first proposed it, the Dominant Kinship Dyad hypothesis as an analytical tool has only been applied to a few cases, especially large literate societies and cultures.

I do, however, maintain that we can unveil much of the secret of Japanese society and culture—Japan's successes, failures and perils—by using this hypothesis. With this conviction we shall proceed to examine the Japanese kinship system and to compare it with its Chinese counterpart.

[1] This is not an exhaustive list of all possible dyads. Others are sibling-sibling, older brother-younger brother, older sister-younger sister, older brother-younger sister, older sister-younger brother, older sibling-younger sibling, and so forth. At this state of the development of the theory our considerations are limited to the eight basic ones listed above.

[2] Among physical scientists the term "property" is generally used in place of our term "attribute."

[3] Ronald M. Berndt has expressly dealt with such influences in his contribution to the *Kinship and Culture* volume (Hsu 1971:158-245).

[4] The term "dominant" is borrowed from genetics but the term "non-dominant" does not describe its exact opposite as does the term "recessive." In genetics a "recessive" gene usually does not appear in phenotype, but in the case of kinship a "non-dominant" attribute may be suppressed or merely reduced in importance.

[5] A distinction which I first made in 1959 (Hsu 1959:790-805). The definitions of structure and content have been somewhat revised and broadened here. But the essentials are the same in both publications.

8 •
Mothers and Sons

We do not claim that our Dominant Kinship Dyad hypothesis explains everything in any society and culture. What we believe is that this hypothesis enables us to identify certain crucial qualities of the kinship systems under review by translating them into attributes and relating them to a variety of behavior patterns in the society at large. In this way we make the social and cultural developments of each society more intelligible than before. We must now ask, does our hypothesis of father-son dominance modified by unigeniture and hierarchical and binding relationships between the heir and his brothers explain most of the relevant patterns of Japanese kinship and culture?

The Sub-dominance of the Mother-Son Dyad

We indeed have something to add to the picture. We can best begin by quoting a comment of Takao Sofue on the first version of this book:[1]

> Dr. Hsu's conclusion that Japan is simply a father-son dominated society is in error . . . it is true that in Japan the father has a strong authority, and patrilineal lines are emphasized; but I have to point out that at the same time in the affective aspect, the mother-son relationship is very important. The traditional pattern of interpersonal relationships among family members in Japan is that the father is autocratic and aloof, and children (especially sons) try to avoid their father or even are hostile to him. As a reaction to this resentment against the father, they have a sympathy with the mother and hence the mother-son relationship tends

to be tinged with sentimental and emotional color.

This pattern is most commonly found in rural families of the northeastern part of Japan, where the patrilineal tie and father's high status are most strongly stressed, and among urban families of the lower-middle class (merchants, owners of small shops or factories, taxi-drivers, etc.) or of the lower class (labor workers, carpenters and other craftsmen, etc.). In some extreme cases (mostly with urban families) the father spends much money for gambling or for women, and is violent to his wife and children. In such cases, the wife's status itself is quite insecure and, as a result, her relationship with the son, particularly with the eldest son, becomes excessively close. She feels that the eldest son is an only sympathizer for her, and that he will be her only supporter in later life. As a result the eldest son receives an emotional overprotection from the mother, and their relationship is characterized by a mutual dependency. Among the urban families of the upper-middle class (or, new middle class which consists of mostly white collar workers) the wife is hardly in such an unhappy and miserable situation, for their status is gradually becoming higher since the War, mostly as a result of the Western influence. However, the mother-son tie is still intense, as is indicated by Vogel.[2]

This close relationship between the mother and the son, and the weak ego of the Japanese which may have resulted from it, were very often discussed from the psychoanalytic point of view, too. Takeo Doi, a senior psychiatrist at the Tokyo St. Luke's Hospital, pointed out that Japanese word *amae* is a special term to mean the psychological state "to depend and presume upon another's benevolence," and this is "generally used to describe a child's attitude or behavior toward his parents, particularly his mother."

He speculates that this *amae* exists in the Japanese continually even in the period of adulthood, and should be a key concept for understanding Japanese personality structure (Doi 1956, 1960, 1962, 1963). William Caudill, psychoanalytically oriented anthropologist at the National Institute of Mental Health, discovered the overrepresentation of eldest sons among the Japanese psychotic patients, which should be related to the eldest son's dependent relationship with the mother (Caudill 1963). He also points to the fact that Japanese male schizophrenic patients show physical assault most often against their mother, and interprets this as caused by their strong desire for *amae* with the mother (Schooler and Caudill 1964). He also stresses that one of the factors strengthening this desire should be a traditional sleeping arrangement that parents continue to sleep in the same room as their children very frequently until the children leave home.[3]

My own data of the Sentence Completion Test collected from several hundreds of both urban and rural junior high school students in various parts of Japan (Sofue 1965), and my study of neurotic students of a university in Tokyo (Sofue 1964) suggest the same general feature as mentioned above, which tends to create a "mother complex" and a "dependent personality" leading in extreme cases to maladjusted college life. Today this "mother complex" is a very popular topic repeatedly discussed in Japanese newspapers, journals, etc. Taking these facts into consideration I would like to conclude that although in Japan the father-son relationship is explicitly dominant, . . . the father-son and mother-son relationships should be closely related to each other and must be regarded as both sides of one shield."

We cannot agree with Sofue that the father-son and mother-son relationships are "both sides of one shield" and therefore both dominant. In fact, what Sofue is describing here conforms well to the age-old *yen fu tsu mu* (roughly, stern father; kindly mother) model in Chinese society so well known to Confucian scholars. In both China and Japan the filial duties to mothers are as important as those to fathers, in repayment for the great debt the children owe their elders. In spite of this the father-son dyad is the backbone of the social organizations of both countries. For while the sons' duties, ritual and otherwise, extend from fathers to fathers' forebears for many generations, they do not even extend from mothers to mothers' parents.

However, given this similar father-son dominance, there are still indications that the mother-son dyad has a greater importance in Japan than in China. We must therefore describe the Japanese kinship system as father-son dominated, but with a mother-son bias, or sub-dominance,[4] by which we mean that the mother-son dyad is only second in importance to the father-son dyad. This mother-son sub-dominance emerges not by way of social design but as a consequence of social circumstances.

One of these circumstances is unigeniture, which we have outlined earlier. Sofue's statement confirms the possibility of a functional relationship between unigeniture and mother-son sub-dominance. For it is with the eldest son or heir that the mother tends to be "excessively close."

Sofue alludes to the other circumstance only in part. He thinks that a father's high status leads to an overbearing attitude towards his wife which in turn leads to the wife's excessive attachment to her son for personal salvation. I think social segregation of the wife and her husband is more relevant to the issue, and this segregation seems to be greater in Japan than in China.

Few perceptive observers of Japan could fail to notice this difference. Chinese and Japanese societies have traditionally disapproved of the kind of public togetherness that American spouses enjoy. It is fair to say that most American husbands have little social life outside the company of their wives. But even in old China, when the sexes were more separated than they are today, wives were always introduced to their husbands' friends when the latter were entertained at home. Since coming into contact with the West, educated Chinese in the universities and the government and even in the business world behave very much like Americans. On the other hand, the Japanese have almost never entertained their friends at home. Instead, male Japanese get together with their male friends or colleagues in restaurants and *geisha* houses without their wives. The Japanese desire for Westernization has apparently had little effect on this pattern. In addition to restaurants and *geisha* houses, Japanese men today go to *majong* parlors and golf courses and take weekend excursions with colleagues from their departments; all these activities take place without their spouses. This pattern holds true even in the universities. I worked for one year as a visiting professor in Kyoto University. The most astonishing thing to me as an university-educated man from China, was the absence of social contact even among faculty wives in Kyoto University and elsewhere. It is reasonable to assume that greater social distance from their husbands has compelled Japanese mothers more than their China sisters to seek closer ties with their sons, especially the son who is the heir.

The Attributes of the Mother-Son Dyad

According to our formulation outlined in Chapter 7, the intrinsic attributes of the mother-son dyad are discontinuity, inclusiveness, dependence, diffuseness and libidinality. The first two of these attributes have been dealt with earlier. We must now briefly explain the other three in order to make our subsequent discussion clearer.

Dependence is obviously present in the attribute of authority inherent in the father-son dyad. But there is a basic difference between the son's dependence on his father and his dependence on his mother. Intensive interaction between a father and his son usually occurs some months or years after the son's birth when the latter is less ineffectual and helpless than when he first began life with his mother. In Parsons' terms,[5] the father-son dyad lies one step further in the process of role differentiation than does the mother-son dyad. This involves not only far less dependence on the part of the son towards his father, but also a dependence characterized by an increasing degree of mutuality. The nature of the dependence has changed from need based on sheer inability to comprehend or perform any task, to need for guidance, channelling, the wisdom of experience, or punishment; in this latter situation reciprocity is more and more possible. The father-son relationship becomes characterized by "instrumentality" rather than "expressiveness." (Parsons 1955:45).

In the mother-son relationship, dependence is more likely to occur in its pristine state; in the father-son situation, authority is the characteristic attitude. The attribute of authority is much higher on "instrumentality" and "power" in Parsons' terms than dependence is. Conversely, though "power" and some "instrumentality" are not totally absent in the mother-child relationship, these attributes (especially "instrumentality") tend to be overshadowed by dependence. At the stage in which he is dependent on his mother, a son is not very competent in carrying out specific tasks, nor can he offer much to the mother; this situation changes as the boy grows older and comes under the tutelage of his father. A son is unilaterally dependent upon his mother but tends to maintain a mutually dependent relationship with his father.

At the same time the mother-son dyad is characterized by much greater diffuseness than the father-son dyad. That is to say, the son, being an infant, relies upon his mother for a variety of undifferentiated needs. His mother is the sole agent who satisfies all his needs, a condition that I have described elsewhere as mutability (Hsu 1963:175-189). This mode of need satisfaction is antithetical to what a boy will experience in later years when he will rough-house with playmates, learn the three Rs from teachers, go to doctors when he has bodily discomforts, attend movies or dances with friends, etc. A boy's growth process involves acquisition of both the knowledge and taste for differentiating needs as well as the techniques and resources for this differential satisfaction. The younger the infant the less his ability for differentiation, the more dependent he is upon his mother, and the more mutable the world is to him.

The attribute of libidinality is present whenever the partners of a relationship are of different sexes. But this attribute is likely to be stronger in the case of the mother-son relationship than that of the father-daughter or sister-brother dyads because of greater physical intimacy at a time when the son is least capable of differentiating his place in the social system. Our libidinality is similar to Parsons' "expressiveness" insofar as the latter includes a sexual component. But diffuseness and dependence, two other attributes of the mother-son dyad, each possesses an importance in the mother-son relationship that the more general term "expressiveness" cannot help us to appreciate.

Although we derive the word libidinality from the Freudian term "libido," we do not intend to equate it with the latter. The Freudian libido is understood as raw psychic material of a sexual nature, the fountainhead of all psychic energy which, through socializing mechanisms such as repression or sublimation or identification, becomes greatly modified, warped, diverted, or driven out of consciousness.[6] Libido is strictly a matter of personality dynamics. Without denying the validity of such psychological mechanisms to account for what goes on in the psyche of the individual, we must point out that our attribute of libidinality describes a certain general type of interpersonal activity. It is expressed in various societies in diverse ways, and is very much affected, as are the other attributes we have mentioned, by the prevalent cultural conditions. Consequently, we have no need, for example, to invoke the psycho-analytic concept of repression to explain its absence. For our purposes, the term "absence of libidinality" means simply that libidinality is not present, not that it has been driven underground by repression.

Finally, our attribute of libidinality must be separated from the attribute of sexuality which is exclusive to the husband-wife dyad. Sexuality refers to something quite specific, with clearly defined objects. The attraction between two lovers is characterized by sexuality. The attraction existing between certain types of entertainers and their public, between the temple *lingam* (male phallic representation in India) and its worshippers, and even between certain pieces of art and their viewers, contains libidinality.

Of course infantile sexuality is likely to be more diffused than the sexuality of adults, but this does not remain the case for long. Where sexuality is an operative attribute, the resulting emphasis is primarily heterosexual. This is the main reason for the great popularity of the concept of the Oedipus Complex in some cultures. However, here too, we are not dealing with psychoanalytic sexuality but with sexuality as a characteristic of a certain general type of interpersonal relationship in a given society. Its presence or absence in a society or culture will be judged by concrete evidence, not by psychoanalytic theory. However, our hypothesis stipulates that a culture having sexuality as a dominant attribute in its kinship system will ascribe greater importance to the Oedipus Complex and other psychoanalytic explanations of behavior than a culture in which sexuality is not a dominant attribute.

A Balance Sheet of Attributes

Taking the mother-son sub-dominance theme into account does not greatly alter our picture as far as the attributes affecting inclusion and continuity are concerned. Unigeniture, by undercutting the attributes of inclusiveness and continuity, has given greater importance to the attributes of inclusiveness and discontinuity. But, the strong and binding hierarchical relationship between an heir and his brothers in the dōzoku probably reinforces two opposing elements of the father-son dyad: inclusiveness (all brothers can be in it, though the relationship terminates for those who move away) and continuity (the link between an heir and his brothers is an extension of that between a father and his sons).

Mother-son sub-dominance, by increasing the weight of discontinuity but reducing that of exclusiveness, has merely added to the degree of disharmony noted before, namely that between continuity and inclusiveness on the one hand and discontinuity and exclusiveness on the other.

However, mother-son sub-dominance has reinforced the attributes of authority and dependence. It has reinforced the attribute of authority from the father-son dyad already made stronger by the power of the father to name the heir and by the markedly hierarchical and binding relationship between the heir and his brothers. Submission to authority is an essential component of dependence, especially unilateral dependence. Mother-son sub-dominance enlarges the scope of the attribute of dependence because, for reasons already explained, unilateral dependence involves more dependence than mutual dependence. Table 4 shows the balance between these attributes.

Father–Son	Unigeniture with power by father to select heir	Strong and binding hierarchical relationship between heir and brothers	Mother–Son
Continuity	Discontinuity	(Continuity)	Discontinuity
Inclusiveness	Exclusiveness	(Inclusiveness)	Inclusiveness
Authority	Authority	Authority	(Authority)
(Mutual dependence)	(Mutual dependence)	(Mutual dependence)	(Unilateral dependence)
Asexuality	Asexuality	Asexuality	Libidinality
		(Diffuseness)	(Diffuseness)

NOTE: The attributes in parentheses are less intense than those not in parentheses.

TABLE 4:   Balance of Attributes

Greater submission to authority and greater unilateral dependence explain, of course, some of the Japanese-Chinese differences. The Japanese have consistently shown greater fanaticism than the Chinese in submission to their leaders. The Japanese have exhibited a greater sense of discipline than the Chinese in their family and national life. Finally, the Japanese in all walks and stations of life, far more than their Chinese counterparts, have always adhered stringently to rituals and ceremonial details handed down from the past.

However, the attributes of diffuseness and libidinality are totally new elements. It is these attributes we must now discusss.

[1] The first version of this book was published as part of Francis L. K. Hsu: Hikaku Bunmei Shakai Ron (Sociology of Comparative Cultures), Tokyo, Baifukan, 1971. pp. 265-365. The quote here is taken from a larger comment by Sofue and published in Francis L. K. Hsu (ed.), *Kinship and Culture*. Chicago: Aldine Publishing Co., 1971. pp. 284-289.

[2] See Vogel 1963: 229-252.

[3] See Caudill and Plath 1966.

[4] The question may arise as to whether the importance of the mother-son dyad in Japan was not an older Japanese pattern which was later overshadowed by the Chinese father-son dominance. However, this line of inquiry will not be pursued at the present time.

[5] See Parsons 1955: 47-55.

[6] A United Methodist pastor told his Evanston, Illinois congregation Palm Sunday that on Monday he would begin a total fast to dramatize the need to end the war in Vietnam (reported in Chicago Sun Times, March 27, 1972). He said he was inspired to engage in the fast, not only by the New Testament but also by Mohandas K. Gandhi. Some who heard the announcement said he (the minister) must be obsessed with the death wish. Others said he was acting out his professional frustrations. Still others said he was sincere but misguided, or that he needed a kick in the pants. "Death wish" and "professional frustrations" are psychoanalytic explanations which are more commonly used in America than in China or Japan.

9 •

Diffuseness and Libidinality

In our analysis of the mother-son dominated way of life in India (Hsu 1963), we noted the enormously wide scope of Hindu culture: monotheistic belief exists side by side with polytheistic practices; emphasis on the theoretical and abstract is found alongside emphasis on the practical and concrete; religious abstention and asceticism coexist with extreme license and what outside observers often regard as lewdness ostensibly practiced for religious purposes. These and other conflicting patterns in the same culture are not the usual differences between ideal and reality, so often proposed by anthropologists to explain incongruities. Instead they are genuine and dissimilar elements in the ideals and again, dissimilar elements in the reality, all of which are held to be true and acted upon without apologies. I regard such facts as the most important evidence for the attribute of diffuseness.

Japanese patterns of life present the same kind of startling contrasts: a people who devote so much energy to excellence in different pursuits yet frequently speak of the impermanence of life; they practice a multitude of rituals, yet many Japanese emperors retire to monasteries in middle age;[1] a society where self-effacing and other-worldly monks frequently took up arms to fight rival sects and intervene in political struggles; a culture that puts such a high premium on art and flower appreciation but also positive merits on suicide.

A most spectacular contrast is that between the extremely effi-

cient Japanese public transportation systems and the extremely confusing and inefficient way of numbering their streets. The numbering
system is very ancient and the Japanese have thoroughly resisted its
modernization. When we found a house in the small town of Ashiya
with the address "26 Yamate Cho" in 1964, we naturally assumed that
our house was the only one bearing that number. But we were mistaken. The day after we moved in a police officer from the nearest
police station paid us a visit. He gave us a diagram of our area showing
the precise location of our house, the names of our immediate neighbors and where their houses were and the route to the nearest police
and railway stations. The officer even wrote the following information on a piece of paper which he handed to us. Assuming correctly
that we had no command of the Japanese language, the note said that
the master of the house to our left was a Dutchman married to a
Japanese wife who could speak English and who would be glad to
help in case of need.

Why was all this necessary? With my background of having lived
the first part of my life under the threat and oppression of Japanese
militarism, and having read all sorts of accounts of how the Japanese
secret police worked in Japan and her occupied territories, I did
entertain momentarily the suspicion that this officer's visit was the
usual Japanese way of keeping tabs on non-Japanese. Soon our suspicion was dispelled because we saw how the officer's gesture was in
the circumstances a reasonable necessity. It turned out that "26 Yamate Cho, Ashiya" does not refer to a single house, but to all the houses
in an area of several square blocks. Question: how do you find a
particular house? Answer: by knowing its exact location in that area!

This is the way to locate addresses not only in Ashiya, but in all
Japanese cities, including Tokyo and Osaka and other towns. The
American Occupation authorities put up, for their own convenience
I am sure, wooden street signs marking central Tokyo into A, B, C
streets to the end of the alphabet. In 1964 I arrived in Tokyo just in
time to see the M and P street signs near the Imperial Palace being torn
down. And Japan reverted to a mode of operation where one has to
know the exact location of the address he is seeking or he has to be
equipped with an area diagram, or he has to go to the police station,
ask for directions every step of the way or find a guide who knows
exactly where Matsuyama san's house is. Even some well-known
places are no exception. For example most taxi drivers take you to the

famed International House because they know its location by heart. But a few of them still had to consult the street diagram that the hostel gave me. We could go on to enumerate other examples of cultural diffuseness, but must be satisfied with only one more. This involves the unsystematic (diffused) and highly unoriginal (dependent) way in which the Japanese have adopted and incorporated foreign languages, primarily Chinese and now English.

The Japanese Use of Chinese

Japan began to borrow written Chinese from approximately the 6th century A.D. Before she developed her own syllabaries in the 9th and 10th centuries, the Japanese either used the Chinese language in its entirety, in accordance with grammatical rules of literary Chinese, or employed Chinese characters more or less as phonetic elements to write Japanese as it was spoken under Japanese grammatical rules. The *Kojiki (A Record of Ancient Events)*, compiled in A.D. 712 illustrates both these usages. The book frequently switches from one mode to the other and then back to the first without warning and without any apparent logic. The differences between the two modes are perfectly clear to many Japanese, for until quite recently, Japanese school children learned two sets of grammar, so that they could read both Japanese and classical Chinese and write treatises and poetry in both styles. But the unsystematic mixture in the *Kojiki* texts is only symptomatic of the even more unsystematic mixture found in the Japanese language in general.

Until World War II, a variety of Chinese characters were used in Japanese writing. Since then the number has been reduced to a total of 1850 known as *tōyō kanji* (or "commonly used Han characters"). The task of fitting monosyllabic Chinese characters into a highly inflective Japanese grammar has always been a difficult one. Conjunctives, case indicators, and many verbs and adjectives are usually written with Japanese syllables, while nouns (and many verb roots) are frequently given in Chinese characters. The following passage, taken from a book entitled *Noiroze* (Neurosis) by Dr. Masaaki Kato is quite typical:

人間でも動物でも、行動の自由を極端に
制限されると、二つの型の反応を示す。
一つは欲求をみたすことを妨げるものを
つき破ろうとして、手あたりばったりな
（試行錯誤）運動をすること であり
これを「運動乱発」という。もう一つは
全く自発性を失い、動く ことをやめ
た 状態 で、これを 「擬死反射」
という。

(Kato 1959:45)

(Both human beings and animals will exhibit two types of reaction when subjected to extreme restraint in their freedom of action. One type is to attempt to break free from the restraint by trial and error, in what might be called "random movements." The other is to exhibit a total loss of initiative, so that movement is absent. This is called the "death feigning reflex.")

There are twenty-three nouns in this paragraph (underlined with straight lines) but only six of them are written entirely in Japanese script (*koto* three times, *kore* twice, and *mono* once). Each of the expressions underlined by wavy, dotted or double straight lines is respectively, an adjective verb, an adverb, and a verb as well as an auxiliary verb. Most of them are combinations of one or more Chinese ideographs as roots and some Japanese syllables as auxiliary elements.[2] It should be noted that, although the title of Dr. Kato's book is given in the Japanese transliteration of the English term "neurosis," the other scientific terms such as "random movement," etc., are coined by combining Chinese ideographs on the basis of meaning.

Although the lack of regularity here is already confusing, the confusion is minimal when compared to its potential in other situations. I shall indicate some of the variety of ways in which Chinese is used in Japanese below.

The first way is to use Chinese characters according to their accepted Chinese meaning. My estimate is that something like 70% or more of all Japanese nouns are written in this way.

A second way is to use Chinese characters for meanings that are somewhat related to, yet significantly different from, the Chinese originals, so that a Chinese who knows only Chinese is likely to misunderstand. Thus the concept of "ambiguity" is represented by two Chinese characters *"ai mai"* which in Chinese refer only to an illicit relationship between a man and a woman. The concept "discount," as in reduction of price in merchandise, is represented by two Chinese characters *"katsu in"* (but pronounced *"waribiki"*), which in Chinese means "to cut" and "to pull." The concept "secure" or "satisfactory" in Japanese is written with three Chinese characters *"dai jō bu"* which in Chinese mean "great or strong man." The concept "to study" in Japanese is represented by the Chinese characters *"ben kyō"* which in Chinese means "forcing." When I began to learn Japanese I realized that a great deal of forcing was necessary in order to achieve success, but I still do not think that forcing and studying have any semantic connection.

I was indeed baffled when I read in Japanese papers an account of Edgar Snow's interview with Chairman Mao in which the latter described the atom and hydrogen bombs as "Master Chang's tiger." I had to delve into dictionaries to find that the Chinese characters "Master Chang" for the Japanese means "papered" (or *hariko*).[3] One can go through Japanese texts and find hundreds of such examples in which the Japanese usage has some connection with the Chinese usage but which is often either obscure or liable to be misunderstood from the Chinese point of view.

A third way of using Chinese characters is to treat them phonetically. Thus the Japanese word for bath *(furo)* is written with two Chinese characters: the first means wind in Chinese and the second is a surname; the Japanese for green grocery *(yaoya)*, is written with three Chinese characters meaning "eight hundred store"; the Japanese for recommendation *(sewa)* is two Chinese characters meaning world and speech; the Japanese for trouble *(jama)* is two Chinese characters meaning crazy and devil; the Japanese for double-suicide *(shinjū)* is two Chinese characters meaning heart and center, and so forth. These, except for *yaoya*, are examples in which the Chinese characters are read in the Chinese way *(on yomi)*.

In contrast, a fourth way is to use Chinese characters with Japanese pronunciation *(kun yomi)* to signify purely Japanese meanings. The Japanese expression for "interesting" *(omoshiroi)* is a good example. The expression consists of two Chinese characters for face and for white plus the vowel "i" ("i" being a common Japanese vowel ending for an adjective). Now, the Japanese spoken word for "face" is *omo* and for "white" is *shiroi*. The resulting Japanese term *omoshiroi* means "interesting." The two Chinese characters (face and white) have no relation separately or together, to any Chinese expression which even comes close to meaning "interesting."

The Japanese term *mimai* (sympathy for sickness or misfortune) illustrates the same point, though with some variation. The first Chinese character, "mi" means to see or to visit and the second one "mai", means to dance. "Sympathy" may indeed have a logical connection with "visit," but its relationship to "dance" is obscure. And the pronunciation of both characters is Japanese.

Related to the above is a fifth situation: using Chinese concepts made up of one or more Chinese characters in writing while using their Japanese equivalents in speech. The concept of go-between or matchmaker is a good example. The two characters which the Japanese use to indicate "matchmaker" derive from a Chinese expression for "middle man" (though not "matchmaker," for which the Chinese have another, related expression). However, the Japanese word, *nakōdo*, has little linguistic connection to the Chinese characters. This would be like an American writing the Chinese characters, *ta tsu chi*, but reading them, "typewriter." The problem here is not that the Chinese characters and their Japanese counterparts are used interchangeably, but that they unsystematically play separate but often equivalent roles in the same language.

We have already mentioned the absence of any reason for explaining why some Western terms such as "random movement" are expressed by putting four Chinese characters together but other Western terms such as "neurosis" are expressed in phonetic transliterations. In the same way, one wonders why the Japanese concept of love is usually expressed by the Chinese term *ai* and for donor, master, or husband only by the Sanskrit term *dana (pati)* and with reference to the secular world only by the Sanskrit term *saha*, or why the kinship terms in speech do not correspond to the kinship terms in writing. For example, while the Chinese term *gibo* means only "adopted mother" in China, it means "mother-in-law," "step-mother," and "foster mother" in Japan.

The readings of Chinese characters are most confusing. In general there are at least two readings for each Chinese character, but frequently there are many more. Thus, the Chinese character signifying birth or life can be pronounced in Japanese as *shō, sei, ha* (eru), *i (kasu), na (rasu), uma (reru), u (mu), nama, fu,* and *ki.* There do not seem to be any rules governing when a Chinese character is read in what way. Even the one basic principle (of which my Japanese teachers told me early in my struggles with the language), that the Japanese reading applies to a Chinese character if the latter is used singly and Chinese reading applies to two or more Chinese characters in combination, is often broken.

English in the Japanese Language

We have by no means enumerated all the confusing features of the Japanese language, but we should now conclude our examination by noting the haphazard manner in which the Japanese have always used European words in transliteration, even in the early days of contact with the West. Words like *pan* (from the Portuguese meaning bread) and *arubaito* (from the German "Arbeit," but meaning supplementary employment) are well known. But while there is good reason for "gas," "skirt," "stereo," "white collar," "salary man," "type," "bourgeoisie," "slogan," etc., to appear in phonetic transliterations (because these concepts or articles were all imported), there is no good reason whatever for "picnic," "hiking," "vacation," "open-car," "service," "ranking," "color," "apron," etc., to be treated similarly. Of late, even the English word "wife" (*waifu* in Japanese) has been used in place of its traditional equivalent.

The English term "wife," rather than the traditional *tsuma* or *nyōbō* is, I understand, often used by a husband who aspires to sophistication (sometimes the German term "Frau" is used, too). I have also been assured by some merchants that advertising with English words is a good sales device. At a certain superficial level these reasons seem sound enough. The same drive or need to express sophistication can be found in the use of academic transliterations from English. Hence such words as "role," "group," "implication," "life cycle," "frame of reference," "member," "data," etc., are used in scientific treatises even though perfectly good Japanese terms can be coined with Chinese ideographs. The problem is the lack of rules which govern such adoptions.

At this point one may say that the Japanese admiration for Western (especially American) cultures and institutions and their desire to simulate the admired objects motivate this borrowing (just as at another time in her history the objects of admiration and simulation were Chinese culture and institutions). Again we seem to have found a plausible explanation, but once more contrary facts stare us in the face. Why are many Japanese modern scientific terms *not* phonetic transliterations but rather terms composed of Chinese characters? In this latter class we find the terms for habit, regulation, ready situation, individual, value-attitude system, social process, bicycle, automobile, train, symphony, electricity, foreign telegraph, geometry, oxygen, democracy and even atomic bomb and air raid. Many of these Chinese character-based terms were coined shortly before or after the Meiji Restoration in 1868, but many of them, especially those currently used in the social sciences, are recent additions.

The ordinary Japanese cannot always sort out the confusion. From my room in the Otani in Tokyo during a short visit, I could see a big neon sign:

不 二 サ ッ シ

I thought the Japanese letters "sashi" represented the Chinese characters "sa tze" (sand paper) and concluded the sign was an advertisement for sandpaper of Fuji brand. I asked the next bell boy who came in the room. He agreed with me. But we were both wrong. The neon sign was really telling prospective customers about window sashes of Fuji brand.

This complete lack of consistency in the Japanese method of incorporating foreign languages stands in sharp contrast to the highly predictable way in which the modern Chinese, most of whom have also been accused of "worshipping the West," have approached the same problem. A few foreign words found their way into the Chinese language by way of engineering or literary fancy. Thus the common Chinese expressions for "motor" and "humor" are transliterations from the English. There were attempts to use the transliterated forms of such words as "inspiration," "democracy," and "dictators," instead of their Chinese equivalents, but they never were very successful. In Canton and Hong Kong the terms "taxi" and "insurance" are transliterations from the English, but to the best of my knowledge none of the transliterated terms enjoyed wide or continued circulation in China except for the word "motor."

The Chinese as a rule prefer Chinese equivalents for Western terms, made by combining native Chinese characters. When Dr. Sun Yat-sen wrote his famous *Three Peoples' Principles* he did not use "te mo ke la shi" and "ti ke tuei tue" respectively for democracy and dictator, but "min chu" and "tu ts'ai." The use of transliterations for "taxi" and "insurance" is identified with overseas Chinese in the south. In Taiwan today a taxi is known as "chi ch'eng ch'e" (metered vehicle), a brake is called "sa ch'e" (stop car), and insurance "pao hsien" (protection from risk). The Chinese term for proletariat is "lao tung," a word also used by Vietnamese and Koreans.

In addition to a lack of consistency in creating vocabulary, we find in Japan almost total absence of rules regarding pronunciation of Chinese ideographs. It is also not clear when to use *kanji* (Chinese characters) and when to use *kana* (Japanese syllables). Looking over a variety of materials such as novels, newspapers, popular journals, and scientific books, the only regularity I find is that the endings of sentences and especially paragraphs tend to be in *kana* (e.g., such as "*desu*," "*narimashita*," "*shiteorimasu*," or "*dekimasen*"). In fact, from the non-Japanese point of view the ending "*desu*" and its variants seem to occur with monotonous frequency.

I have asked many Japanese why Japan did not drop *kanji* altogether, for most other languages of the world operate very well with phonetic scripts. One common Japanese answer to this query is that there are so many homonyms in Japanese that the Chinese ideographs are essential for discriminating among them.

There is a certain truth in this point of view. For example, the syllable "*shō*" can mean nature, disposition, smallness, commander, prize, business, quotient, chapter, ministry, charge, honorable name, victory, just or exact (as in "just at six o'clock"), etc. These different meanings could indeed create some ambiguity if the syllable "*shō*" was used by itself, and sometimes the Japanese listener does have to ask which "*shō*" is meant; the speaker then replies, for instance, "*shōten no shō* (the *shō* as in a shop)." But, this sort of explication is also a common Chinese practice and is not peculiar to the Japanese. Besides, the syllable "*shō*" can be used, according to Sanseido's *New Concise Japanese-English Dictionary* (1959), in at least 296 rather unmistakable ways in combination with other syllables. It is hard to accept the existence of homonyms as a good reason for retaining *kanji*.

Recently a distinguished Japanese offered me another reason for maintaining *kanji*. He says that the use of Chinese characters saves time. For example, the expression "*seikatsu*" (life) consists of only two ideographs in *kanji* but needs four syllables in Japanese.

This answer is not very satisfactory. Shorter *kanji* expressions are available for concepts typically written in *kana* such as *wareware* (we), *iroiro* (various), *shitagatte* (according to), *tatoeba* (for example), and, of course, *yukiataribattari* (haphazard). There is no evidence that Japanese writers wish to save time where these terms are concerned. The real reason for this perplexing situation, it seems to me, is the unsystematic (diffuse) and unoriginal (dependent) way in which the Japanese approach their language.

Comparing the Japanese approach to language with the attitudes of the Chinese, the Hindus and the Americans, we find the Chinese most resistant to transliteration and adaptation, while the Hindus and Americans are similar in that they are somewhat less resistant but both tend to derive most new words from their ancestral languages (Sanskrit for the Hindus and Greek or Latin for the Americans) whereas the Japanese are the most non-discriminatory in adopting foreign words and concepts.

However, while the Hindu approach to language assimilation is not similar to that of the Japanese, the Indians exhibit an extremely strong attribute of diffuseness as regards their epics and scriptures. *The Ramayana* and especially *The Mahabharata* are conglomerations of anecdotes and elements from different sources and historical times. There are so many different kinds of scriptures that I know of no learned Hindu who is even able to give an account of the total number, let alone know all of them to any great extent. The Hindu concern for systematization is so small that no effort has been made to deal with the many contradictory rituals prescribed in the multitude of scriptures. They simply exist side by side.

In the midst of this confusion of beliefs and rituals, the Hindu's fixed point of reference is his guru (spiritual guide), who dictates ritual details and demands an unquestioning obedience, just as the fixed point of reference for the Japanese is his master in religion (as we shall see in a later chapter), his lord in *bushidō*, his *Iemoto* in trades and professions and his *oyabun* in modern firms and factories.

Hindu caste raising efforts are most successful when rationales for them are found in ancient texts. In Japan, status raising efforts (for business sales or academic disciplines) are accomplished by the incorporation of large elements of a prestigious new language. But the Japanese businessmen and intellectuals seem to be ambivalent about this process, for they incorporate in a haphazard manner, sometimes coining new terms composed of Chinese characters and sometimes resorting to transliteration of Western terms.

The Question of Libidinality

The theory of mother-son sub-dominance also raises the question of the attribute of libidinality. Can we find evidence for this attribute? The answer is yes. This attribute expresses itself in Japanese society and culture through a generalized emphasis on sex appeal through the widespread production and appreciation of the arts.

Like the Chinese the Japanese consider tea their most popular drink. With their predilection for *iemoto* came various "schools" of tea ceremony. The tea ceremony is often performed by an ornamented, beautifully dressed girl. The fact that sometimes the tea ceremony is performed by an old lady only shows that the psychology involved here is generalized and not one of specific sexuality. The woman does not have to be an actual, desirable sexual object; a mere suggestion of sex will do. It should also be noted that traditionally men have been the true masters of the tea ceremony; nowadays many young girls study the art, but it is still practiced by men as well.

Prostitution is universally understood to be based on the sexual act. No Chinese poet or social thinker ever claimed otherwise. The Chinese had prostitutes who were differentiated according to class: the first class girls would only agree to sleep with their customers after the latter had made a few "social" visits and lavished presents on them and their establishments, while the second and third class girls made the objective easier. But there were no Chinese ladies who developed the skills of singing and dancing and entertaining and then claimed that their charm and company were for sale as art objects, but that their bodies were not for sale as sex objects. These are precisely the claims of the Japanese *geisha* and their promoters. Many Japanese *geisha* do, in fact, give their bodies to wealthy customers, but aided by the institutional and theoretical elaboration explained above, the Japanese have made it possible for old *geisha* to continue selling their studied professional talents and company without seeming ludicrous.

Add to these observations the fact that nearly every taxi driver in Japan has some female doll (nowadays usually European in looks) hanging from his rear-vision mirror, the fact that the Japanese have elongated the head of the Chinese God of Longevity to such an extent that it resembles the Hindu *lingam* (phallic representation; see Plates A, B, C and D), and the fact of the occurrence of festivals like the annual Hadaka Festival in Okayama where, before midnight, hundreds of completely nude young men jostle against each other for several hours on the small platform of the Saidaiji temple for the benefit of men and women spectators. We now see some clear expressions of diffused sexuality.

The ubiquitousness of art and artistic motivations in Japan is equally easy to perceive. For example, calligraphy which had already become an art in China (as contrasted to the modern-day United States, where the quality or style of hand-writing is without artistic significance), underwent extensive proliferation in Japan. In both China and Japan calligraphy is an essential part of any good painting, and a calligraphic work can stand alone as an object of art. But the *sōsho* or the cursive script developed to a much higher degree in Japan than in China.

The creation of both porcelain and pottery was a highly sophisticated art in China; some T'ang (A.D. 681-907) and Ming (A.D. 1368-1644) items are priceless treasures of museums and private collections the world over. However, the skilled potters and porcelain makers in China were considered craftsmen who worked to turn out expensive or common wares for the society at large. I know of no Chinese masters in the field of ceramics who attained a position of artistic prominence similar to the masters of *Bizen Yaki* fame near Okayama in Japan and no Chinese concept arousing so much artistic challenge and mystery as does the delicate Japanese *shibui.* Furthermore, fine ceramics were associated in China with the expensive tastes of the higher classes. The vast majority of the people including peasants and workers used very crude wares. One of the most striking features of Japanese life is the widespread use of "good" Japanese porcelain and especially pottery in "average" homes. In the United States, if one buys inexpensive things one must be satisfied with inferior quality in their design or decoration. In Japan, very artistically refined and exquisite wares can be bought in some of the most unlikely places for very little money.

The Japanese home is another interesting phenomenon. A very humble Japanese home is still likely to have a *tokonoma* (recessed alcove) with its *kakemono* (hanging scroll), flower arrangement, a low table, *shoji* (sliding paper doors) with their simple lines, and neatly spread *tatami* (straw matting), with one or more *zabuton* (cushions) on the floor. The bedding and pillows are neatly stored away during the day and there is also likely to be a *tana* (shelf) for the display of family "treasures"; a prize, a certificate of merit, a *bonsai* (dwarf plant), a photo, or sometimes an incongruously cheap plastic or metal statue of Western origin. The homes of the rich are likely to have attached to them extensive gardens with their lovely rocks, stepping-stone paths, stone lanterns, artificial ponds, trees, etc., but the basic arrangement of their interiors is not very different from that found in humbler homes.

This picture sharply contrasts with the traditional situation in China. In most of China the farmers and workers, even those living above the poverty line, dwelt in homes that were as a rule not at all artistic. They gave better protection against the elements than Japanese houses, but their interior furnishings were without elegance. The huge well-to-do homes would have big immaculate gardens cared for by servants, but their interiors would look crowded. I have seen expensive homes with parquet floors, reflecting Western influence, in which a bundle of hams or pressed ducks would be hanging from the dining room ceiling for no other reason than that this was a convenient and airy place for temporary storage. Wealthy homes would have straight-backed armed chairs and vases; they might have scrolls crowded together on the walls; but they would not show that concern for spatial arrangement and simple harmonies characteristic of the Japanese. The homes of the Chinese poor simply had less of everything, and showed even less signs of care or artistic concern.

If we allow ourselves the luxury of an over-simplified contrast between the Chinese and Japanese well-to-do homes, we might say that while the former are first for status and second for comfort, with no thought for art, the latter are first for art (show) and second for status, with much less thought for comfort. The last observation is not as fantastic as it might seem to some. The poor heating in Japanese homes is notorious, and nothing vexes a Chinese guest in a Japanese home on a midwinter morning more than finding upon his return in a bathrobe and pajamas from the family washroom, that his hostess has rolled away all his bedding and opened wide all the windows in his room.

Finally, the non-Japanese observer cannot fail to be impressed by the Japanese love of flowers. The Japanese genius for flower arrangement (*kadō* or *ikebana*) is world famous. Previously we described some of the most important schools of flower arrangement and their organizations. But even people who do not enroll in one of these schools probably make the annual rounds of "chrysanthemum viewings" and especially spring "cherry blossom viewings." A non-Japanese simply has to visit some such place as the Heian Shrine (in Kyoto) in May to realize how very much flowers move the Japanese. And this Japanese appreciation for flowers is not simply a fad or a matter of conformity. It has lasted for centuries and continues today. It affects equally the rich and the poor, men and women, the scholar and the less literate. Its strength has increased not decreased with modernization. In fact while visiting Japanese factories I have again and again seen a vase of flowers on the floor near some greasy and ugly engine, put there by some unknown worker.

Dominance vs. Sub-dominance

The attributes of a sub-dominant dyad are strongly influenced by those of the dominant dyad. In the Japanese situation, diffuseness and dependence (mother-son attributes) are kept in check by authority and, to a more limited extent, by continuity (father-son attribute). For example, dependence among the Japanese tends to be mutual rather than unilateral. This is to say, the dependent party is less likely to wait helplessly for orders and succor from his superior. Instead, while he derives benefit from his benefactor, he does a great deal to benefit the superior in return. This is the the essence of mutual dependence in contrast to unilateral dependence. It is, as we saw in the chapter dealing with *iemoto*, one of the key elements in the relationship between a master and his disciple.

Japanese society and culture also exhibit controlled diffuseness rather than unfettered diffuseness. That is to say, although the scope of Japanese life patterns (including language) is wide and full of incongruities, the actual tasks for various individuals are extremely specific, and very clearly designed and executed. There is no evidence of diffuseness in them. Such precision is, as we also saw in the chapter dealing with *iemoto*, characteristic of the products and the proccesses of learning and production in that secondary grouping.

However, although Japanese subordinates show extreme deference to their superiors, the former can sometimes alter the course of events by invoking (or acting on behalf of) authorities higher than their immediate superiors. The May 15, 1932 insurrection, in which a number of army radicals (mostly of company ranks) attacked the metropolitan police headquarters in Tokyo, the Mitsubishi Bank, the Seiyukai headquarters and electric transformer stations in many parts of the city, is a typical expression of this approach. During this eruption, Inukai, the Prime Minister, was assassinated and Count Makino, lord keeper of the privy seal, was gravely wounded.

This was no ordinary rebellion in the sense that Westerners would understand it. The rebels wanted a more militaristic policy leading to greater territorial expansion than the majority of the officials in power was willing to grant. The rebels issued a manifesto calling attention to the so-called dangers confronting the nation and urging the people to take up arms to "save" Japan. They specifically demanded the liquidation of the political parties and *zaibatsu* (financial cliques) and the punishment of delinquent bureaucrats and advisers to the throne. For, the rebels maintained, *these officials had failed to carry out the Imperial Way as the Emperor would have wished it.*

The insurrection forced the resignation of the cabinet. The party government gave way to a series of cabinets dominated by the military. The assassins were given exceptionally light sentences in the subsequent trial, during which the accused were not treated as criminals but as "misguided patriots." All this, in spite of the fact that the

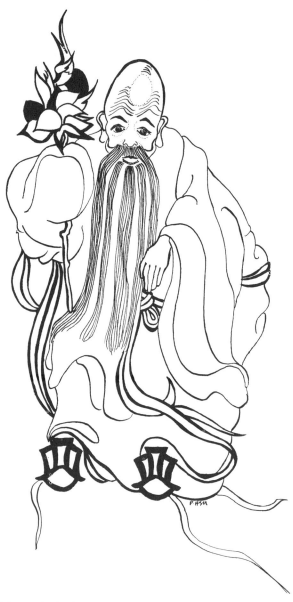

Plate A: Chinese God of Longevity

Plate B: Japanese God of Longevity

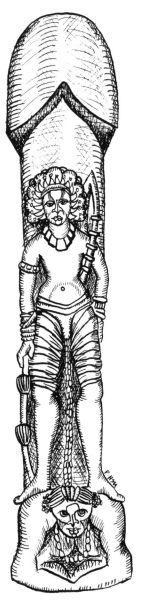

Plate C: The Hindu lingam of the God Shiva

Plate D: Madonna and child

acts of violence perpetrated by the low ranking army officers were not followed by a popular uprising. And the Emperor was not asked whether or not he agreed with the rebels nor did he ever issue a statement clarifying his views.

Such an event, including its rationale, reception, and results, could not have occurred in China or India. Throughout Chinese dynastic history the emperor was indeed the highest authority on earth. That authority might be usurped in which case the emperor or his dynasty would fall. But it could not be merely assumed and acted upon by someone else in his name without his permission and his authority and dynasty would remain unchallenged by such an attack. In India some men at lower levels (in the caste, in the military, in the government) could indeed invoke the will of Atma or higher authorities of secret texts to justify deviation from the norm. But any such conflict in India was likely to concern far vaguer issues than the rate of national expansion or armament.

Libidinality in Religious Symbolism

Do we have any evidence that libidinality (an attribute of the mother-son dyad) is similarly overshadowed by asexuality, an attribute of the father-son dyad? Indeed we do. This fact may be gauged from religious symbolism. Here a four-way comparison is most instructive (see Plates A, B, C, and D).

Plate A is a common Chinese representation of the God of Longevity. It is found in numerous Chinese books and paintings. It adorns the ceremonial wall of many Chinese homes whenever the birthday of an old man or an old lady is celebrated. Plate B is a common Japanese representation of the same god. The most unusual feature in the Japanese version, from the Chinese point of view, is the enormous elongation of the god's bald head.[4]

Plate C is a Hindu representation of the *lingam* of the God Shiva. This is the form found in Gudimallam, Madras, 1st century, B.C. (according to Basham 1954: plate facing p. 105). Later representations of the *lingam* in Hindu temples are usually not so realistic, except in the great Shiva temple in Benares. They tend to be simple rod-like forms rounded on top, similar to the Japanese God of Longevity's head. But as a rule they each also have the female sexual organ *(yoni)* represented at their bases so that the two elements symbolize male and female principles in congress. The Nativity scene in Plate D is familiar to all Westerners and to Christians everywhere. It symbolizes the Virgin Birth, a concept later extended to cover Mary's Immaculate Conception.

To the Chinese, whose kinship system is marked by the absence of the attribute of sexuality or libidinality, the sexual element is not a point of contention, to be glorified, denied or disguised. Consequently, it has either no place in religious representations (as in Plate A) or is present as a matter of course, as when some gods have spouses. The Chinese Kitchen God is usually associated with his wife, and both are objects of worship. But many Chinese gods (of War, of Literature, of Wealth, etc.) have no spouses.

The Japanese, Hindu and American symbols are concerned with the sexual element. To the Japanese, in whose kinship system libidinality is only a subordinate attribute, the phallic symbol is only the elongated head of an old god who cannot by any stretch of the imagination be associated with sexual prowess. But this deity is only of minor religious importance in Japan, as is its counterpart in China. To the Hindu, in whose kinship system libidinality is a dominant attribute, the sexual reference is explicit or even glorified. The *lingam* or *lingam* and *yoni* in combination is a major religious symbol in India. Numerous temples house them, and there are rituals, prayers, and scriptures offered for their adoration, worship and explication. However, the representation is incomplete because no expression is given to the consequences of the sexual union. The Western symbol of the infant Christ and his Virgin mother embodies not only a preoccupation with sex but also with its result.[5] This is commensurate with the attribute of sexuality in a husband-wife dominated kinship system.

Furthermore, a most interesting point that emerges from this comparison is the fact that, while the God of Longevity in China and the God of Blessing in Japan grant pure blessings without further complications, the *lingam* and the Virgin Mary and the Christ Child are associated in India and in West with destruction as well.

In the Hindu case, Shiva is not only known as both Creator and the Destroyer, but he also suffers from the obvious aggression of his wife, the *Mata* of Mother Worshippers. For when Shiva's consort appears in the ferocious form of Kali, she has a black face and a garland of human skulls around her neck, and her husband's naked body lies under one of her feet. Hindus say this is why Kali is also invariably represented as having her tongue hanging out, for she was astonished by what she had mistakenly done (stepping on her husband). The West has gone much further in this connection. The Virgin Birth and Immaculate Conception are not enough. Christ has to be destroyed in order that He may atone for the Original Sin.

Superficially, the four patterns of religious symbolism seem to form a continuum, from the Chinese case in which the sexual element is absent to its Western counterpart in which sexuality is central. Qualitatively, the Chinese, Japanese, and Hindu patterns belong to one group, deeply separated from the Western pattern, which exists in a class by itself. Even between the Chinese representation which says nothing about sex and the Hindu one in which sex looms large, the differences are still quantitative. The Japanese representation should be placed midway between the two. But in all three cases sexuality is treated as objective fact, like hunger or physical danger. It is relevant in some human situations, not relevant in others. But it is not a problem to be defended or explained, for its presence or absence is self-evident.

The Virgin Birth is distinct from the other three because it involves a denial of sexuality. Since such a denial contradicts reality, explanations are important and primeval guilt has become the basic foundation for its justification. I do not imply that guilt in mythology is the same as an actual sense of guilt in an individual's psyche. But I do think that the wide circulation of the former and its extensive use in church and popular education are highly commensurate with Puritanism, a uniquely Western development totally unknown in the East.[6]

This distinction has a strong bearing on patterns of human interaction, especially among members of the same sex, that will become clearer as we once again look at the *iemoto.*

---

[1] In sharp contrast to the rulers of China, only one of whom retired because of a broken heart.

² The signs are used as follows: ———— noun; ∧∧∧∧∧ adjective verb; ‒ ‒ ‒ ‒ ‒ adverb; ════verb and auxiliary verb. The part of speech termed "adjective verb" is a Japanese grammatical peculiarity, which is non-existent in English. However, some Japanese grammarians deny the existence of adjective verbs. In this case the adjective verb is separated into two parts of speech: noun and auxiliary. In English the function of auxiliaries is in most cases performed by prepositions.

³ The present Chinese meanings of the word "chang" are a surname, a sheet (of paper), or to spread (a flag). It is possible that its ancient Chinese meaning could include paper (as in papered tiger).

⁴ In China this deity is one of the household gods and exists side by side with the Kitchen God, Gate Gods, God of Joy and Bliss, etc. I am not aware of any special temple dedicated to him. In Japan this deity is commonly known as Fukurokuju (blessing, wealth and longevity) or Fukurojin (old immortal of blessing), and as one of the Shichi Fuku Jin (Seven Gods of Blessing). The other six are: Daikoku, Ebisu, Bishamon, Benten, Hotei, and Jurojin. I am also not aware of any Japanese shrine specially dedicated to him. On the other hand, Daikoku, and especially Ebisu, are honored in many shrines. The latter is variously thought to be the God of Prosperity, of Trade, of Sailors, of Fishing, etc. One of the largest shrines dedicated to this god is the Ebisu Jinja in Nishinomiya, near Osaka. A set of statues of Shichi Fuku Jin is placed next to the *butsudan* in many homes.

⁵ The central theme of the Virgin Birth and Immaculate Conception is, of course, a denial of sex. But the psychological link between explicit denial of and preoccupation with the same object may be amply illustrated by the following Chinese tale: A poor farmer suddenly inherited a fortune of 300 ounces of silver. There being no banks or safety deposit boxes in his village, he dug a deep hole in his backyard and buried them. Still fearing that someone would discover the treasure, he put the following sign beside the hole: "There are no 300 ounces of silver here."

⁶ After writing these lines, I came across a book entitled *Nihonjin to Yudyajin* (Japanese and Jews) by Isaiah Ben-Dasan (1970). In this book the author explains why the Japanese and the Jews did not possess or pay attention to the myth of the Virgin Birth. Noting that the myth was a non-Jewish attribution to Jesus principally due to the work of Luke, Ben-Dasan gave two reasons for its absence in Japan. First, the importance of unbroken "lineage," which runs through all Japanese institutions including *iemoto* and the imperial house, is in direct conflict with the idea of Virgin Birth, which would have broken that continuity. Second, the Japanese place a high mysticism and romantic emotionalism to sex (in contrast to nomadic peoples) and they see children and parents as inseparably tied to each other. Both of these are, too, incompatible with the notion of Virgin Birth (Ben-Dasan 1970:137-141). At least two of Ben-Dasan's observations, emphasis on "lineage" continuity as in *iemoto* and the unity between parents and children, are in line with the main thread of our analysis. These features are, of course, even more characteristic of the Chinese than the Japanese. However, unless we add the dimension of kinship content, they alone lack explanatory power with reference to India.

10 •

The *Iemoto* and the Individual

All human beings live in a society. Those who claim they prefer solitude or who extol the virtue of solitude form not only a tiny minority of mankind, but usually use solitude as a means for enhancing their positions among the multitude. Most holy men in India claim long periods of solitude and austerity in the forbidding Himalayas as a basis for their "powers." The Lord Buddha claimed to have reached enlightenment after six years of practicing asceticism in the forests. Jesus Christ was alone in the wilderness for over 40 days during which time he powerfully resisted various temptations. These facts remind us of the Pacific Northwest American Indians, among whom it is the custom for every youth to stay alone for several days in the wilds until he sees an apparition of "his" guardian spirit, the possession of which is part of his manhood. As for Thoreau of Walden Pond, he described his two years of solitude in 14 volumes of his *Journal*. One may say that Thoreau's primary interest was to start a sect of believers in solitude with himself as its founder and chief priest.

However, each individual does not relate to all his fellow men with equal intensity or in the same way. He confides in some, deals superficially with others, and may only be vaguely conscious of the existence of still others. Upon inspection we find that human beings relate to each other in two basic ways: through role and affect.

135

Role and Affect

The main ingredient of role is usefulness. "What can I do for you?" "He can't help me." "Will you hire me?" "In this fight God is on our side." The amount of alimony should support her "in the style to which she is accustomed." Such comments as these and thousands of other sentiments familiar to us express the nature of roles.

In every society human beings are more or less formally known according to the roles they perform: skilled and unskilled labor, white collar and blue collar workers, dentists and diamond cutters, janitors and politicians, warriors and witch doctors, mothers' helpers and merchants, and many others.

The main ingredient of affect is feeling. "Do you love him?" "There is nothing I wouldn't do for that woman." "He is a loyal friend." "He inspires confidence in his followers, who are devoted to him." These and thousands of other statements express the nature of affect. Love, hate, rage, despair, endurance, sympathy, hope, alienation, anxiety, forbearance, loyalty, betrayal—these are kinds of affect variously known to all mankind.

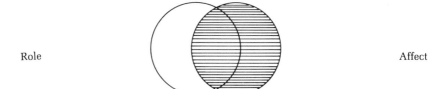

Role   Affect

DIAGRAM 7: Role and Affect

Both role and affect are essential for human *solidarity*. And they usually overlap (see Diagram 7). A man may hate or love his job, be loyal or disloyal to his spouse, feel secure or insecure vis-à-vis his colleagues. In these and other connections, affect determines how a man performs his role. A mother's relationship with her infant child is marked more by affect than by role. A street car conductor's approach to his job collecting fares is marked more by role than by affect. However, a mother who loves her baby but is totally ignorant of child care is not a competent mother, just as a street car conductor who has no pride in his work will not do it well or stay in the job long.

However, while usefulness or role is calculable and rates for role transactions are measurable, feeling or affect is far less calculable and rates for affective interactions are far less clear. For one thing, in all societies the former can be gauged in terms of cowrie shells, money, or some other medium of exchange. But no such precise tools or measurements are available for the latter.

An even more basic distinction between role and affect is found in the history of their evolution: as societies have grown in complexity, the number and variety of roles have also grown. In fact, role differentiation is the major concomitant of the growth in societal complexity. For example, each candidate for national office in the United States today is supported by an army of experts including speech writers, public relations men, technicians, and foot soldiers of which small town politicians of yesteryear would never have dreamed. American giant corporations often have larger numbers of workers and more diversified specialists on their payrolls than the governments of many small member states of the United Nations.

This development is inevitable. The number and variety of laws have increased, as have bureaucratic departments, problems of production, and the size and complexity of machines. Every modern giant jet plane has about 2 million parts. Computers have been developed not only to coordinate the parts of machines, but also to deal with human problems such as job matching, job performance, communication, and even mate selection.

On the other hand, while our roles have evolved in number and proficiency with the complexity of society, our affect has not. We still entertain the same kinds of feelings as our ancestors who lived two or three thousand years ago, namely, love, hate, rage, despair, endurance, hope, anxiety, forbearance, sympathy, loyalty, betrayal, and so forth. The list was short before and it is not much longer today. Like the ancients we still cannot reduce affective interactions into calculable quantities nor regulate them with some form of exchange. In fact, we consistently brand any intrusion of the role-based mediums of exchange into the affective sphere as prostitution or as bribery, and describe its futility by saying "you can't buy friendship or love." That is why great literature (fiction, poetry) and great art (painting, sculpture) and even great philosophy and ethics survive the ages, for we moderns feel the same agony and joy and the same loyalty and duplicity as the ancients. We can relive their lives through what they have written and if they, were alive today, they would be able to discuss with us our problems with our children, parents, friends, enemies, sweethearts and spouses. But old books of science and technology are useless except as curiosities or as material for histories of science and technology. Not only the ancients, but our fathers and even our older brothers would find catching up with our present generation's achievements in science and technology impossible or at least extremely arduous.

The Separation of Affect from Role

The escalation of role differentiation with the growth of societal complexity has given rise in the West, especially in the United States, to a significant phenomenon: the separation of affect from role.

In traditional small workshops all members of the family used to work together as a team, and each worker had the opportunity to see the fruits of his labor from start to finish. In many cases the workshop was also the place where the products were sold.

In such a situation role and affect greatly overlapped with each other. Each member of the work team had two affective ties: with his co-workers as members of the same family and with the tools and the products because they could be identified as *his* personal tools and *his* products.

As workshops became larger and larger compartmentalized factories with giant assembly lines, the worker's affective ties to his tools and products were lost. And as the worker was removed from family labor and became part of a large production team, the traditional bases for affective ties with his co-worker also vanished. That is to say, role became separated from affect (see Diagram 8).

These Western developments are viewed by Western social observers as universally inevitable; that as societies become more industrialized, human beings will become more impersonal towards each other. Alex Inkeles, a sociologist, describes what he calls the "industrial man" which is based on his proposition:

> that men's environment, as expressed in the institutional patterns they adopt or have introduced to them, shapes their experience, and through this their perceptions, attitudes and values, in standardized ways which are manifest from country to country, despite the countervailing randomizing influence of traditional cultural patterns (Inkeles 1960:2).

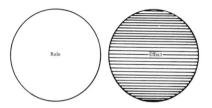

DIAGRAM 8: Role Separated from Affect

However, an examination of Inkeles' evidence in support of this proposition shows his data to have come primarily from the United States, the Soviet Union, Germany, Italy, Mexico and Australia. Except for a brief and insignificant Japanese sample, all data were obtained from Western societies. But in fact, the case of Japan directly contradicts Inkeles' main proposition. Instead of separating role from affect, Japanese employees in large, modern industrial and commercial establishments seem to exhibit as much devotion to their places of work and their employers as did their predecessors. This is the secret of Japan's economic miracle which the world has yet to understand.

Why have drastically altered conditions of work not led to a separation of role from affect in modern Japan? For an answer to this question it is necessary first to delve into the reasons why they have separated in the West.

Psychosocial Homeostasis (PSH)

Here we must digress slightly by examining how the human individual operates as a social and cultural being. For this purpose I have developed a Psychosociogram (PSG), and the notion of Psychosocial Homeostasis (PSH; see Diagram 9). PSG and PSH are respectively the synchronic and diachronic aspects of a non-Freudian view of how the individual sees himself and relates to the world. Briefly, since a more detailed discussion is found in another publication (Hsu 1971), the thickened circle in the diagram separates the individual's inner from

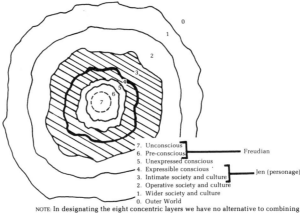

7. Unconscious ⎤
6. Pre-conscious ⎦──────── Freudian
5. Unexpressed conscious
4. Expressible conscious ⎤
3. Intimate society and culture ⎦──── Jen (personage)
2. Operative society and culture
1. Wider society and culture
0. Outer World

NOTE: In designating the eight concentric layers we have no alternative to combining psychic terms with social ones. This is the nature of the beast, so to speak. This diagram may remind those readers who have seen similar ones used by Kurt Lewin in his contrast of American and German interpersonal relations (Kurt Lewin 1948:21). However, the differences between Lewin's scheme and mine will soon become evident. Lewin's diagrams are tied to the traditional notion of personality and show only what occurs within it while our diagram aims principally at illustrating the interpersonal process.

DIAGRAM 9: Psychosociogram (PSG) of Man

his outer worlds. The individual relates to the outer world selectively. Thus most human beings relate to layers 1 and 0 marginally or not at all. Similarly, only certain portions of the individual's inner world are significant psychic bases for his behavior. Thus, most human beings in the normal course of events, mobilize little of the contents of layers 6 and 7.

The more universally important parts of the PSG (Psychosociogram) are layers 2 and 3 in the individual's external world and layers 4 and 5 within him. Layer 2 contains his role relationships and layer 3 his affective ties, while the contents of layer 4 are mobilized for day to day living and those of layer 5, though usually kept to the individual himself, certainly have significant and conscious bearing on his behavior.

Whether the individual comes into contact with many other human beings or few, he must stand in a relationship of intimacy with some. By intimacy I refer to an interpersonal condition in which, ideally, all parties can afford to let their guards down, can communicate their worst troubles to each other without fear of rejection, and can count on comfort, sympathy, and help from each other without the onus of charity (Hsu 1971:26).

For this reason layer 3, where the individual forms his affective ties, and layer 4, which houses his expressible conscious, are termed the *human constant* (or *Jen*). These two layers form the minimum requirement for every human being. Besides role relationships, every human being needs some affective ties to other human beings with whom he can communicate much of his conscious thought and feeling.

The concept of Psychosocial Homeostasis (PSH) is inspired by biology. It refers to the fact that, every individual tends to maintain a satisfactory level of psychic and interpersonal equilibrium, within the human constant, or *Jen*, in the same sense that every physical organism tends to maintain a uniform and beneficial physiological stability among its parts (Hsu 1971:28).

As in the case of physiological homeostasis, deficiences in the maintenance of PSH are met with the principle of compensation. For example, if other human beings are not available for affective ties, the individual may resort to animals or material things or supernatural creatures as substitutes.

PSH Among the Chinese

Human beings in every society begin life with parents (and usually siblings as well) who are the first inhabitants of his layer 3. For the Chinese, whose kinship system and culture tell him that his self-esteem and future are tied to his first group (continuity, inclusiveness and authority), his parents and siblings, the latter are not only the first but also the permanent inhabitants of his layer 3. Even though a majority of Chinese households are not the giant structures emphasized in the traditional Chinese ideal and portrayed in Chinese novels such as *The Dream of the Red Chamber*, the Chinese individual tends to have close relatives nearby, and to interact frequently with them. They are likely to engage most of his attention and command his respect, or to respect him depending upon his place in the kinship organization. They are his principal source of aid in times of distress and need. In addition, the Chinese individual is likely to be strongly concerned with knowledge, artifacts and rules of conduct emanating from the kinship sphere. Hence, filial piety is the cornerstone of all morality, ancestral land is the basic attachment, and the individual is enjoined not to be adventurous as regards the rest of the world.

The last injunction is commensurate with the fact that the Chinese individual does not have to move far afield into the outer layers (layers 2,1 or 0) of his possible human network for intimacy, since the latter commodity is readily and continuously accessible to him. He can satisfy the requirements of his psychosocial homeostasis without going to the other layers. If for any reason he gets to the outer layers at all, he is most likely (1) to seek previously unknown but existing ties, therefore kinship or locality ties; (2) to develop pseudo-kinship or kinship-like ties; (3) to continue his ties with his kinship and local group at home; and (4) to fulfill the requirements of layers 2,1, and 0 as far as it is necessary for him to find his place in them. He will do what is necessary to keep his role position or improve it. He would not initiate any dissent that might disrupt the establishment in any layer. In fact, he can be counted on to modify his views if that modification appears to be confluent with the dominant tendency in a particular situation. (There is measurable psychological evidence that Chinese subjects possess greater persuadability than American subjects. See Godwin C. Chu 1966:169-174.) He can do this because he has little investment of affect in these layers since he has no need to resort to the inhabitants of any of these layers for psychosocial homeostasis. He can relate to them in relatively impersonal terms befitting a variety of situations under which he and they must deal with each other. He can afford not to be curious or anxious about them; he is unlikely to have the urge to improve or help them; they are no threat to him and unless they engage in physical acts of aggression against him he is able to ignore them completely. He can meet them or he can leave them. Hence the Chinese, throughout all of their history, have developed no missionary movements, no significant religious persecutions, and few secondary groups outside of their kinship system. China had some famous travelers and conquerors. But the famous travelers were either in imperial service or religious zealots who were bent on *bringing back to China the complete teachings of Buddha.* There was no Florence Nightingale, no St. Francis Xavier, Lawrence of Arabia, or Carrie Nation who was intent on changing the world. As for Chinese imperial conquests, they were not followed by colonial settlement of Chinese people (Hsu 1968) interested in spreading Chinese ideas or their way of life.

The Chinese have little need to include deep psychic discoveries in their PSH. This is clear whether we look at their art, literature, philosophy, religion, or folklore. In spite of the fact that the Chinese have produced a large body of written literature over the centuries, they have only one simple-minded utopia (Hsu 1970:215). Their gods and ghosts are human-like creatures with human frailties. They are unconcerned with the meaning of life and death (Hsu 1970: 357-364). Their art and literature dwell almost exclusively on the external relations of the world and never explore the intricacies of the mind (Hsu 1970:17-41). Even today psychoanalysis is not popular with the Chinese in Hong Kong and Taiwan.

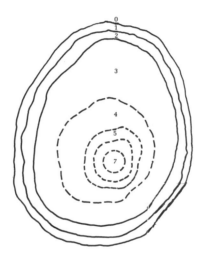

DIAGRAM 10: The Home Body

Diagram 10 entitled "The Home Body" portrays the typical mode of PSH of the Chinese individual in his society and culture.[1] For him layer 3 is larger than any other layer. The father-son dominated kinship system is the individual's primary, automatic and continuous source of intimacy. Over the centuries the Chinese have developed a remarkably centripetal civilization, self-satisfied, uninterested in emigrating to other lands or in the conversion of non-Chinese peoples (layer 0). In fact, a majority of the Chinese were little interested in their own government (layers 2 and 1), doing what was in the long run reasonably required of them by their rulers but settling most of their disputes through locally administered justice undergirded by kin-ship ties. They had few non-kinship secondary groupings and no purely cause-oriented organizations at all. The self-contained and non-dynamic nature of layer 3 of the Chinese proves to be the chief stumbling block to a central government bent on modernization via democracy or totalitarianism (Hsu 1968, 1970).

PSH Among Westerners

The Westerner also begins his life with parents and siblings. These too are the first inhabitants of his layer 3. But since his kinship system and his culture tell him that his self-esteem and future depend upon how well he can stand on his own two feet, his parents and siblings are only temporary occupants of his layer 3. He does not, of course, invariably leave them or they him as he grows up but his relationships with them are voluntary, especially after he marries or reaches legal maturity. Consequently, his layer 3 tends to be filled with individuals other than those with whom he began his life.[2] Since these individu-als are non-kin, he has to go out to search for them and to establish some sort of link with them to maintain his psychosocial homeostasis.

This necessity to search for his circle of intimate companions makes the Western individual's problems more complicated. For one thing, the new inhabitants of his layer 3 are likely to be his peers. Having defined his adult status as one of freedom from overpowering elders, he is not about to choose to be at the mercy of anyone like them. But relationships with unrelated peers are bound to be more unstable and to require more constant attention than relationship with par-ents. Parents are like dogs; one can kick them in the teeth and they will still come back for more. No one can take his peers for granted to that extent. He and they are likely to compete for the same things. His desire for mastery over them is matched by their need to dominate him. He has to satisfy his peers as much as they have to satisfy him.

Consequently, the problem of maintaining psychosocial homeo-stasis is much more difficult for the Western individual than for Chinese. He attempts to solve it in a variety of ways. He may have to explore layers 2 but especially 1 or 0 for new frontiers, other people, and other worlds to which he can affectively relate. He will need to convert or incorporate some or all of the inhabitants from these layers into his layer 3. He will do this in search of his own identity and fulfillment and to prove himself, or he may come to rely solely on his inner self for definition and guidance, exploring his inner world, his anxieties, his own unconscious (layers 6 and 7), sometimes using drugs if he thinks them necessary.

There are several consequences to both of these routes to psychosocial homeostasis. To begin with, by either route, the Westerner's yield of interpersonal intimacy is precarious or scarce. He often receives no more than the illusion of intimacy, by way of intense but fleeting interactions with other human beings.

Secondly, when the individualistic man follows the route of self-exploration, he finds the tasks of maintaining psychosocial homeostasis a considerable one. He has to go through the agonies of what his parents and possibly also his siblings once allegedly went through themselves. He has to experience a privatized exposé of these "atrocities" committed against him. He has to be freed from his overpowering parents and siblings in order to pursue precarious relationships with unrelated peers in layers 2, 1, and even 0.

Thirdly, since his exploration of layers 2, 1, and 0 is linked with maintaining psychosocial homeostasis, the Westerner needs to shower affection on the objects of his exploration. Here the main barrier to his satisfaction is the nature of the objects in layers 2, 1, and 0. He may live among them but they are not intimate enough with him for affective sociability. He may be their friend but they are too deeply enmeshed in other concerns to give him affective security. And while they may marvel at his weapons and fear him like the plague, they will not readily accord to him any affective status, for he is not likely to be an object of their respect and love. In other words, they do not need him for their PSH the way he needs them for his. Under these circumstances it is not enough for the individualistic man to relate to the objects of his exploration in layers 2, 1, and 0 in role terms. He must bring them into the glow of his affect. He must not merely conquer them physically but must also convert them to his value system and his way of looking at things. He needs to educate them, improve their health and sanitation, change their moral standards and save them from witchcraft and paganism, uproot them from their kinship and local bondage so that they will need him for their PSH.

Fourthly, conquest and conversion of the world in the individualistic man's terms is really an unending and even impossible task. For since individualistic and unrelated peers are in sharp competition with each other, each of them needs to stake out a human "territory" for himself; as a result, these peers are inevitably and constantly at "war" with one another. We all know how sectarian differences separate missionaries and even generate hatred between them. It is therefore not unusual for the individualistic man to turn his attention instead to material wealth, animals, and objects from the inanimate world. This course of action has some advantages but it is also fraught with perils. On the one hand, control over material wealth may serve as a means of control over men. The difficulty is, of course, that the possessor of wealth cannot be sure how those who dance around him and concede superiority to him really feel about him. On the other hand, control of wealth, animals, and things can camouflage the lack of intimacy with fellow human beings.[3] In the individualistic man's competitive circumstances, the control of wealth, animals, and things is easier than relating to other human beings. It involves no surrender of any part of his autonomy. He can emote towards wealth, animals, and things in the manner best suited to himself and he has no need to be concerned about how they feel about him.

With this in mind we can see that the well-known Puritan work ethic is a similar approach on the part of Western man to maintain his PSH. Work too, like wealth, animals and things, is an object on which the autonomous man can lavish his affect without fearing the problem of reciprocity. On the one hand, work enables him to manage his affect, to transform it into tangible returns which he can control. On the other hand, his affect towards work enables him to reduce his human contacts into calculable units of production. This is the basic psychic ingredient of what we know as depersonalization. This is why the Puritan ethic sees sexual activity as work (reproduction). In this view, even the most intimate of human relationships is reduced to a mere means for the acquisition of some other end.

However work, no less than things, is a poor substitute for real human intimacy. Not surprisingly rebellious American youths have followed a diametrically opposed direction. In and out of communes, they place togetherness and love on a pedestal and eschew work and wealth. In other words, the Puritans want all role and no affect, but for the modern day anti-establishmentarian youth, the order is reversed.

The individualistic man's affective investment in animals and things as substitutes for human beings is likely to be much stronger than that of his Chinese counterpart whose requirements for psycho-social homeostasis are easily and simply met. The Chinese have traditionally valued industry and frugality, but the work ethic never stood by itself. It was always understood in the social context of working for someone and for something. The Chinese will travel to learn, to trade, as a matter of family obligations or for sheer sensory pleasure. The individualistic man may be moved by some of these reasons but he is much more attracted by the notion of "conquest" of the Himalayas for instance, or of the four seas. The difference between the two approaches is similar to that between regular eating because one is hungry and compulsive eating because of some deep-seated emotional need. In the first case eating will stop once hunger no longer exists, while in the second case the action tends to be endless since emotional needs are much harder to satisfy.

Consequently, if one travels to a certain secluded monastery on a well-known mountain because one wishes to see its famous scenery and appreciate its beautiful architecture (as Chinese scholars and officials were wont to do), then the mode of getting to the destination is purely one of means and of secondary importance. If one can get there more comfortably in a sedan chair or an automobile, then so much the better. But the physical trip will have no personal success-failure connotation to the Chinese for he is not conquering what he finds. He is merely resorting to the best means to enjoy what he finds. This contrasts sharply with the approach of the individualistic man, for whom the means to achieve the end often becomes the end itself or overshadows it. The mountain and the scenery do not have to be famous already. He will be the first to make them famous. Anyone can visit the spot in sedan chairs or automobiles, but he will be the first to get up there on a bicycle. Furthermore, once he has done it, he will have little interest in doing it again, especially in the same way, for he needs to look for "firsts." He must look for a higher mountain to climb, a more hazardous means of climbing it. This situation stands in sharp contrast to the Chinese who longs to visit a famous spot precisely because some well-known man has been there before. If the well-known man was gifted and left some impromptu poems on the walls of the temple (another favorite gesture of Chinese scholars and officials), he would like to do the same. For he seeks the glorious shadows of some "ancestors."

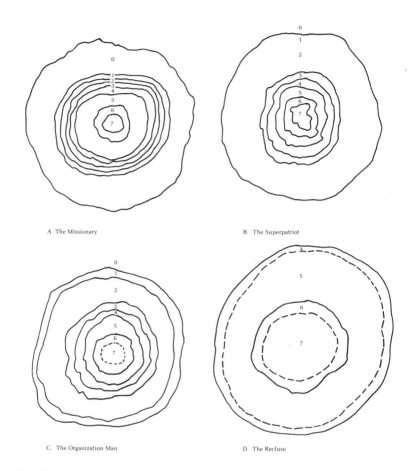

A The Missionary   B. The Superpatriot

C. The Organization Man   D. The Recluse

DIAGRAM 11: A Variety of Modes for Maintaining PSH

Diagram 11 schematically represents *a few* of the possible PSH patterns typical of the Western individual in his society and culture. The reader will be interested to note that, contrasted to its Chinese counterpart, the outcome of the Western approach is extremely diverse. This diversity is rooted in the internal impetus for change inherent in the Western kinship system. It has expressed itself in Western history as revolutions in many fields (political, religious, economic, cultural, artistic, social, educational, etc.), in the form of dispersion of dissidents from the mother country to set up independent societies (European emigrants were not only proportionately numerous but have formed numerous independent nations elsewhere, including the U.S.A., while Chinese emigrants were not only proportionately fewer but have never set themselves up as separate political entities, except once in northern Borneo for less than ten years; Singapore is a modern phenomenon and a political accident), and massive and continuous missionary movements (nearly all the world's missionaries are Westerners; Hsu 1970:224-276). This diversity expressed itself in Western literature through depiction of characters whose chief source of personal fulfillment or happiness (real or imagined) has been to wage war against themselves or others: Holden Caulfield in *Catcher in the Rye* or "the old Man" in *The Old Man and the Sea* or Captain Ahab in *Moby Dick* are a few of the many examples. Such characters, however, are wholly lacking in Chinese fiction—a condition described by one astute student of Chinese literature as "psychological poverty" (Hsia 1961:503). Even the Western *Gulliver's Travels* by Jonathan Swift contrasts sharply with its Chinese counterpart *Ching Hua Yuan* (*Tale of the Mirrored Flower*) by Li Ju-Chen. The hero of the former novel went through all his strange experiences alone, while the Chinese novel describes its hero usually in the company of several constant companions, including his brother-in-law.

The husband-wife dominated kinship system of the West does not supply the individual with a primary, automatic and continuous source of intimacy. Accordingly, over the centuries Westerners have developed a remarkably centrifugal civilization, always searching for the self and/or for the unknown, intensely preoccupied with abstract issues (such as truth or the nature of God), or trivial and concrete details (such as the liturgical quarrels which divide followers of the same Christ), or gold, or remaking the rest of the world in its own image (layers 1 and especially, 0).

This Western tendency was not brought about by Christianity. Alexander the Great in his zeal to fuse the East (Middle East) and West (Greece) carried out the following acts shortly before he died: "Undeterred, yet deeply shaken by the incomprehension surrounding him, Alexander persisted in his views. After the ordeals of the retreat from the Beas and the terrible crossing of Gedrosia (the Baluchistan desert), on arrival in Susa he organized the marriage of ten thousand of his followers to Iranian maidens. And at Opis, in Mesopotamia, on his way to Babylon and his premature end, he gave one last, vast banquet, in which all joined him in a symposium and the drinking of a "loving cup" to the union of mankind and universal *armonia* (concord)." (Prince Peter 1965:7).

No parallel to Alexander's acts can be found in Chinese history. The most that any Chinese conqueror did was to suppress seeds of rebellion cruelly as for instance Ch'in Shih Huang Ti (the first emperor of Ch'in, whose reign began in 221 B.C.) who reportedly buried alive the country's best scholars and burned most of its written works.

Alexander's action patterns and those of his Western successors are too numerous to enumerate. But we should note that it is also in the West that individualism and industrialism have originated and been greatly developed. Western individualism did not stop with defending individual rights including privacy. Western man went on to probe the secrets and role of the deep psyche through various means for scientific and utilitarian purposes and for pleasure. There is simply no comparable Chinese interest in this kind of activity. Similarly, Western industrialism did not stop with the accelerated use of resources and mass production of goods. Western man went on to develop theories that economics determine all human thought and relations, or hold the key to the solution of all the world's problems (the human factor being substituted by material objects).

PSH Among the Japanese

To many Western observers, Japan is a prime example of a completely Westernized society and culture in the East. They point to Japan's military potential, nuclear households in suburbia, parliamentary government, interest in Western art, literature, music, and clothing, and emphasize in particular, her colossal industrial achievement. From an observer's economic determinist point of view, the total Westernization of Japan in psychological, social and cultural terms is a foregone conclusion.

I am of the opinion that all these developments, and especially Japan's rapid industrialization, are built on Japan's traditional social structure, not the Western pattern of human relationships. Japan's kinship system is like that of the Chinese, being father-son dominated, but it has two unique features: (a) it is marked by unigeniture or one-son inheritance, and (b) in it the mother-son dyad occupies a position of sub-dominance.

Unigeniture means that the non-inheriting sons have no rightful place in the original kinship group. They have to go outside it to maintain their psychosocial homeostasis. Japanese culture, however, does not mould individuals to be their own masters. Ideologically, Japanese culture allows far less social mobility (vertical as well as horizontal) than is the case in Chinese culture. The non-inheriting sons, instead of seeking fame and fortune on their own, tend to become subordinate and lifelong members of the establishment. The sub-dominance of the mother-son dyad enables the Japanese individual to be much more unquestioningly dependent, pliant and loyal to his superiors than the Chinese individual would be.

These two factors are highly compatible with the Japanese institution of *iemoto*. The core structure of the *iemoto* is a master-disciple (client) relationship marked by mutual dependence. This relationship and its characteristic ideas are not simply economic, political, militaristic, or religious. They can be applied to any field of endeavor, such as running a bean paste shop or a temple or an army or a university.

As we noted before, in essence the core *iemoto* relationship is not dissimilar to the master-disciple link in China. What differentiates the Japanese institution are the following features. Firstly, the master-disciple relationship in the *iemoto* is more inclusive and is marked by a higher degree of superordination and subordination than its counterpart in traditional China. Secondly, each set of master-disciple relationships in the *iemoto* tends to be linked with other sets forming a hierarchical organization often of considerable magnitude. Where farming is the main source of livelihood, the spirit of the *iemoto* tends to express itself in the form of the *dōzoku*. The total size of the *dōzoku* is, of course, limited by the available amount of land and its productivity. But where skills alone are concerned (such as floral arrangements, dance, *kabuki* drama, etc.), the resulting hierarchical organization may consist of millions of members and thousands of local chapters.

Thirdly, an equally important feature is the fact that the spirit of *iemoto* prevails among businessmen, industrial workers, teachers, professors, and students in modern universities where the *iemoto* does not formally exist. Its spirit is apparent in the all-inclusive and nearly unbreakable command-obedience, succor-dependence relationships between the old and the young, the senior and the junior, the superior and the subordinate. It is well known, for example, that there is very little horizontal mobility among professors in different universities, and employees tend to remain for life in the same business firms in which they began their working careers.

Finally, all ties in the iemoto are couched in pseudo-kinship terms. From this point of view each iemoto is a giant kinship establishment, with the characteristic closeness and inclusiveness of interpersonal links, but without kinship limitations on its size.

Therefore, although a majority of Japanese individuals have to move away from their first kinship base, their culture enables them to secure permanent circles of intimacy without moving too far away from it. And the all-inclusive, interlinking mutual dependence among members of any two levels in a large hierarchical organization has the effect of extending the feeling of intimacy beyond those situated in the closest proximity. Under these circumstances, the individual can be interested and even involved in his layers 2 and 1 (though not 0) not because he needs to go that far to maintain a balance in his psychosocial homeostasis, but because he is joined to people in those layers through their links with his immediate and intimate circle. On the highest level, the emperor becomes the head of a hierarchical organization embracing the entire nation. We may with justification describe the Japanese iemoto as being like the Chinese kinship organizations, which include links with deceased ancestors. In the broadest interpretation of the iemoto, the Japanese emperor is comparable to the Chinese head of the living clan and the emperor's ancestors are those of his subjects as well.

The primary Sino-Japanese difference is that the Chinese, in maintaining their PSH, are far more confined to their actual, patrilineal kinship structure whereas the Japanese are not. This is why Chinese men very rarely married matrilocally, as this involved giving up their kinship affiliations and adopting their wives' kinship relationships as their own, while a very large percentage (perhaps in the neighborhood of thirty percent) of Japanese marriages are concerned with precisely this kind of arrangement. This explains why the ancestors of Chinese imperial lines were not the concern of the people at all while those of the Japanese imperial house could be regarded as the ancestors of all Japanese.

To put it differently, for both the Chinese and the Japanese, role and affect are strongly linked with each other. The individual works hard and well not because he uses work to maintain his PSH (so that work is the object of his affect), but because work is only an expression of his feelings (care, succoring, subordination, superordination, devotion, etc.) toward some human beings who stand in specific social relationships to him. For the Chinese, role and affect are linked within the kinship bonds and their immediate extensions, while for the Japanese, whose social organization enables him to move farther afield, they are linked in a much larger human arena, the *iemoto*.[4]

This in my view is the chief reason why Japan responded to the challenge of the West by modernizing her government, industry and armed forces so rapidly and so successfully, while China, caught in the same predicament, lagged far behind.The same linkage was a serious impediment to China's modernization but greatly facilitated Japan's modernization.

To meet the challenge of the West, China has had to make major structural rearrangements in her social organization. The Chinese who were used to depending on kinship and its immediate extensions for sources of intimacy have had to be steered elsewhere. Resistance to this change is so great that the task is far from complete over twenty years after the Communist assumption of power (Hsu 1968). On the other hand, the basic Japanese way of life has remained intact in spite of her outward Westernization; the age-old institution of the *iemoto* is the source and model for Japanese PSH which in turn provides the human foundation for Japan's modern achievements (see Diagram 12).

However, although the institution of the *iemoto* contributed greatly to Japan's rapid modernization and national unity (layers 2 and 1), it does not enable the Japanese to tune-in to universalist aspirations (layer 0) on any equalitarian basis, such as that preached by Jesus of Nazareth or envisaged by many Western political idealists. In moving into layers 2 and 1 the Japanese has not really left the kinship base of layer 3. With reference to the wider world (layer 0) the Japanese will always distinguish between "we" and "they," between "superior" and "inferior," between those who do business with him and those who do not, etc. This is why Japan is not a society in which the non-Japanese can ever achieve acceptance as a Japanese, no matter how well he knows the language and has acculturated himself. As evidence for this conclusion we need only to contrast the Japanese

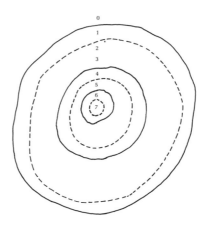

DIAGRAM 12:   Japanese Mode of PSH

non-acceptance of foreigners who are not physically different from themselves (such as the Chinese and the Koreans), with the white American acceptance of immigrant Europeans.

Concomitant with the Japanese need for going beyond kinship boundaries to maintain his psychosocial homeostasis is the much greater Japanese concern with the mind than the Chinese (layer 5). The contrasting nature of Japanese and Chinese art and literature in the two societies is a good indication of this.

In a previous discussion we noted the paucity of interest in psychological exploration in Chinese fiction. Compared with Western fiction we may consider this statement to be true of Japanese fiction as well. However, when we confine ourselves to a comparison of Japan and China, we cannot fail to notice that Japanese interest in psychological matters is much greater than Chinese interest. Contrast for this purpose Japanese literary products such as The Tale of Genji, The Great Mirror (Masukagami), or The Tale of Heike with Chinese works such as *The Dream of the Red Chamber, All Men are Brothers,* or *The Romance of Three Kingdoms.* The Japanese books deal with how the characters feel and think, while the Chinese novels almost entirely confine themselves to what the characters do. Such typically Japanese, aesthetic concepts as *aware* (pathos, compassion), *sabi* (age, antiquity) and even *yūgen* (subtle profundity) are rarely mentioned by Chinese masters. For this contrast we do not even have to explore the many Japanese diaries (such as *The Gossamer Years* [Kagero Nikki] or *The Pillow Book* by Sei Shonagon) which are concerned with the daily thoughts of court women. The greater emphasis on feeling and thought in Japanese literature also expresses itself in the field of poetry. Poetry in China was, until very recently, a pastime of the literati, a small minority of the population, but poetry in Japan has had a wide following of people from all classes. There was nothing in China that even remotely resembled the popular Japanese custom of New Year's Day poetry competitions before the emperor and his consort.

Interpersonal Devotion and Libidinality

There is another dimension to the *iemoto* pattern of human relationships that needs elucidation. This has to do with the differential influences of the three attributes of sexuality (from the husband-wife dominance), asexuality (from the father-son dominance), and libidinality (from the mother-son sub-dominance).

As explained in an earlier publication (Hsu 1971:439-475), the dominance of sexuality has led to a variety of developments in the West. We had the Agape of early Christianity. Then came the belief in the Immaculate Conception (of Mary and the Virgin Birth). Agape was associated with the early Christian love feast and with the Eucharist; the Immaculate Conception and the Virgin Birth are attempts to unite all mankind, at least all Christians, through the sex bond by making that bond a symbolic rather than a physical union.

Modern psychology tells us that the louder the denial of an object, the greater is the preoccupation with that very object. As a result, denial of sexuality has been followed by three lines of development in the West. The first was Puritanism, through which man was able to reduce all human links into role relations because he confined his affect to work. Puritanism came closest to applying the concept of the Virgin Birth to all men. It did so by defining sexual activity as work.

Freudian psychology is a revolutionary movement against Puritanism. It is founded on the concept of the libido, which sees sex as a human bonding or destroying agent. Libido is used to explain how and why the individual seeks (unconsciously or otherwise) to relate and cling to, or repudiate and destroy others.

Nowadays we are witnessing a new Western development. This is the proliferation of sex in all aspects of life: in daily speech, the press, literature, and the motion pictures, in advertising, dating patterns, sex education, and open cohabitation without the benefit of formal ties. All these activities are justified as liberation from "outmoded" conventions and attitudes.

The common denominator in these developments is the preoccupation with sexuality rooted in the husband-wife dominated Western kinship system. This preoccupation has far-reaching consequences on the relations between the sexes and among people of the same sex. In the case of opposite sexes, role relations are always overshadowed by affect, so that males can hardly see females aside from their sexuality. Consequently, no matter how much the ideal of equality is professed, men will tend to discriminate against women in the professions because they feel females enjoy advantages other than role competence. I have dealt with this matter elsewhere (Hsu 1970:42-57).

Of far greater relevance to our present discussion is the relationship between individuals of the same sex—especially American males. American males (in contrast to males in most other societies in the world) avoid all close physical contact with each other and seem to be incapable of forming deep relationships. They only make close bodily contact in emergencies (such as mouth to mouth resuscitation) or in certain sports (such as wrestling). This inability to make close bodily contact is only the external symptom of an inner inability to form deep friendships. American men simply cannot be sentimental or devoted towards one another. They will combine to conquer the external world but they will shun lasting and undying attachments.

The reason for this aversion is the fear of homosexuality. If all affect is sex-charged, any suggestion of it between members of the same sex is suspect. That is why Holden Caulfield, the young hero in J. D. Salinger's *Catcher in the Rye,* bolted out of his favorite teacher's apartment when he found the older man sitting on the edge of the couch and stroking his hair. This is what the other itinerant farm laborers suspected when they questioned Lenny and George as to how long they had been traveling together in John Steinbeck's *Of Mice and Men*. The more American culture is preoccupied with sex, whether by denial or by flaunting it, the less Americans of the same sex will be able to develop and maintain *affective* relations with one another. At first, this inability seems to be confined to males, but we should note that American females also are afraid of walking hand in hand. However, when sex is used as a means for anti-establishmentarianism, militant flaunting of homosexuality between males and lesbianism between females is part of the same picture. Whether in the fear of homosexuality or in the desire to flaunt it, the source, namely preoccupation with sex, is the same.

Were the attribute of libidinality merely a lesser version of sexuality, the impeding effect of the attribute of sexuality on relationships between males in America would also be seen in Japan, at least in some form. In reality, this does not happen. Instead of being detrimental to the solidarity of the *iemoto*, libidinality enhances it. The reason is not merely that libidinality is an attribute of a dyad that is only sub-dominant, but also that libidinality is fundamentally different from sexuality.

Since the Japanese kinship system is father-son dominated, we can expect the Japanese culture to treat sex in the same manner as its Chinese counterpart. That is to say, sex is very much present in certain social compartments of life but entirely absent in others. What the sub-dominance of the mother-son dyad has done is to increase the number of compartments in Japanese life where diffused sexuality is more or less obvious but not so prominent that it becomes ubiquitous. Relations between members of the same sex is one of the compartments where sex is irrelevant. As we noted in Chapter 8, in Japan as well as China and India, sex is treated as an objective fact, like hunger or physical danger. Its presence in some compartments of life is not a problem to be defended, explained, or rejected.

Libidinality is rooted in the earliest period of the individual's development, when unilateral dependence upon the mother for all physical needs is paramount. It is sensuous but non-directive in the way that sexuality is directive. It is not keyed to the consummation of specific acts in the sense that sexuality is. Its presence in the culture heightens the ardor and increases the sensuous elements of human devotion without implying, even remotely, the sexual act.

This is indeed what we find in India where the mother-son dyad is dominant in the kinship system. The extreme physical lengths to which Hindu gurus and their followers will go, in order to indicate the strength of their faith, have been discussed elsewhere (Hsu 1963). What distinguishes the Japanese, in whose kinship system the mother-son dyad is only sub-dominant, is this: whereas the Hindu's objects of worship are many and his line of affiliation is not at all clear, the Japanese tends to lavish his profuse devotion on a certain specified entity, and his line of affiliation is without ambiguity.

We can therefore observe the following contrasts in a four way comparison. The Hindu tends to lavish affect on a variety of gurus whose descent or origin may be obscure and whose role is not precisely defined. The Chinese are more restrained in expressing their affect than both the Hindus and the Japanese. If and when they do express some affect, they are likely to do so within the confines of kinship and local community. The American is most exuberant in lavishing affect in diverse directions, but his affect is reserved for persons of the opposite sex, or work, or things of his choice, not for persons of the same sex and, as a rule, not for those with whom he is linked by work.

[1] In my first publication on PSH (Hsu 1971:23-44) I used a tree-like expression representing these modes. I am indebted to Miss Ann Elizabeth Robinson of Washington, D.C. for this new diagram.

[2] I am aware that the kinship systems in various Western cultures are not uniform. I am also aware that some students (sociologists in particular) maintain that the American type of kinship pattern, for example, is a result of the Industrial Revolution. My answer is that the basis for the husband-wife type dominance in Western kinship systems is symbolized in the Biblical legend of Noah and his sons, and is therefore very old. The generation gap was in existence then. By way of contrast, the Chinese legend of the deluge is also very old and symbolizes the Chinese pattern of father-son dominance outlined here (Hsu 1969:77-88).

[3] In a recent (April 30, 1972) report on why college students have taken to pets, a Swarthmore College psychiatrist says "pets represent honesty, freedom and sincerity.

They are generally friendly, emotionally uncomplicated, and rewarding." A neighboring veterinarian observes that "pets give students something they can love, or reject on their own terms." Here are some comments from Swarthmore students: "Dogs pep things up." "Cats make things feel more like home." "They always have time to play." (*Parade* Magazine, April 30, 1972).

[4] It may seem inappropriate to some but the only Chinese groups that embodied the same set of ideas *across kinship lines* were the secret, gangster organizations such as the Blue Group and the Red Group. Such groups were helpful now and then to anti-government movements, and were of material assistance to Dr. Sun Yat-Sen's Republican Revolution which toppled the Manchu government in 1911. But they remained *outside established society* even after that.

11 ●

The *Iemoto* Pattern in Religion*

*With the assistance of Professor Esyun Hamaguchi.

So far we have dealt with the roots of the *iemoto* found in the Japanese kinship situation, discussing how these roots express themselves in the structure and content of this remarkable Japanese secondary grouping. We must now examine how or whether the same kinship roots manifest themselves in the pattern of Japanese behavior at large, in those groups not specifically designated as *iemoto*. One of the best arenas for this examination is religion, especially Japanese Buddhism, which came to Japan from India, via China.

Buddhism in China

In Chapter 6 we saw the Chinese and Japanese patterns of dealing with departed ancestors. The differences in those patterns reflect their different ways of treating kin and non-kin. With unigeniture, the Japanese define their kinship circles much more narrowly than the Chinese do, for instance. The *ie* or household is primary. Each household maintains a *honke-bunke* relationship with some other households representing the brothers who had left and formed their separate households and their descendants. Their genealogical records link them together more loosely than the Chinese, for although these records may indicate depth ties they tell little of horizontal ones. After separation from the *honke*, the *bunke* have to seek other resources for livelihood, and consequently, non-kinship affiliations become more and more important. The ancestral spirits of each kinship group are mingled with those of kinship groups unrelated to them.

The Japanese pattern is not the same as that found in the Christian West. The souls of Westerners lose their worldly connections under a universal God. The souls of Japanese merge into sectarian Buddhism but at the same time remain ancestral spirits under one specific and supreme national ancestress, Amaterasu, at least on a high ideological level. In the Christian West the individual has the ideological basis for possible unity with all Christian mankind, but Japanese ideology allows for unity with other Japanese only. On the other hand, whereas the Chinese ancestral spirits remain identified with the particular kinship group of their origin (though some of them, due to their personal worldly merit, may become gods to serve as administrative gods in other localities under the Supreme Ruler of Heaven) and never lose that connection, Japanese ancestral spirits tend to lose this very connection because they merge with other spirits originating from diverse kinship groups. The Japanese system provides the individual with an ideological basis for solidarity with a much wider circle of families that, in turn, are united under the royal ancestress Amaterasu, while the Chinese system provides only for permanent solidarity within each kinship group.

This pattern of separation of the ancestral spirits from their kinship moorings and their projection into a wider social framework is duplicated in the *iemoto* of Buddhism. Hence I have entitled this chapter "The Iemoto Pattern in Religion."

Indian Buddhism, being a protestant movement within Hinduism, possessed many Hindu characteristics and introduced new ideas as well. It emphasized the impermanence of human bonds and the need to sever all worldly connections. It preached the unity of all things and the doctrine of transcendentalism. The Buddhist guru, like the Hindu guru, could be from any stratum of society, including the Untouchables. Buddhism was tolerant and conciliatory towards other creeds. But the most distinguishing feature of Buddhism was the doctrine of castelessness. Kings and robbers would be treated alike and all who wished could reach salvation in the present life. There would be no need to wait for many reincarnations as prescribed in Hinduism.

When Buddhism reached China it underwent great changes.

First of all, the Chinese, instead of believing in the unity of all beings, considered humans to be superior to animals. Secondly, while many Chinese Buddhist temples were built away from society, Buddhist monks and scholars composed and wrote commentaries on what the Japanese Indologist, Hajime Nakamura, called "spurious" *sūtras* such as the *Ta Pao Fu Mu En Chung Ching* (The Scripture on the Repayment of Parental Kindness) (Nakamura 1964:269). Even the deceased abbots of Chinese monasteries were worshipped in temple altars exactly like ancestors in family homes.

There were other peculiarities to Chinese Buddhism. Since the Chinese valued hierarchy they dwelled on the Lord Buddha's greatness not only in terms of his religious achievement but also in terms of his high birth as a prince. And Chinese Buddhism, in contrast to Indian Buddhism, submitted to the authority of the Emperor.[1] Finally, there has simply been a scarcity of Chinese Buddhist religious teachers (in contrast to an abundance of gurus in India) who wielded great personal influence and authority over their followers. Buddhist monks were hired to recite scriptures or incantations for the blessing and profit of the living and for the repose and succor of the dead, but for little else. In fact, the social ranking of monks and priests in the public view was not much higher than that of soldiers and even prostitutes. It was not uncommon to see posted on the lintels of the gates to Chinese homes the sign "Sheng tao wu yuan" ("Monks and priests not welcome"). These were Chinese families that did not wish to be solicited by men of the cloth. They posted their signs in the same spirit that many American public and private buildings sport similar signs against door to door salesmen or canvassers for various causes.

Not only did I fail to find anything corresponding to the Chinese attitude in Japan, but I was greatly astonished by the high esteem in which monks and priests are held. Many Japanese celebrate various anniversaries with their family priest. I have seen many pictures of Japanese family gatherings (with men, women and children) which included a priest or two. This would have been unthinkable among the Chinese.

It has been said that Buddhism enjoys such high social esteem in Japan because it was first espoused by Japan's ruling classes. This argument does not bear close examination. Why did the ruling classes of China not espouse Buddhism when it was first introduced? Even more important is the fact that, when some particular Chinese emperor became too zealous about Buddhism, as Hsien Tsung of T'ang dynasty (A.D. 618-906) did, for instance, his officials objected. The emperor wanted to send a delegation to India to seek to bring Buddha's remains to the Chinese capital. The leader of the objectors, the literati-bureaucrat Han Yu, was even punished by demotion, but this did not help the Buddhist cause in China. And emperors of other Chinese dynasties did not follow this T'ang example. The high social esteem accorded Buddhism in Japan goes much deeper than the actions of some leading individual or group.

Characteristics of Buddhism in Japan

Buddhism in Japan shares many of the characteristics of Buddhism in China but the Japanese have introduced new elements into the religion or given old elements new emphases. Like the Chinese, the Japanese emphasize specific human bonds over the universal, but in quite their own way. To begin with, while acknowledging the importance of filial piety, some Japanese Buddhist sects nevertheless preach that one must turn his back on his parents in order to believe in the *Dharma* (law). Nichiren, founder of a major Buddhist sect (Hokke shū, also known as Nichiren shū) and a zealous devotee of the *Lotus Sūtra*, distinguished "low filial piety" or devotion to parents from "high filial piety" or devotion to Buddhist universalism (Nakamura 1964:422).

From this initial divergence, Buddhism in Japan assumed characteristics unknown in China or India. While the Chinese considered humans higher in status than animals, the Japanese held ranks among humans to be practically inviolate, so that those of lower birth could not in fact ascend to a higher position. Therefore, the followers of a sect would glorify the high births of their leaders. When the leader was of common birth the followers tended to fabricate a different genealogy for him. Certain temples became more important than others because they housed the graves of the founders or were headed by direct descendants of the founders.

Like its Chinese counterpart, Japanese Buddhism was subordinate to the power of the state, but this subordination was of a more extreme form. As contrasted to the Chinese type of negative obeisance, Japanese Buddhism developed a positive support of the imperial family and a sense of ultra-nationalism. This kind of intimate relationship between the monastic orders and the state was totally absent in China and only occasionally seen in ancient India.

Another peculiarity of Japanese Buddhism is the tendency to resort to military power in defense of sectarian creeds, a tendency unknown in China. This tendency has been documented ever since the Heian period (A.D. 794-1185). Large temples, which owned sizable estates, employed priest-soldiers to achieve the temples' demands. This tendency was also prevalent in some Shintō sects. The balance of the war between the Genji and Heike clans in the 12th century is said to have been seriously tipped by the switch of support of one group of priestly soldiers. In the 15th and 16th centuries the Ikkō and Nichiren sects fought against the feudal lords. At one time the chief abbot Rennyo of the Shin sect summoned the priests and their families and exhorted them thus:

> Our destiny is predetermined by the deeds in our previous lives, so you should not be afraid of death. You should fight. (Nakamura 1964:494).

However, the most important characteristic of Japanese Buddhism is sectarianism. As contrasted with the situation in India and China, a great number of sects in Japan are segregated, exclusive, and closed bodies. Nakamura notes by way of illustration that, for example, the Zen and Jōdo schools which in China were in complete harmony "without any sense of conflict, form in Japan separate sects, which are incompatible with each other" (Nakamura 1964:486). This sectarianism is based, primarily on the absolute devotion to a specific religious leader.

At the core of Japanese sectarianism is the doctrinaire emphasis on faith, and the object of Japanese religious faith is typically human.

> In general, Indian religions and Chinese Buddhism are contemplative, focused on the vision of truth. In such religions, faith is merely the first step toward entering the innermost recess of the religion. It is simply preparatory. However, when these sects were introduced into Japan, faith came to be recognized as the very essence of religion. Therefore, Japanese Buddhism is, above all, a Buddhism centering around faith. The Japanese emphasize purity of faith. (Even the Zen sect, in which faith is comparatively less esteemed, exhibits this trend in Japan.) This faith is of two kinds: (1) faith in a certain real person (founder, teacher); (2) faith in an ideal person (a specific Buddha or Bodhisattva). In practice, however, both appear so commingled that it is difficult to

differentiate them. In either case the focus is on a specific individual. (Nakamura 1964:459)

Though Nakamura is quite right in observing that although the two kinds of objects of faith tend to be commingled in practice, they are sometimes separated. Take the Pure Land (Jōdo) sects for example. Faith in an ideal being provided the foundation for these sects. They put their sole emphasis on the 18th of the 48 Vows of Amida Buddha, namely, absolute dependence upon another's (Amida Buddha's) strength for salvation, by practicing thankful and repetitive recitations of the Nembutsu.[2]

However, as time went on, faith in an actual person as teacher or founder became the backbone of the organizational development of Buddhism. The original Pure Land Doctrine of Hōnen (1133-1212) was based almost exclusively upon the teachings of one Chinese master, Shan-tao (Japanese, Zendō; 613-681). The next great leader, Shinran (1173-1262), was absolutely devoted to his master Hōnen. "As far as I, Shinran, am concerned, the sole reason I have faith is that a good man explained to me that in order to be saved by Amida I had only to recite the invocations (nembutsu). I do not know whether the nembutsu is actually the means to rebirth in the Pure Land, or whether perhaps it is the road to Hell. Even though I were cajoled by Saint Hōnen that I should go to Hell through nembutsu, I should do so and not regret it." (Nakamura 1964:450). After the death of Shinran in 1262 his direct descendants and followers were so devoted to him that they organized a new monastic order, Jōdo-shin-shū (the True Pure Land Sect), one of the head temples of which is the Hongan-ji in Kyoto. The Hongan-ji order initiated by the devotees of Shinran "has developed into a large organization on a nationwide scale, not as a free and open association of the believers, but rather as a closed order with the 'pope' as its central authority" (Nakamura 1964:482). The successive "popes" of the Hongan-ji order (Shin-shū sect) were really the lineal offspring of Shinran.

In some instances, this devotion to a particular founder from a particular family went so far that "enlightenment" became a certificate conferred on a devotee after he had received the necessary secret instructions. The Myōshin Temple sect acts in precisely this manner (Nakamura 1964:485).

It is interesting to note that the tendency to make religious attainment hereditary was not always endorsed by all the Buddhist leaders. Shinran himself was against it. Shinran himself never intended to set up a new sect of his own, but only wished "to elucidate the true purport of his master Hōnen's teachings" (Nakamura 1964:450). To him every disciple was merely "a disciple of the Perfect One (Buddha)," and he believed that "we are all fellow-disciples practicing religion together." For, he emphatically affirmed, "I, Shinran, have no disciples to be called mine" (Nakamura 1964:482). In spite of this, his followers proceeded not only to make him the founder of the Hongan-ji order (Shin sect) through their absolute devotion to and dependence upon him as the final authority, but also accorded his lineal descendants the same veneration as heads of the order. This is exactly the way the Japanese *iemoto* was founded and developed. This was and is today, commensurate with the way diverse groups of Japanese have exhibited their devotion to the emperor, their feudal lord, their superiors or their boss. Even Japanese thinkers have been noted for disregarding "universal laws in favor of the authority of a specific individual" (Nakamura 1964:449).

The sectarianism in Japanese Buddhism takes a violently exclusive turn in some instances. The Nichiren sect of Buddhism has been most extreme in this regard. We have already mentioned how Nichiren followers were exhorted by their masters to fight to death. The four-point maxim of Nichiren to his followers went thus: "Those who practice invocation to Amitābha (Amida Buddha) are due to suffer continuous punishment in hell; the Zen sect is the devil; the Shingon (esoteric) sect is the ruin of the country; the Ritsu (discipline) sect is the enemy of the country." The "non-alms-giving-or-taking faction" of this sect even forbade the giving of alms to or taking of alms from non-believers of the Lotus Sūtra (Nakamura 1964:483), the sole scripture Nichiren prescribed for himself and his followers.

The Japanese pattern of absolute, external devotion to a specific religious leader and his lineal descendants is different from what we find in China, India, or the West. The Chinese have no conception of this kind of devotion. To begin with, no Chinese Buddhist order allowed its monks to marry, so the latter could not have blood descendants. Furthermore, the attribute of continuity in their father-son dominated kinship system limits the Chinese from serious involvement outside the webs of kinship and their local community. They simply could not have subordinated duties and obligations to specific persons in kinship and local links to those required by non-kin persons. In Chapter 4 we noted some Chinese instances in which filial devotion to parents was transferred to loyalty to the emperor. But these were exceptions and the lineal descendants of the emperors were not objects of devotion for the sons and grandsons of their loyal ministers. As for religion, the denomination of a Chinese temple usually depended upon the resident priest and was subject to change from time to time.

The Hindu exhibits absolute devotion to his *guru*. But there are so many *gurus* in any one sect that none would be regarded as the sole source of salvation. The attributes of discontinuity and diffuseness in the Indians' mother-son dominated kinship mean that their teachings are bound to be vague and their theological affiliation uncertain. They exemplify nothing similar to the Japanese custom whereby the teachings of one absolute master were regarded as a kind of an inheritance, to be kept within a sect "family" and secretly transmitted from generation to generation, and from the head temple to the branch temples in strictly hierarchical fashion.

Of course, since, with a few exceptions, Hindu holy men do not marry, they cannot bequeath their "secrets" to their descendants. But is it not reasonable to suggest that most Hindu holy men are celebate while most Japanese priests are married and raise families precisely because, as I have indicated elsewhere (Hsu 1963), mother-son dominance gave the Hindu a freedom from kinship ties that it did not give the Japanese, among whom the mother-son dyad is subordinate to the father-son dyad?

Westerners, with their attributes of discontinuity and exclusiveness derived from a husband-wife dominated kinship system, are most inclined to sectarianism characterized by militancy, violence, clashes with or in support of the state, and discrimination and persecution against non-believers or believers of other creeds. Like India, but unlike China and Japan, the West has always accorded high prestige and power to celebates. But unlike Indians, Chinese, or Japanese, Westerners do not on the whole regard individual religious leaders as ultimate and absolute objects of devotion, and they certainly never consider religious leadership to be inherited along kinship lines. Hence, while Luther might have enjoyed veneration by his followers in his own life time, his descendants have never been similarly honored because of his position.

The Japanese approach to their religious leaders is commensurate with the facts of father-son dominance and mother-son subdominance in kinship: it is sectarian, sometimes militant (a result of discontinuity and exclusiveness), exhibits extra-kinship ties with kinship-like permanence (showing discontinuity and continuity), emphasizes non-rational submission to ritual formulae or objects (a result of diffuseness),[3] and exemplifies absolute devotion to a master and his lineal descendants (showing authority and continuity). These are the essential elements that make Japanese sects like the *iemoto*.

In the case of Zen Buddhism, the special *iemoto*-like exclusiveness and the hierarchical and non-rational link between master and disciple have taken a new turn. Zen is more popular in Japan than it ever was in China, the country of its origin. Through the Japanese, Zen Buddhism has attracted world attention and there is no Chinese exponent of any form of Chinese religion who can even begin to claim any sort of world fame comparable to that of the Japanese master of Zen, Daisetz Suzuki.

I submit that the development of Zen in Japan has owed a great deal to the *iemoto*-like characteristics of Japanese society. Zen masters have to communicate their religious experiences to others by symbolic or actional expressions because "Zen has no thought-system of its own; it uses Mahāyāna terminology liberally; it refuses to commit itself to any specified pattern of thinking. Nor is it a faith, for it does not urge us to accept any dogma or creed or an object of worship" (Suzuki 1967:122). Yet when we try to understand these symbolic or actional expressions we generally get something like the *koan* (riddle) dialogue or analogies. In spite of myriad publications and lectures on the subject, I doubt if many people in the East or the West really understand the meaning of the *koan* dialogue. To a majority of mankind the *koan* will remain simply a kind of non-sequitur, some clever, more often, simply pointless. Zen exponents are full of analogies. The following is one from Suzuki:

> "The Zen master is adept in the use of a medium, either verbal or actional, which directly points to his Zen experience and by which the questioner, if he is mentally ripe, will at once grasp the master's intention. The medium of this kind functions "directly" and "at once," as if it were the experience itself—as when deep calls to deep. This direct functioning is compared to one brightly burnished mirror reflecting another brightly burnished one which stands facing the first with nothing between them."(Suzuki 1967:126).

But two mirrors facing each other with nothing in-between reflect only each other. What we are left with is still the two mirrors (or the master and his disciple) in a certain relationship and whatever that juxtaposition means, but nothing else.

Consequently, the central contribution of Zen is, it seems to me, an elaboration or escalation of intuitive techniques for binding a large number of human beings together under the absolute authority of one master, into one school or congregation. Hence, in the Zen sect, no less than in others, "it is not the difference in the religious faith or doctrine but *merely such specific factors of human relationships* as the inheritance of the master's endowments that account for the split of the religious school into multitudinous sects and factions" (Nakamura 1964:484).

A final characteristic of Japanese Buddhism is the particular nature of the Japanese congregation. As noted before, Japanese sectarianism is built on the custom of a specific congregation belonging to a specific temple of a specific sect. This is similar to the pattern of Christianity in the West, but different from the religious patterns of the Chinese and even of the Hindus. Except for the Christians and Moslems among them, the Chinese have no concept of a congregational religion whatsoever. It is simply a Western misunderstanding to refer to the Chinese as Buddhists or Taoists. The Chinese as a rule do not belong to any organized temple. The individual Chinese goes to whichever house of gods that seems most convenient at the moment and offers the best results; furthermore, he goes from one to another as an American would go from one shop to another searching for the best prices or most attractive merchandise. The Hindu is more certain about his places of worship than the Chinese but he is not any more constant. Hindu temples do not have exclusive membership lists and many devout Hindus will have no compunction in praying at tombs of Moslem holy men, for instance, if their gods seem powerless.

However, whereas the unit of membership in Western churches is the individual, in Japanese Buddhist temples (otera) or Shintō shrines (jinja) it is the household (ie). The relationship between the danka (parishioner family or household) and its temple is determined by custom and tradition, and not usually determined by individual conversion. The danka family depends upon its temple to perform its funeral services and other Buddhist rites such as continual prayers for the dead and care of the family tombs. The temple priests are paid for these services, and the *danka* also makes contributions of money for building, reconstruction, repair and other maintenance costs of the temple. Before the Tokugawa period the *danka* system operated on a voluntary basis. But the Tokugawa government not only adopted the *danka* system but also expanded and enforced it, so that each individual's religious faith "had to be guaranteed by his temple. Those who were confirmed as not pagan were registered in the denominational census-register" (Nakamura 1964:486-487).

Hence, I was not surprised at the results when, in the course of one year's field work in Japan (1964-65), I asked about the temple affiliations of approximately 550 families in different parts of Honshū from Akita to Kure as well as in Kyūshū and Shikoku. Only one per cent replied that they did not know the denominations of the temples with which their families were affiliated. A few said they were not *danka* of any temple. The rest not only knew the denominations of the temples of their affiliation but also the names and locations of their sect's *honzan* or main temple.[4] The *danka* system is thus another link between Japanese kinship and the Japanese way in religion.

The results of our inquiry seem obviously different from those of some other studies. According to the Institute of Statistics the number of Japanese believers for the years 1953, 1958, and 1963 fluctuated between 30% and 35% (Institute of Statistical Mathematics 1961: 180-193 and 1964:106-176). According to the questionnaire returns distributed among the males in the age group 20-40, the percentage of believers is even smaller, 18% (Basabe et. al. 1968:9 and 22). Of course, our responses came from persons of both sexes and all age groups, not just young males. But even more revealing is the fact that these studies (especially the Basabe study) asked about what the individual himself believed, while our inquiry dealt with the denominational affiliation of his *ie* as well as the *ie* of his origin. When the details of the Basabe data are examined, it is found that his three groups ("believers," "indifferents," and "negatives") overlap a great deal. For example, more of his "believers" agreed (42.3%) than disagreed (23.1%) with the statement "Actually there is no such thing as an afterlife, but because people want an afterlife, they believe in it" (Basabe 1968:59). Then, on all three questions concerning the existence of God, the "believers" agreed and disagreed with nearly equal frequency on two of them. On the third question, "God really exists, regardless of whether a man believes in Him or not," the percentage who disagreed with it was three times as high as those who agreed (45.7% to 15.7%; Basabe 1968:37).

The *iemoto*-like character of Japanese sects is not unrecognized by some Japanese scholars. Morioka, whose particular attention has centered on the Shin sect founded by Shinran, notes how each local temple is a kind of *ie*, and how the local temples stand in a relationship to their *honzan* (head temple) much like the *bunke* (branch families) relate to their *honke* (head family), thus forming a sort of religious *dōzoku* (Morioka 1955:42). The fact that priests are married and bequeath their religious mantle and residential priesthood in both head and branch temples makes the religious organization a real *dōzoku* in practice, not merely by analogy.

The mutual dependence between the *honzan* and the branch temples in the Shin sect is very real. The former confers upon the local temples the *Nyōgō Scroll* certifying that they share the main statue of Amida Buddha with the *honzan*. In turn, the local temples offer various services as well as large monetary contributions to the *honzan*. This *honzan*-local temple relationship continues through renewal of the certification and appointment for succeeding residential priests (Morioka 1955:42-43). As each sect gets larger the tendency is to expand the organization beyond the *dōzoku* model in the direction of the *iemoto* model. The Honpa-Hongan-ji branch of the Shin sect is one such example. It is a huge hierarchical organization. At the bottom are the *danka* or believer households. The next rung in the heirarchy are the *kumi* or local units of temples. Then come the *kyōku* or prefectural parishes. And finally at the very top is the hongan-ji, presided over by its abbot.

These points by no means exhaust the distinguishing features of Japanese Buddhism in contrast to Chinese Buddhism. Yet they are sufficient to show how the same creed underwent drastic transformations when it was introduced into a society with a different kinship system. The Buddhist creed as it began in Hindu India was egalitarian, non-violent, and focused on other-wordly salvation through escape from the cycle of reincarnation. In China it was subordinated to filial piety and imperial authority and remained outside regular society. Chinese monks were celebate and were accorded very low social esteem. In Japan, Buddhism pushed filial piety in the kinship sphere into a lower order of importance. Japanese Buddhism formed an essential and extremely prominent part of the social structure. Monks in most Japanese Buddhist sects married and raised families, in contradiction to the original Buddhist rule and to their Chinese counterparts. This made it possible for succession in most monastic orders to be restricted along blood lines. Japanese Buddhism evinced strong sectarian tendencies and provided active support for the imperial house and for militarism.

Even among the general population, kinship affiliation tends to ease itself imperceptibly into religious affiliation. Certainly the *danka* relationship, which links the individual with his non-kinship Buddhist temple through the *ie*, is enormously more significant to the average Japanese than it would be to the average Chinese. A Chinese individual's affiliation to his ancestral spirits remains forever on the same basis—namely kinship, whereas a Japanese individual's affiliation to his ancestral spirits changes from the kinship basis (a primary grouping) to a sectarian basis (a secondary grouping), with which his links tend to be definite and continuous.

Yet, in spite of this shift, a Japanese individual's affiliation in a religious sect involves no rejection of kinship. He gives himself to the pseudo-kinship Buddhist sect not as an equal or a free agent but in a spirit of devotion towards the particular founder of a particular sect, in the same way that the traditional Chinese has been tied to the ancestors of his own kinship group.

"Old Wines in New Bottles"

The *iemoto*-like characteristics of Japanese religion persist in the many pre- and post-war "new religions." Statistics concerning the number of adherents of these new sects vary a great deal; one of the causes of this variation is the fact that the leaders of each group tend to inflate their following. Nevertheless, what is clear is that the number of these new religions and the size of their collective following are impressive, especially when we contrast their absence in neighboring China before 1949. Furthermore, we have clear and incontrovertible evidence of the success of some of the new religions, such as the Soka Gakkai, in contemporary Japan.[5]

However, in spite of their exuberance or numerical strength, these are not really "new" religions, in the sense of a revolutionary departure from the past, but essentially "old wines in new bottles." The most cogent substantiation for this conclusion is to be found in three areas:

(1) pattern of leadership succession
(2) organizational relationships among functionaries and between functionaries and the congregation
(3) ideological departure from the past.

(1) Pattern of Leadership Succession. In a book entitled *The New Religions of Japan* (Thomsen 1963), the author describes in some detail 13 new religions, and provides us with a good deal of information on leadership succession. In the following paragraphs I shall indicate patterns of leadership succession where the facts are known. The extracts are from Thomsen's book except where otherwise indicated.

> *Tenrikyō.* Founded by a woman Nakayama Miki in 1837. Succeeded on her death in 1887 by Master Iburi, who was a carpenter before he became Miki's disciple. After Iburi's death in 1907, "the Nakayama family again took over, the present leader being Miki's great-grandson" (35-36).

> *Kurozumikyō.* Founded by Kurozumi Munetada. No specific information on succession, but I presume him to have been succeeded by his lineal or blood descendants since this is one of the 13 Shintō sects, and the "Kurozumi family had furnished priests to Okayama Prefecture for generations" (61).

> *Konkokyō.* Founded in 1859 by Kaware Bunjiro, posthumously honored as Konko Daijin. "According to the rules of Konkokyō, the leader is to be elected in democratic fashion by all ministers of the religion, but it is emphasized that the Patriarch must be a blood relative of the founder" (71).

> *Soka Gakkai.* Founded in 1931 by Makiguchi Tsunesaburo. Succeeded by Toda Jodai (unrelated to founder) who was Director General under Makiguchi. Toda was succeeded after his death by Daisaku Ikeda, the present leader. Ikeda is the son-in-law of the Vice-Chairman of Soka Gakkai's Board of Directors (Brannan 1968:86-87).

> *Reiyukai.* Founded in 1925 by Kubo Kabutaro with a woman, Kotani

Kimi. Upon Kubo's death, Kotani Kimi assumed the leadership. Kotani "does not have the personality of Kubo, and she has been involved in financial scandals which have hurt the reputation of Reiyukai. . . . Many of the leaders of the religion look forward to the time when Kubo's son, Tsuginari, who in many ways has the charming personality of his father, will succeed to the leadership of his religion" (110-111).

Rissho Kosei Kai. Founded in 1938 by Niwano Shikazo in collaboration with a woman, Mrs. Naganuma Masa. After Mrs. Naganuma died in 1957, Niwano became the sole leader.

Omoto. Founded about 1898 (or thereabouts) by Deguchi Nao, a farmer's daughter without education, in collaboration with a school teacher, Ueda Kisaburo. Omoto was based on revelations received by Nao. Before starting the religion jointly, Ueda was adopted into the Deguchi family and became Deguchi Onisaburo. Nao claimed Onisaburo was the messiah God promised her. Onisaburo later married Nao's daughter, Sumiko. Onisaburo was joint leader with Nao; then sole leader after Nao's death; then was succeeded by his wife Sumiko (Nao's daughter) after his death in 1948. Sumiko died in 1952. Present leadership shared by Deguchi Eiji and Deguchi Isao, two blood descendants (132).

Ananaikyō. Founded in 1949 by Nakano Yonosuko, a disciple of Onisaburo, one time leader of Omoto. Nakano "has chosen a young woman as his successor and given her his own family name. Her name is now Nakano Yoshiko, and she holds the title of Superior of Ananaikyō. Besides her, Nakano has adopted about fifteen young women and men and has placed them in organizational positions in the religion" (144).

Seicho no Ie. Founded in 1928 by Taniguchi Masaharu. He was a member of Omotokyō, broke away from it and was then interested in Ittoen for a while. No information on succession yet.

Sekai Kyusei Kyō. Founded in 1934 by Okada Mokichi, who was a member of Omotokyō and broke away from it. His widow Okada Yoshiko succeeded him as leader in 1955. After her death Okada's married daughter Fujieda Itsuki became the leader. Mrs. Okada held the title "Nidai Sama" (second generation leader) and her daughter holds the title "Sandai Sama" (third generation leader; 176-177).

P. L. Kyōdan (Perfect Liberty Religion). Founded in 1946 by Miki Tokuchika, after seed of it was planted in 1912 with the founding of Tokumitsu Kyo by Kanada Tokumitsu. Miki Tokuchika's father, Miki

Tokuharu, was one of Kanada's disciples. Miki Tokuharu "had been a Buddhist priest of the Obaku Zen sect. After the death of Kanada in 1919, Miki Tokuharu planted a shrub called *himorogi* at the place of Kanada's death. He worshipped it for five years in accordance with the instructions given him by his master. At the end of the five years he claimed to have received the revelation promised by Kanada before his death. Miki then established a religion known as Hito no Michi (the way of Man) in 1924." It was quite successful but it was suppressed by the government after 1937. In 1938 Miki Tokuharu died. Tokuchika, founder of P. L. Kyōdan in 1946, began as leader of his father's religion, Hito no Michi, which was banned by the government again in 1945 (184-185).

Tensho Kotai Jingu Kyō (Odoru Shūkyō or dancing religion). Founded in 1945 by a grandmother Kitamura Sayo. She designated on May 27, 1951 the baby girl born to her son and his wife as her successor. The girl ever since has been given the title Ohimegamisama (Princess Goddess).

Ittoen. Founded in 1928 (ca.) by Tenko-San. No present information on successor.

This brief analysis of the 12 cases on which we have some information reveals the following facts about leadership succession in the major Japanese new religions: 4 cases of patrilineal descendants, 1 case by the widow, 1 case by the widow and then the son, 2 cases of daughters, 1 case of the widow and then a daughter, 1 case of an adopted daughter, 1 case by "blood relative of the founder," 1 case involves marriage to the Vice-Chairman of the Board of Directors. The overwhelming importance of kinship in religious leadership succession is undeniable. In most cases lineal descendants are the successors. The use of adopted children and *mukoyoshi* is also quite consistent with what we saw in the Japanese kinship system of the *dōzoku* and especially in the *iemoto.*

Even the case of the Soka Gakkai falls within the accepted pattern. It is interesting that the present President, Ikeda, wants to be addressed as *"Sensei"* (Teacher), because he feels that *"Kaicho"* (President), the proper title for his position, ought to be reserved exclusively for Makiguchi, the deceased founder and Toda, Ikeda's immediate predecessor (Brannan 1968:86). It is also interesting that Toda's "tape-recorded voice still speaks to his followers on important occasions; and all important decisions and other noteworthy tidings are brought to his grave at Taiseki-ji" (Thomsen 1963:85).

(2) Organizational Relationships. Each of the new religions has a headquarters, usually with one or more imposing architectural edifices, that fulfills the function of the honzan. To this honzan the followers repair in pilgrimage, for education and to offer their wealth and their voluntary labor. The Grand Kōdō (lecture hall) at the Soka Gakkai headquarters at Mt. Fuji, erected at a price of 400,000,000 yen (about U.S. $1,250,000) with a total floor space of about 9,900 square meters, is among the most impressive buildings. The mammoth Daiseido (grand temple) in the headquarters of the Rissho Kosei Kai in Tokyo is even more impressive. It has a total floor space of 22,840 square meters, accommodates 550,000 people, and cost about 1,600,000,000 yen (about U.S. $5,000,000).

The new honzan deal with the new local temples (sometimes called "chapters") as if the latter were bunke. The membership of some new religions such as the Soka Gakkai is conceptually based on individual conversion, but statistics show that its basis is still the household.[6] The Soka Gakkai is perhaps the most aggressive of the new religions, and has adopted many novel activities such as massive gymnastic displays, but its basic system of human relationships remains strictly hierarchical. For example, the member of Soka Gakkai who brings in a potential convert is his "introducer" and after the conversion, becomes the new convert's "immediate superior in their kumi (unit)" (Murata 1969:147-148).

Of course, with greater mobility, the impact of America and things American, and with much wider economic opportunities than before, one would expect many Japanese followers of these more disciplinarian sects to resist or resent their closed and exclusive and often harsh nature. Some cases of Soka Gakkai drop-outs have been reported. For example a faction under Masaki Sakura that broke away from the Soka Gakkai in 1960 claimed fifty members. One woman dropped out of Soka Gakkai because, "having worked day and night for the organization in an official capacity she had finally lost her husband and her children because they could not tolerate her fanaticism" (Brannan 1968:83). A man dropped out because the Soka Gakkai did not benefit his business as his persuaders had promised. Another quit because of "hypocrisy of so many leaders whom he had met" (Brannan 1968:84). I myself met two similar drop-outs.

The fact remains, however, that Soka Gakkai has prospered, and is flourishing today more than ever before.

(3) Departure from the Past. A striking contrast between Japanese and Chinese Buddhism is not merely that the former is sectarian, but rather that sects have so greatly proliferated in Japan. One historian of Japanese religion speaks of "the formation of a number of new and independent branches coming out of Hiei-zan during the thirteenth century" and regards that outburst of sectarianism as the ancestor of all Japanese sectarianism (Anesaki 1961:76). But that was not the only burst of Japanese sectarianism. In 1966, the Japanese Ministry of Education officially recognized 376 religions, and, according to Basabe et al., "a majority of the authors on the subject are in accord in affirming that at least some 150 pertain to the category of new religions" (Basabe 1968:7).

Yet the new religions of today, such as the sects that have split from the traditional religious groups of the past, have merely introduced new styles in buildings, new communications media, new techniques for getting more converts, new youth programs, and new international missionary activities. They have not deviated significantly in the basis of their faith, in the elements of their human organization and in their larger objectives. Most of the new religions are still, by and large, Japanese religions for the Japanese, even on the theoretical level. For this reason, Christianity has not prospered in Japan any more than in China. Since World War II the Catholic Church has increased its number of converts more than the Protestant churches, but the total number of Japanese who profess Christianity remains about one half of 1 percent of the total population. These facts lead us to recall our conclusion on mother-son dominated Hindu India:

> The result is a society and a culture remarkably dynamic in appearance but which in the long run undergoes little real change. Castes and sub-castes will divide and redivide. Schisms and protestant movements will always mark the religious scene. But none of them will be a decisive and permanent break with the traditional context and framework (Hsu 1963:226).

However, father-son dominance in the kinship sphere enables the attribute of continuity to outweigh diffuseness, and mutual dependence to outweigh unilateral dependence. Unigeniture, hierarchical bonds between the heir and other brothers, and freedom to incorporate unrelated persons into the *ie* combine to foster the *dōzoku* and especially the *iemoto*. Instead of being centrifugal in outlook like the Hindus, the Japanese are centripetal, except that the outer boundary of their centripetalism is not the inflexible kinship group (as among the Chinese) but the more viable *dōzoku* and especially the *iemoto*. The *iemoto* is thus an expression of Japanese centripetalism, in contrast to the Hindu caste, which is but a practical check against rampant diffuseness.

On the basis of this analysis we must take issue with Norbeck that "religious changes" in Japan "have lagged behind changes in social life and other aspects of Japanese culture" (Norbeck 1970:82). Japanese religions have indeed changed very little, but this imperviousness to change is commensurate, not discordant, with the strength of the *iemoto* pattern in Japanese society and culture. The *iemoto* pattern governs the most basic element of the individual's existence in Japan, namely, his relationship with his fellow men, in work no less than in play, in conflict resolution no less than in approaches to the supernatural. The slowness to change is equally evident in the Japanese attitude toward caste and caste-ism, to which we shall now turn.

[1] A Chinese pattern observed by Moslems and Jews in traditional China. The same pattern has prevailed among the Christians in China since 1949. There was never any contest of power between church and state in Chinese history, a conflict extremely common in the West.

[2] "Namu Amida-butsu," often shortened to "Nanmanda" which means roughly, "homage to the Buddha Infinite," is a ritual formula, as confession of faith with gratitude to the Buddha of the Western Paradise, Amida.

[3] The relationship between diffuseness and emphasis on non-rational rituals is discussed in *Clan, Caste and Club* (Hsu 1963:179-191) and also in Chapter 12 of this book.

[4] About one-third of the many university students (not included among the 550 families indicated above) with whom I had contact said that they did not know the denominations of their temples nor care about them.

[5] According to *Religion Year Book* (1966), some 29,000,000 Japanese are members of "new religions," including those of Tenrikyō, each of which claims a membership of 500,000 or more (quoted in Basabe 1968:7). Of these at least 15,000,000 belong to one of them, the Soka Gakkai. The total number is much larger if we include those "new religions" with memberships less than 500,000.

[6] In 1969 the Soka Gakkai claimed its membership to consist of 6,876,000 *shotai* or households.

12 ●

Caste and Caste-ism

In *Clan, Caste and Club*, my analysis indicated that caste, the most prevalent secondary grouping in India, is the Hindu's solution to a dilemma. This dilemma is generated, on the one hand, by diffuseness and the impermanence of the kinship situation and, on the other, by the tendency of human beings to align themselves in groups to satisfy their needs for attachment, for status and to make social organization possible (Hsu 1963:179-180). Hindu castes express themselves as arbitrary boundaries isolating one group of human beings from another. The arbitrary boundaries are fortified by diverse and ever multiplying symbols and rituals. Castes constantly divide into new caste groups for the purpose of claiming superiority over other castes. Finally, both the entrenchment behind arbitrary walls and the everlasting search for superiority over others based on some new or higher authority are commensurate with a social organization characterized by mother-son dominance in kinship and by unilateral dependence and diffuseness (Hsu 1963:162-191).

We can see nearly all the elements characteristic of the Hindu caste in the Japanese *iemoto*. The Japanese *iemoto* closely resembles the Hindu caste in its hierarchic nature, in its artificial boundaries, in its great emphasis on rigid and detailed rituals, and in the continual proliferation of new *iemoto* or sectarian groups.

In view of the fact that the *iemoto* in Japan seems to fill a role similar to the Indian caste, does this mean that caste is completely absent in Japan? The answer to this question is "no," for we know that

181

the *Eta*, an untouchable group, does exist among the Japanese. However, since the *Eta* is a relatively small group in proportion to the total population (3,000,000:100,000,000), does this mean that the *Eta* phenomenon is merely an anomaly of "peripheral interest" (Norbeck 1970:83-89), a survival from the past having no functional link with present day Japanese society and culture?

Class and Caste

Before we proceed, we need to make clear our understanding of certain terms which have become confused because of misuse. Class and caste are both inherently vertical ways of grouping members of a society, as contrasted, for example, with clubs and schools which are inherently horizontal linkages. That is to say, when we speak of class or caste we cannot avoid the implication that one class or caste is above or below another. This implication is not inevitable when we speak of different schools among philosophers or different fraternities.

However, class and caste differ a great deal in the clarity of their relative boundaries. Membership in different classes usually depends upon a definition of class. There is far more room to maneuver and the margin for confusion is much larger in the case of class as opposed to that of caste. In the U.S., class membership is more likely to be determined by income rather than origin (so long as one is white), while in England, social origin with its corollaries such as manners and speech, still carries more weight. When traditional Chinese spoke of *shang teng jen* or "uppermost class men" they actually meant those with impeccable character—although the men were also as a rule users of the writing brush rather than wielders of the scythe. Caste, on the other hand, is always linked with birth and origin, even though there is a common rationalization to explain why certain castes are lower than others in occupation, either of the caste members themselves or of their forebears. For example, Hindus often told me that Untouchables were people who clean latrines and handle corpses at burning ghats. When I first arrived in the U.S. in 1944, some American scholars told me that the low position of the American Negroes resulted from the fact that they were descendants of slaves. In other words, class membership has largely to do with what one does, while caste membership deals with what one is. Change in the former is thus much easier than in the latter.

A second difference between class and caste is that members of a caste tend to be organized in some fashion, whereas those of the same class often are not. In traditional India, each sub-caste (jati) in a local area was governed by a panchayat. The caste panchayat and the village panchayat were often not clearly distinguished from each other, and they sometimes crossed each other in jurisdiction even when they existed as two separate organizations. But, the important fact is that they were both organized. On the other hand, we can find hardly any evidence that class in pre-modern times was ever organized. In fact it has been said, and with some plausibility, that "class consciousness" was created by Marx. Certainly, labor movements are a modern phenomenon. Servants of the aristocracy used to scorn those who labored for lower ranking masters.

The third difference between class and caste is, in my view, the most crucial. In some text books its has been said that vertical mobility is possible between classes but not between castes. This is simply not true. Vertical mobility is possible in both. Crossing from Black to White is a well-known phenomenon in the United States. The true difference is that successful vertical mobility from a lower class to a higher one leads to personal pride and social reward, whereas caste crossing is wrought with personal perils and social opprobrium for those who attempt it. Thus "from log cabin to the White House" or "Horatio Alger" stories are good for vertical mobility in class, but not for caste crossing. One can gloat over how far one has risen in class, but one cannot divulge one's caste origin if the latter happens to be lower than the caste membership presently claimed. To divulge a lower caste origin will surely involve not only being shunted right back to the lower caste but also, in most instances, punishment as well.

This fact provides the essential drama for novels like Kingsblood Royal by Sinclair Lewis and Hakai by Tōson Shimazaki. In each case the story focuses on the psychological and social problems of a hero whose publicly known caste is different from the one of his origin. There would have been no such problems had class and not caste been the issue.

Caste and Caste-ism

Caste may exist openly, accepted as part of a society's ideal, and incorporated into its indigenous cultural and legal framework. Or it may exist as an observable reality but regarded as contradictory to the society's ideal and rejected in its indigenous cultural and legal framework.

There is, however, a third pattern. This is found where caste is seen as a clear reality in a limited sphere of a society and a caste-like approach to human relationships prevails in the rest of it. The latter condition is what I call caste-ism. Caste-ism exists if social groups exhibit separatism, caste-like hierarchical strife, and a denial of individual mobility from one group to another, even though the groups are not called castes.

We may thus envisage a continuum with class differentiations at one end, caste differentiations at the other and a situation of caste-ism in the middle. At the caste end of the continuum, mobility in an individual's life is totally denied. At the class end of it such mobility is taken for granted and rewarded, however rarely such mobility may occur. But the intensity of caste-ism in the society and culture is measured by whether the castes take on class-like characteristics or whether classes take on caste-like characteristics.

Kinship and Caste-ism

It is part of our hypothesis that caste-ism in Hindu India (the tendency for each group to insulate itself behind rigid walls and to claim superiority over other groups similarly insulated) is a functional outgrowth of the diffuseness of human relationships and a value orientation with an emphasis on the supernatural. In addition to diffuseness, the mother-son dominated kinship system of Hindu India also generates the attribute of unilateral dependence, which reinforces submission to a hierarchical arrangement in which fissionary efforts lead only to more claims to a higher place in the same hierarchy.

In the Chinese father-son dominated kinship system, on the other hand, caste-ism has no ground for development since the Chinese system is characterized by the attributes of continuity and inclusiveness but not diffuseness. The Chinese individual is so permanently linked to his forebears and descendants, and contemporaneously to his extended family, that he is not free to seek other forms of affiliation.

If the attribute of diffuseness is overshadowed by those of continuity, inclusiveness, and exclusiveness in the Japanese situation, since the mother-son relationship occupies only a position of subdominance, we shall have good reason to expect some caste-ism in Japan, but nothing to the extent found in Hindu India. This is indeed what we find.

The *Eta* as a distinctly untouchable group has existed in Japan for over a thousand years. Their main concentration is in the older settled areas of Japan including Osaka and Kyoto, but some of them also live in Tokyo and nothern Japan. There are no official statistics regarding the *Eta* but their number is generally assumed by scholars to be about 3,000,000.

The Japanese have kept the *Eta* out of the mainstream of society for centuries (Price 1966). Traditionally, the colloquial and semi-secret expression among the Japanese when referring to an *Eta*[1] was four out-stretched fingers signifying four legged animals. Strictly speaking the outcasts were formally separated into the *Hinin* (not human) and the *Eta* (much dirt), but this distinction is not clear to a majority of the Japanese. Under Emperor Meiji the *Eta* caste was formally abolished and they were publicly declared to be *Shinheimin* (New Citizens) placed in a comparable position with *Heimin* (Citizens). Nowadays they are officially designated as *Mikaiho Burakumin* (Unemancipated People)[2] but colloquially the term *Burakumin* alone is sufficient. All this has not really altered the inferior status of the *Eta*, and we are reminded of the new terms for India's Untouchables such as *Harijan* (God's people) initiated by Gandhi and "Scheduled Castes" used by the Indian government. Although some Japanese have told me that discrimination against the *Eta* is weaker since World War II, the *Eta* today are still not accepted as Japanese, rarely if ever rise in employment, even if they find employment, continue to be segregated in residence and burial, and certainly cannot intermarry with Japanese. Japanese laws today do not forbid the latter, but the strength of the custom remains. I must add that this discrimination has no basis in physical differences. The *Eta* cannot be visually separated from other Japanese. I tried to pin down some such differences in Kyoto, Osaka, and the suburban town of Ashiya, and I failed. Nor did I find any Japanese who could assure me of the existence of such differences.

The existence of such a distinct caste group in Japan is especially striking when we note the total absence of caste in China. The usual Japanese rationalization for the orgin of *Eta* is conventional enough: their ancestors were slaves or were holders of *sengyō* (shameful or mean calling) or even were Korean prisoners. But the Chinese not only practiced slavery according to the law until 1911,[3] they also forbade descendants to the third generation of holders of certain occupations from taking the Imperial Examinations.[4] Yet in spite of their emphasis on ancestor worship and genealogy, the Chinese never had a permanent caste composed of the descendants of slaves or men of base occupations. They absorbed those people along with foreigners, including Mongols, Koreans and tribal people, such as the Min Chia and Miao of the southwest, into the general population. For the hallmark of being Chinese has always been an individual's degree of Sinicization mostly in terms of language and culture, not origin.

Conversely, ever since the first emperor of the Chin, Chin Shih Huang Ti, brought all China under one empire (221 B.C.), the Chinese have not known a permanent aristocracy or a continuously prominent group of literati-bureaucrats. My own research on prominent Chinese families both at the local level and at the national level reveals that family prominence as a rule did not last over three generations; the duration was usually shorter. Since their first publication in 1948, my conclusions have been borne out by more extensive research (Hsu 1948:256-289 and Hsu 1971:297-315). In other words, two-way vertical mobility among the classes was a long-standing reality in traditional China.

Although the total number of *Eta* in Japan comes out to some 3% of the population, the significance of the Japanese approach to the *Eta* is far more important than the actual numbers involved. Had Japanese society permitted the Chinese type of mobility, the *Eta* would have been completely absorbed, especially since they do not differ from other Japanese physically, linguistically or by custom.

What is of great importance here is the Japanese discouragement of mobility among social classes. The Japanese borrowed the traditional Chinese concept of a four class structure (scholar, farmer, artisan and merchant, in that order of rank) and the Japanese use the same Chinese ideographs for these classes, with the exception that the

Japanese mean warrior or *samurai* by the Chinese ideograph for scholar (pronounced *shih* in Chinese and *shi* in Japanese). Hence, we have *bushido* or the way (*dō*) of the military (*bu*) scholar (*shi*). Above this four-fold class structure is the aristocracy with the Imperial Family and its lineal descendants at the apex.

The rigidity of this class structure was most pronounced under Tokugawa rule. The Shōgunate sanctioned it by demanding registration in order to maintain the status quo "in the name of national law and order" (Embree 1945:20). The Japanese were prevented by law from attempting any kind of movement from one class to another. This rigidity was not a Tokugawa creation. Its roots were strong in traditional Japanese society as we mentioned in the preceding chapter; an exalted social rank was an important source of power even for religious leaders. The Japanese approach to social class, in contrast to the Chinese attitude, is indeed characterized by caste-ism. In contrast to the Chinese, the Japanese never had a "from-rags-to-riches" tradition. And this caste-istic approach to social class had positive effects, one of which was that those on higher rungs of the ladder of hierarchy did not slip down as easily as their counterparts in China. Social, political and economic prominence in Japanese society was of longer duration than in Chinese society. Unigeniture and the adoption of non-kin heirs undoubtedly had a strong bearing on this, but the caste-istic approach is not without significance here.

The Japanese class structure has undergone some changes, especially since World War II. "Conventional criteria such as incomes, occupations, and levels of education may conflict, especially when these are related to subjective self-appraisals and non-subjective appraisals of social placement. The old makers of class-dress, demeanor and expressed attitudes and values—have become blurred and are unreliable as guides" (Norbeck 1970:93). According to the estimate of a Japanese sociologist, in 1965 the uppermost stratum should have made up 3 percent of the Japanese population; the upper-middle class, 18 percent; lower-middle class, 19 percent; intermediate stratum, 32 percent and lower class, 28 percent (Odaka 1964). But the *Eta* remain outcasts. For example, the *Eta* or *Burakumin* "appear never to have been subjected to active proseltyting (sic) by either Christian sects or any of the new sects . . . perhaps simply because they are outcasts" (Norbeck 1970:94). This fact fits well with the Japanese approach to religion dealt with in the last chapter.

The Japanese caste-like approach toward non-Japanese in Japan follows closely this caste-ism in social classes. Previously we mentioned one popular Japanese notion about the origin of the *Eta* —that their ancestors were Korean prisoners. This seems to be a myth. But the fact that such a myth exists in Japan and not in China, is significant. In fact, the Japanese non-acceptance of foreigners can be clearly seen. It was in Japan and not in China that Koreans, Ainus, Okinawans and Formosans were treated like lower castes (Norbeck 1966:183-199). I have been told that, before World War II, restaurants and other public places in Kobe and Osaka used to post signs that Okinawans and Koreans were not welcome.

The treatment of Koreans in Japan since World War II by the Japanese government is, of course, drastically different from what it was before 1945, but the attitude of the Japanese people is another matter, even towards Koreans who were born and raised in Japan, who attended Japanese schools and speak Japanese fluently. For example, in a small village of about 100 households, some twenty miles from Kyoto, William Newell found its Korean residents (who were forcibly brought to Japan as supplementary labor during the war) physically segregated from the Japanese, not represented in the village council, barred from burying their dead in the Buddhist graveyard, and whose children sat at the back of the classrooms (Newell 1967:220).

Newell observes that what the Japanese fear is that if non-Japanese obtain admission to the small local group which forms the basic unit of Japanese society, the "moral" foundation of the group will be undermined. "Group success, according to the Japanese way of thinking, is based on group solidarity and integrity, and the admission of an outsider even if he appears to be totally integrated is introducing a risky element" (Newell 1967:225). The Chinese minority in Japan fares much better. Apart from economic strength, the Chinese "have a sense of cultural superiority which results in a strong desire not to go to Japanese schools" and "they live in sufficient contact with each other in sufficiently large numbers to form and to maintain a social system which does not depend on Japanese largesse to keep it operating" (Newell 1967:225).

What Newell has described is what we have designated as Japanese caste-ism. And his conclusion is very helpful.

In general, Japanese recognize the rights of minorities to exist even inside Japan and grant them full status as minorities. As long as they remain minorities like the Chinese who do not wish to become Japanese, then no special difficulties will result. . . . But as soon as individuals demand the right to become entirely Japanese losing their non-Japanese background, then the particular groups which they wish to join close up and exclude them in order to protect what they conceive as their special character (Newell 1967:225-226).

All this stands in sharp contrast to the situation in China. It is well known that as the centuries rolled by, many different racial or ethnic strains amalgamated with the Han Chinese. At the time of Confucius the people inhabiting what is largely the Hunan province had short hair and tattooed bodies—customs not followed by the Han Chinese. Throughout later Chinese history, the Han Chinese were invaded at different times by Mongols, Kitans, Jurjins, Manchus, and various Turkic peoples. There were many individuals with non-Chinese names who later adopted Chinese ones. The Chinese never attempted to place them in distinct groups for special and inferior treatment. Just as the Chinese were never given to sectarian quarrels in religion, similarly they also never segregated racial minorities. The Chinese have always distinguished people of southwestern China in terms of whether they were *Sheng fan* or non-Sinicized barbarians or *Shu fan*, Sinicized barbarians. The latter were considered and treated as Chinese.

Caste-ism is widespread in Japanese society. The term *murairi kankō* which describes the practice of segregating outsiders and newcomers from the village community, is a custom unknown in China. Newcomers in a Japanese village are required to offer some amount of rice (e.g., two and a half bags of rice in Nagao, Saga Prefecture) to the *buraku* and to stay for several years before they are treated as real members of the community. These newcomers, who are called *iribito* or *iriudo*, have no right to share the benefits of the common properties (communally owned lands and money) of the *buraku*. Newly established *bunke* are similarly treated for a while, though the requirements that they need to fulfill are usually less than those demanded from recent immigrants to the *buraku*. This exclusive attitude toward newcomers and new branch families is greater among *buraku* provided with communal lands than in *buraku* which have no common *buraku* properties. However, there also exists some sort of *murairi kankō* in villages which have no communally owned lands. The newcomers are usually supposed to offer a bag of rice or a bottle of *sake* to the *buraku* and to be formally introduced to members of the community.[5]

Another expression of Japanese caste-ism is found in marital alliance. Both the Chinese and the Japanese traditionally held arranged marriages to be the norm, though Japanese girls seem to have enjoyed somewhat greater freedom in this regard than their Chinese counterparts. In both societies, the matchmaker played an essential part in all marriages. In both societies, parents had the final authority. And in both societies it was the parents' duty to ascertain the desirable qualities of the prospective bride or groom and the "matchability" of their respective houses of origin.

However, while the traditional Chinese inquiry covered at most *san tai* or the three ascending generations of the ancestry of the prospective bride or groom (in most cases it did not go that far back), the Japanese investigation covered far more genealogical territory; this was an attempt to prevent marital alliances with any person tainted by *Eta* connections, however remote. Furthermore, contact with the West has led modern educated Chinese to free themselves of arranged marriages and to relax the mutual investigation of the ancestral backgrounds of the prospective bride and groom, but this has hardly been the case in Japan. As early as the 1930's Chinese college graduates married generally more or less by personal preference but most of their Japanese counterparts are still married by family arrangement even today. Many Japanese, especially the younger ones, will voice the desirability of self-choice, and there are city-village as well as men-women differences in such responses (see e.g. Matsumoto 1960:17-18), but the responses do not, according to my observations always match with performance.

Furthermore, and this is a more important fact for our discussion here, Japanese today resort to genealogical investigations as a prerequisite for marriage and employment. I cannot say what percentage of Japanese of what social classes rely on such investigations. But I can testify that such genealogical investigating services are doing a booming business in Japan exactly as credit bureaus prosper in the United States. Like the American credit bureau, the Japanese genealogical service has in some instances introduced modern technology such as modest computers to aid their work. There are no comparable developments in Taiwan, Hong Kong, or Singapore. The new social order in the People's Republic of China tends to move the Chinese even further from their traditional marital and employment requirements.

In Chapter 10 we noted the lack of horizontal mobility for occupations and professions. Even Japanese university faculty members and certainly Japanese employees of business and industry tend to remain in the same organization in which each began his working career. That, too, is a clear expression of caste-ism. The pattern is true for employees in government no less than in private firms. We shall examine this pattern and its implications in Chapter 13, "Iemoto and Industrialization." Each Japanese has life-long security once he is taken on by a firm as a "regular worker." From that point onwards seniority, measured by the number of years of service, determines his advancement. His lack of desire to change his place of employment is matched by his employer's desire to retain his services.

A few other facts point to a caste-ist spirit. The Japanese status differences between males and females are more pronounced than among the Chinese. The loneliness of emigrants from Japan who return to their home villages (Nakane 1967:61) stands in sharp contrast to the reception accorded Chinese emigrants when they return to their home villages. Japanese orphans whose fathers died when they were still young are liable to discrimination at the local level "because such an orphan might lack the moral background derived from parental instruction" (Newell 1967:225). This attitude, too, is alien to the Chinese.

Caste and Caste-ism: A Comparative View

However, the caste system has not permeated and affected the foundation of the entire Japanese social organization the way it has in Hindu India. Many Japanese, writers and others, do speak of the impermanence of life, but Japanese society and culture has not developed an other-worldly view of life with an emphasis on reincarnation as a long term means for ascending the caste ladder. Instead, Japanese society and culture are remarkably concerned with the here and now, with the mutual dependence between a master and his disciples, a superior and his subordinates and the Emperor and his subjects. Continuity of father-son dominance in the Japanese kinship system inevitably checks the diffuseness of the mother-son sub-dominance.

Conversely, since diffuseness is overshadowed by continuity, Japanese civilization has produced no indigenous religious or philosophical protests against ritualism, against caste-ism in connection with the Eta, or against the rigidity of the iemoto system. What we saw in Indian history was the rise of many protestant movements within Hinduism (such as Jainism, Buddhism, and Sikhism) which aimed at reforming the whole social structure, but which in the end either became castes in the mainstream of Indian life or left Indian society altogether (Hsu 1963:186). What we have seen in Japanese history is the emergence of many separate leaders who did not aim at reforming the whole structure, but who instead began by building up a personal following, and ended by becoming heads of different iemoto-like groups or sects. What occurred in iemoto-like sects has been the exact parallel to what has prevailed in groups that actually call themselves iemoto.

This general relationship among diffuseness, caste-ism, caste-like behavior and protests against caste-ism finds support also in United States data. The attribute of diffuseness does not figure in the American husband-wife dominated kinship system. But, husband-wife dominated kinship leads to the continuous disintegration of parent-child ties because maturity of the individual means independence from the parents. Husband-wife dominance therefore prevents the kinship group from ever developing into any extensive and supportive entity as was the case in China. The individual is forced by necessity into joining or forming other groupings where he can satisfy the requirements of his PSH. However, unlike the Japanese non-inheriting sons, who leave their parental homes because of unigeniture and/or ambition but not because maturity means independence from parents, American youngsters often find it necessary to reject their parents in order to assert themselves and to symbolize their manhood. Consequently, when Japanese men leave their kinship-based first groups, they seek dōzoku in rural areas and kinship-like iemoto in urban centers, where their relationship to superiors is primary. But when their American counterparts leave home, they tend to seek groups where they can operate as peers.

The relationship between superiors and inferiors is one that is already well-defined the moment it comes into existence. But the relationship among peers is one that is much more amorphous (diffuse) and some clear principle to govern it has yet to be worked out. The pecking-order type of mechanism well known among Western sociologists and psychologists is certainly important. Wealth or physical attraction or talent must also come into play. There is in a peer relationship, much more room for free competition, for uncertainty as to one's role and for the fear of failure. Caste-like behavior will take place because, while those who are fortunate enough to advance can break out of one category after another, those who are not so fortunate (as a rule the majority) must attempt to fortify themselves behind existing status walls or push others down in self-defense or for the illusion of advancement.[6]

The attribute of diffuseness in the American situation, which emerges not from the basic kinship constellation, but from inevitable emeshment in peer relationships, provides the foundation for caste-istic tendencies in the United States.

However, the attribute of volition and the ideal of complete freedom of the individual are commensurate with the tendency on the part of a majority of Americans to be dissatisfied with the *status quo*, so that many on the lower rungs of the ladder, or those who have been deliberately suppressed, are bound to protest. Their protests are not only likely to be directed against their status as individuals ("I belong to category B not C") but more often against the system as a whole ("There should be no discrimination in employment or residence or club membership according to race, color or creed.").

Consequently the universalistic, protestant movements in the United States promise to lead and have led to more evident structural modifications in the caste situation than they had ever achieved in India. However, the same universalistic, protestant movements have also given stimulation to the formation of more exclusive caste-like clubs in the United States. The escape from inner cities to suburbia is but one such example. Table 5 summarizes our analysis so far.

Our analysis demonstrates three things. First of all, it links the phenomenon of caste with patterns of kinship. Secondly, it shows an inverse relationship between caste-ism and the human sources of Psychosocial Homeostasis (PSH). That is to say, the more readily and continuously available the human source for PSH, the lower the tendency toward caste-ism. Thirdly, it should clarify some confusion in anthropological thinking as to how much caste is a dilemma in various societies today. Myrdal concludes that the inequality suffered

China	Japan	India	United States
Absence of the attribute of diffuseness in kinship and elsewhere.	Diffuseness is a subordinate attribute in kinship.	Diffuseness is a dominant attribute in kinship.	Secondary diffuseness is derived not from kinship but from later peer relationship.
Class mobility in the long run.	Class assumes caste-like characteristics.	Class distinctions overshadowed by caste differences.	Class mobility high, though many individuals and groups never rise.
No caste, no caste-ism and little evidence for caste-istic behavior.	Eta, caste-ism and much caste-istic behavior. No universalistic protests against caste or caste-ism. Proliferation of caste-like *iemoto* or pseudo-*iemoto* not by fission but by growth.	Whole society organized into castes and strongest caste-ism. Profusion of dispute over individual caste affiliation and the relative position of castes in relation to each other on the caste ladder. Fissionary tendencies. Some universalistic protests against caste and caste-ism. Protestants become new caste groups. Proliferation of new castes within the total caste framework and hierarchy.	Caste and caste-ism refuted in the indigenous cultural ideal but profusion of caste-istic behavior. Some caste crossing and dispute over relative position of castes, but greater prominence of anticaste, universalistic protests. Great structural changes in society resulting from anti-caste, universalistic protests. Proliferation of exclusive, caste-like clubs.

TABLE 5:   Diffuseness and Caste-ism

by American Blacks is an American dilemma because it is inconsistent with the egalitarian nature of American culture (Myrdal 1944). Writing after Myrdal, Oliver Cox maintains that such a dilemma is non-existent in India. "The difference between the racial attitudes of whites and the caste attitude so far as the social ideals of each system are concerned, is that whites *wrongfully* take the position of excluding groups from participating freely in the common culture, while castes *rightfully* exclude outsiders from participating in their *dharma* (moral duty)" (Cox 1945:367).

Berreman disagrees with both views. He argues along two lines. On the one hand, quoting Spiro (1951:34), he thinks there is no American dilemma because "discrimination against the Negro is not in violation of Southern ideal norms." On the other hand, Berreman insists that "if there is an American dilemma, as Myrdal has described it, there is also an Indian dilemma . . . since India's constitution, like America's, espouses principles of equality and among India's intellectual and political elite there is widespread advocacy of and even conformity to these principles—more widespread, one might note, than in the elite of the Southern United States today" (Berreman 1966:297). The net result of Berreman's position is that there is no difference between the caste situation in India and Black-White inequality in the United States.

I think both of Berreman's arguments fall short of the mark. It is perfectly true, as Spiro noted, that "discrimination against the Negro is not in violation of ideal norms" *in the Southern United States*. But the Southern United States is not the whole of United States society and is not the prime force behind American national policy today. A bloody Civil War was fought over the slavery question and it was the North, not the South, that won. Not only is the widespread ideal of American society today egalitarian, but its legal, educational, economic, and social developments, especially in the last 20 years, have moved inexorably toward a greater reduction of the customary *de jure* and *de facto* inequality. In both respects the American scene contrasts sharply with what we see in the contemporary South African Union.

Furthermore, while it is also true that India's modern constitution is egalitarian in principle and that India's elite supports that constitution, the entire weight of Hindu customs and the sacred literature supports the Hindu caste system. The ideal and reality of life in local communities *all over India* are in support of the Hindu caste system. This statement holds true whether we look at Sirkanda, according to Berreman's own ethnographic report (Berreman 1960:125), or elsewhere. And finally, even the Hindu elite who support the egalitarian principles of the Indian constitution tend to adhere to caste customs when they deal with personal matters such as dining and marriage.

The difference between the Indian caste situation and the United States' Black-White situation is not a matter of degree, as Berreman would have us believe. The American constitution and the principles of equality and freedom embodied in the American legal framework arose from within Western and American societies, and were not imported from outside. The Civil War was made in America, not inspired by some colonial masters. (Of course, those who championed the cause of racial equality were opposed by others deeply committed to the opposite point of view. This resulted from the nature of American society, in which extreme fissionary and protestant tendencies are two primary characteristics, as I have explained in my book *Clan, Caste, and Club* [Hsu 1963:192-231]. The egalitarian principle among free men, not the hierarchical principle of the caste system, is the basis of American kinship usages, employer-employee relations, and interpersonal relationships in general.)

This is not the case in India. The modern egalitarian Indian constitution is not rooted in India's past but represents a major Western intrusion. It has yet to find its psycho-socio-cultural roots in India. It is still incommensurate with India's kinship system and interpersonal relationships in general. There simply is no Indian dilemma comparable to the American one.

Once this is understood it becomes clear that caste is likewise not a Japanese dilemma. The organization of the *Eta* for advancement (such as the *Kaihō Renmei* or *Kaihō Dōmei)* is a modern phenomenon, which developed under Western influence. This is also true of other movements such as the *Kaihō Undō* of the League of Korean Residents in Japan. The *Eta* persists as an untouchable group because caste-ism is commensurate with the basic Japanese approach to human relations. This is why Emperor Meiji, who succeeded in seizing power from the Tokugawa Shōgunate and who sponsored Japan's modernization in the economic and military spheres, failed to emancipate the *Eta*.

Internal Impetus to Change

In some of the foregoing chapters we noted a contrast in dynamism among the several societies in question. We found that Chinese society was least dynamic because few non-kinship groupings ever developed; Hindu society is more dynamic, because non-kinship caste groupings have proliferated, but it harbors little potential for change because the caste groupings all have the same objectives, though they may use different means to achieve these ends; the club groupings of the United States aim at diverse objectives, resort to different means, and the individuals climb different ladders.

In view of our present analysis, it becomes clear that, as far as the potential for change is concerned, Japanese society is several steps ahead of Hindu India, but quite behind the U.S. The non-kinship *iemoto* or pseudo-*iemoto* aim at achieving different objectives, resort to different means, and the members of different *iemoto* climb different ladders. They therefore provide far more basis than Hindu castes for industrial and military (or technical) modernization. But they provide no comparable advantage for social modernization, because they are organized along father-son lines and limited by the super-father, the Emperor, who in turn is descended from a super-mother, the Sun Goddess Amaterasu.

It is a striking fact that Japan achieved world prominence before World War II in industrial and military affairs but changed very little in her traditional social relations: between parents and children, between husbands and wives, between masters and followers, between employers and employees, and between Imperial House and its subjects. This, despite the fact that the literacy rate was nearly one hundred percent, and that Tokyo was (and still is) the largest city in the world.

Long ago the late Dr. Hu Shih noted this contrast in connection with his study of the differences in the modernization processes of China and Japan. He quoted a most sympathetic interpreter of Japan, G. C. Allen, who said: "If the changes in some of the aspects of her (Japan's) life have been far-reaching, the persistence of the traditional in other aspects is equally remarkable. . . . The contrasts between these innovations and the solid core of ancient habit are as striking as ever they were." Dr. Hu then addressed himself to the following question: "Why has Japan, after seven decades of extraordinarily successful modernization yet failed to break up her 'solid core of ancient habit'?" (Hu 1940:115).

Hu's answer was that Japan's modernization was initiated by a ruling class which exercised central control but had only very limited vision. Members of this class understood "certain superficial phases of the Western civilization," but failed to note "many other phases" of it. Consequently, much of traditional medieval culture is artificially protected by a "strong shell of militant modernity" (Hu 1940:116). And Hu's hope for the future of Japan was that the "solid core of ancient habit" in Japan might yet some day be broken down by "the element of freedom" (from Western culture).

Now we understand that the startling contrast of a "solid core of ancient habit co-existing with military and industrial modernity is not so much due to the central control of any single ruling group as to the prevalence of the *iemoto* and *iemoto*-like groups, and the pervasiveness of the kin-tract principle of human relationships. The *iemoto* is the fountainhead of all-inclusive hierarchies within each of which clear lines of superordination and subordination are part of the natural order. We have already noted that the Emperor Meiji led Japan to industrial and military modernization but failed to abolish the *Eta*. He succeeded in the former because he had the basic Japanese approach to human relationships supporting him, but that approach was against him in the case of the *Eta*. And Hu's hope that the Western element of freedom might some day break the "solid core of ancient habit" is obviously misplaced. It belongs to the same category of post-World War II political optimism or sociological projection that modern Japan is somehow going to develop into a Western-style democracy or that the industrial facts of life will compel the Japanese to progress through stages of social development similar to those experienced by the West.

The psycho-cultural foundation of modern Japanese military and industrial development did not include such ingredients as individualism, free enterprise, equality, and freedom. The legal and institutional changes in the direction of individualism and freedom, encouraged by the United States since its defeat of Japan have not so far made basic inroads into the power of the kin-tract principle in human relationships. This is not to say that Japanese society and culture will never change. But fundamental changes affecting a society's pattern of satisfying the PSH needs of its members does not come about easily nor is it a foregone conclusion. As far as Japan is concerned, it may mean, as Dore has observed, that the Japanese will be able to "create a new sort of society and a new sort of political regime in which the old forms of dependence are subtly combined with the new" (Dore 1958:393).

[1] For some excellent descriptions and analyses of the *Eta* in relation to ordinary Japanese, see George DeVos and Hiroshi Wagatsuma (1966). This is a symposium containing works by Cornell, DeVos, Fukumoto, Norbeck, Price, Sasaki, Wagatsuma and others.

[2] Meaning undelivered from class discrimination.

[3] I have seen sporadic cases of slavery in mainland China as late as 1943, along with footbinding.

[4] Some of the occupations on the list were prostitutes, actors, buglers, executioners and chiropodists.

[5] I am indebted to Professor Teigo Yoshida of Tokyo University for this information. (Also see Yoshida 1963.)

[6] These are the real roots of racial and other prejudices in the United States. (See Hsu 1972:241-262.)

13 ●

Iemoto and Industrialization

Not recognizing or refusing to admit the primacy of man's relationship with his fellow men, the power of particular cultural traditions to shape and sustain that relationship, and the resultant differing patterns of PSH for the individual in various societies, Western scholars have tended to treat the spectacular economic achievements of Japan with the same sort of explanations they have used concerning developments in their own societies. Their arguments proceed along two directions: on the one hand, the same economic achievements must be rooted in human values similar to those prevailing in the West, or, that even if the Japanese did not begin with the same human values, the conditions of modern industrialization must have necessarily forced them into Western ways of seeing themselves and reacting to the world around them.

In the foregoing chapters we have seen how the patterns of kinship, *iemoto* and the kin-tract principle are commensurate with the Japanese pattern in religion and social stratification. The net result of the *iemoto* pattern in religion and caste-ism is essentially conservative. Changes are relatively superficial. Some structural rearrangements in the form of suburbia, *Eta* improvement organizations, or foreign missionary ventures have occurred, but the content of human relations, the way the individual feels about himself and about the world around him has not.

We are now ready to show that what is true for other aspects of modern Japanese development is equally applicable to her economic miracle, a subject with which we began our present inquiry. In this chapter we shall take a look at the Japanese employee and show how his approach to his work and his relations with his employer are different from those of his American brethren. We shall then show that such differences are possible because the Japanese economic miracle is rooted in the *iemoto* pattern and not in those Western values commonly associated with Western industrialization.

The Japanese Worker

The Japanese worker operates, even today, at some disadvantage in comparison with his U.S. counterpart. The economic facts are obvious.

More than half of the workers in Japan's manufacturing industries (compared with about a quarter in the U.S.) are employed in factories with 1 to 99 workers, while only 20 percent (compared with twice that many in the U.S.) are employed in factories with 1,000 or more workers. Those in smaller factories not only have to contend with less efficient tools of production, but they must also accept wages lower than those paid in larger factories. The wage disparity between large factories and small workshops is still considerably greater in Japan than in other industrially advanced countries. For example, in 1949 the wages in small British workshops were only 16-17 percent lower than those in very large factories with 1,000 or more workers. But in 1958 Japanese wages in workshops with less than 100 workers were two-thirds to one half lower than those in factories with 1,000 or more workers. However, by 1967 this disparity was considerably reduced (Rō Dō Shō 1967:18-19).

Japanese wages, moreover, are still lower than those offered in most industrially advanced countries. In 1967 Japanese hourly wages were less than one-fourth the amount of wages paid to U.S. workers, half of those for British workers, and 5 percent lower than those of French workers. In spite of these disadvantages, the index of productivity of Japanese labor has consistently risen faster than the rise of real wages. For example, the productivity rose by 50 percent from 1965 to 1968, while the real wages during this period rose by only 27 percent.

This high productivity is due primarily to the average worker's loyalty to his employer, who reciprocates in his turn. For both parties the economic facts are not unimportant, but their importance is overshadowed by other factors.

The Japanese worker relates to his peers, employer, and work in ways that are very different from his American counterpart.

To begin with, a very substantial number of Japanese workers are recruited by the factories through the labor boss, on whom the factories depend for labor supply, and on whom workers in search of work depend for finding employment.

The relationship between workers so recruited and their labor boss is that of oyabun-kobun (parent-child or boss-follower), a system well described for the English reader by Bennett & Ishino (1963:40-85). The labor boss may recruit workers for a short term project, in which case the oyabun-kobun relationship is temporary. Or he may recruit workers for on-going work, in which case the relationship is permanent. Whichever the case, the commencement of the relationship was marked by definite ceremonies and such ceremonies were reported as late as the 1950's. The labor-boss is responsible not only for locating jobs for workers, but also for helping them in their private lives, as though they were his children.

Traditionally the oyabun-kobun relationship extended horizontally into elder-younger brother ties, grandfather-grandchild ties, and even uncle-nephew ties. Military occupation authorities and other U.S. inspired reform bodies discouraged the labor-boss system and even made exaggerated claims about its destruction. They saw it as purely exploitative (Bennett and Ishino 1963:121). But its main features, centering in paternalism, a term full of negative connotations for Americans, have persisted to this day. This paternalism is still welcomed, not resented, by most contemporary Japanese workers (Rohlen 1971:91). In fact the term paternalism is not often used in Japanese. It is definitely a Western term, but when it is used in Japan, it is most appropriately translated as onjo shugi, or "kind treatment of employees."

Consequently, while not all regular workers in factories are under the labor-boss system (some would say not more than ten to fifteen percent), all Japanese workers operate within a highly paternalistic system unheard of among, and intolerable to, their American brethren.

For example, many (I think most) workers and sarari men (salary men) live in company dormitories (for single employees) or in company apartments (for married employees) near their places of work (Whitehall and Takezawa 1968:265). They participate in a variety of company sponsored activities and social events and enjoy numerous company provided extracurricular facilities such as sports fields, equipment and various athletic courses.

The Japanese employer is not just someone who impersonally pays his employees for work. He is a sort of senior relative, friend and counselor. Of course, the presidents or their senior lieutenants in large establishments must of necessity be physically remote from thousands of employees. When a labor-boss is not involved, the person to whom the Japanese worker looks for a paternalistic relationship is his supervisor, through whom he maintains a positive identification with the company at large. His general foreman is his formal "guarantor" upon his entry into the company. If he is a minor and charged by the police with a traffic offense the general foreman, as a rule, accompanies him to the traffic court as a parental substitute. Immediate supervisors of Japanese companies vividly report and discuss their concern with and sense of responsibility for the men in their shops.

A panel discussion among immediate supervisors found in *QC to Ningen Kankei* (Quality control and Human Relations, Tetsujiro Kato 1966), the fourth book of a series entitled *Genba QC Tokuhon* (The Workshop Quality Control Reader), leaves no doubt as to the depth and width of this concern. The panel discussion was entitled "Support from the Top and the Bottom," and its eight participants included supervisors from Shin Mitsubishi Heavy Industries, Kawasaki Iron and Steel Works, Takeda Pharmaceuticals, Matsushita Electric Co., Komatsu Manufacturing Co., and Sumitomo Rubber.

The chairman of the panel discussion began with a list of indicators of low morale among workers such as, "lack of concentration on work," "production of defective work," "failure to obey rules governing workshops," signs of "insomnia and alcoholic smells," "objecting to new machinery for the sake of objecting," "no smile, dishevelled hair, no greeting (in the case of women)," and others. He then proceeded to give a list of common causes of workers' poor performance such as "poor health," "indulgence in gambling and leisure," "family problems," "troubles in romantic relationships," "oversensitivity and inferiority complex," "friendship, religious, and ideological problems," and so forth (Kato 1966:14-15).

The participants then related some of their own successful experiences in dealing with the poor morale of workers in their charge. Only a few samples are given below.

"One of my subordinates was engaged to a woman in his home town. Some time ago he went home to arrange the wedding date. But upon his return to the factory he would not engage other workers in conversation nor look at us in the face. He also produced many defective products. (Previously his products had been 100 percent acceptable.) So I gave him a psychological test . . . . The result confirmed that he was not in an ordinary state of mind. . . . I asked him if something was wrong at his home. He then told me that his marriage plan broke up because his ex-fiance had a boy friend. . . . I (temporarily) transferred him to an easy job so that he could relax. In addition, I told him about my own (similar) experience. Successfully overcoming this problem, he not only was married to another woman last spring but also passed the national government license test (for some sort of certificate)" (Kato 1966:15).

". . . I also made use of our company newspaper. I would put an ad in it which read: 'The young men in our shop are looking for brides.' Seeing this our workers began thinking 'Well, our supervisor is very demanding about job performance, but he is concerned with our attaining happy marriages.' In this way our men started feeling very positive about their relationship with me. If there is this kind of trust between the supervisor and his men things generally work out very smoothly."

"The worker's awareness that if he talks to the supervisor he will understand him; and the supervisor who kindly (like a parent) takes care of his men for example, by finding a future spouse for him (or her): These are both important. These in essence suggest that the workers trust in the supervisor. ('If I talk to the *Oyaji* ["father"] [1] he will take care of it.') is indispensable for a good morale" (Kato 1966:17).

"Unless the employees feel 'Our supervisor is concerned with even very personal matters about me' it is impossible to educate present young people into respectable workers" (Kato 1966:18).

The chairman of the panel discussion concluded the session by making the following observations:

"The shop supervisor needs support both from the top and the bottom. To attain this he must lead an orderly life."

"The shop supervisor must be involved in his subordinates' personal life. For example, if the workers feel 'My *Oyaji* (supervisor)[2] understands me, he even tries to find a bride for me,' this is an indication of his deep trust in the superior."

"Thus, it is our conclusion that if these two conditions are satisfied the shop enjoys good morale and the workers develop genuine willingness to do a good job" (Kato 1966:22).

Some recent findings of Masako Osako in a Japanese automobile factory illuminate particularly well Japanese workers' attitudes towards work, towards superiors and towards the company (Osako 1972). This is a plant employing modern mass-production techniques comparable to the best in the United States. It exhibits all six of the main characteristics of mass production jobs as specified by Charles R. Walker and Robert H. Guest (1952) namely (1) mechanically controlled work pace, (2) repetitiveness, (3) minimum skill, (4) predetermination of tools and techniques, (5) minute sub-division of production and (6) surface mental attention.

Western scholars, being obsessed with the economic factor, generally link the worker's loyalty to his employer with wages or the nature of modern technology (Blauner 1964 and Goldthorpe et al. 1968). To her question "When do you feel a sense of satisfaction from your immediate job?" Mrs. Osako received mostly negative answers. That is to say, most of the respondents experienced little or no satisfaction from the performance of their immediate jobs. The workers' feelings about their wages were equally negative. Mrs. Osako asked the following questions: "What do you think of the salary you get in this plant in relation to (1) your company's ability to pay wages and (2) your work load?" Eighty-three percent of the sample viewed their wages as low in relation to the company's ability to pay and ninety-five percent thought that the salary they received was low in relation to their work load.

Yet, in spite of such negative or lukewarm views about their job satisfaction and material rewards, the Japanese automobile workers in question overwhelmingly feel positively about their company. Only 18 percent of Mrs. Osako's respondents say the company "does not do much of anything" for its workers, while 84 percent view their company as "better" or "just about the same" "compared to other places of work." Finally, to the question, "Would you mean to stay in this plant until your retirement?" 48 percent of the respondents gave a positive answer, 34 percent were ambivalent, while only 18 percent answered "no." Mrs. Osako notes that since several respondents in the last group "intended to return to their home because they were the eldest sons," the actual number of those unequivocally negative toward their present job was obviously even smaller.

In an attempt to reconcile the negative attitude concerning job satisfaction and material rewards with the positive attitude towards the company, Mrs. Osako suggests that the Japanese workers differentiate between the job as assembly line men and employment as members of a large company. She draws this conclusion especially in view of the fact that what her respondents liked about their occupation mostly had to do with the prestige of the company, the welfare and recreational activities, good co-workers and friends in the plant community, etc., while what they did not like about it mostly had to do with night shifts, monotony of the job, the heaviness of the job, etc.

I think Mrs. Osako's effort to reconcile the contrasting responses has unnecessarily compartmentalized the Japanese worker's perception of himself and the world. What every living individual seeks is a satisfactory level of PSH according to the cultural orientation transmitted to him through the kinship system. For the PSH of Western individuals, job satisfaction and wage levels have priority over relationships with superiors, co-workers and friends in the plant community. Consequently dissatisfaction with the former means dissatisfaction with the entire work situation.[2] But for the PSH of the Japanese, the human relationships are primary and the order of priority is reversed. Consequently, dissatisfaction with the job and wages is greatly overshadowed by a much more important satisfaction with employer-employee links and with membership in a big company.

In this light we can understand why many Japanese workers and employees do not mind traveling long distances every day to maintain the same employment in the same plant.

The longest commuting I know of is done by an employee of a Tokyo company who lives in Shizuoka. He commutes four hours each way every day. The plant used to be nearer his home, but when it moved away the worker did not want to find other employment.

But even more spectacularly congruent with our analysis and Mrs. Osako's findings is the way Japanese labor is organized. Superficially, Japan has three major unions, each having more than a million members. The Sōhyō (General Council of Trade Unions of Japan) is the largest, with over four million members. The Dōmei (Japanese Confederation of Labor) has nearly two million members, and the Chūritsu Rōren (Federation of Independent Unions) has one million members.

In fact, only the All Japan Seamen's Union is a union in the Western sense. Most other unions are organized strictly within *units of individual enterprise.* Applying the Japanese pattern to the American situation we would have a union for GM plant #354 in Flint, Michigan, and another for plant #24 in Harvey, Indiana. These are not called locals. Each is an independent union with its own powers of settlement.

There is, therefore, much closer contact between union leaders and workers and between employers and employees in the Japanese situation than in its American counterpart. The Japanese employee is rarely fired and less easily laid off than in America. By and large, automation and rationalization have not led to industrial contraction and mass unemployment. The Japanese unemployment rate has been consistently lower than that of the United States, the United Kingdom, West Germany, or Italy, even during recent years. Japanese employers see lay-off or firing as the last resort, never as the first steps, in any adverse economic development.

This reduces the possibility of impersonality since each side sees the other as individual human beings with human feelings and needs; the situation cannot but encourage a positive attitude on the part of labor towards management. In addition to the infrequency of intentional damaging or pilfering of plant property, this positive attitude has led to three outstanding results: (a) greater increases of labor productivity than wages (a fact we noted before), (b) the small labor turnover, especially in the big factories (a fact also noted earlier), and (c) the scarcity of strikes and their resulting destructive effects.

Japanese workers engage in verbal and written arguments and exposés against their employers, but strikes are usually averted by amicable settlements. Every May and every November employees of all large and medium-sized concerns engage in what they call the "Spring Offensive" and the "Autumn Offensive," respectively. These are times when the size of the summer and winter bonuses are decided upon. There will be slogans on the walls, sporadic speeches to small and large gatherings and leaflets denouncing the employers in strong terms. Even if a strike occurs, it will be short. Often the employees of a plant or organization will engage in token "strikes" — during the lunch hour or after closing time. In some instances, the "strikers" sing international labor songs. And symbolic of the *positive* attitude of the workers towards employers and place of employment is the fact that not infrequently a vase with a flower arrangement is found at the entrance of a workshop or next to an oily and smelly engine, brought by some worker from his home.

The White Collar Employee

The Japanese *sarari man* (salary man or white collar worker) identifies even more with his company than the blue collar worker does. He has more reason to do so.

He is recruited shortly after graduation from high school or from college. This commences a life-long career. As the official statement of one bank puts it: "When a person is accepted into the bank as a member, he is not chosen for his skill; nor is he selected to do a predetermined task. Rather, he is regarded as someone with the potential to learn and to be trained to do increasingly difficult work throughout his career with the bank. It is assumed that his stay will be a long one. . . ." (Rohlen 1971:45).

Beginning with a rigorous initial training period lasting anywhere from six weeks to three months, the employee is progressively integrated into the community of his employers and colleagues through ceremonies, company papers, fringe benefits, welfare facilities and company sponsored or oriented activities. The central theme of the initial training usually concerns *seishin*, or spirit, often involving Zen meditation, group living, and twenty-five mile endurance walks.

After this training period, the new employee settles down at his new place of employment, where his life at work overlaps largely with that at play, and where his devotion to the company is thoroughly reciprocated by the company's to him. If he is single he usually lives in a company dormitory. If he is married he is still likely to reside with his family in a company-owned apartment house.

The company hires instructors in English conversation, flower arrangement, judo, and other arts for any dweller of its dormitories who wants to take advantage of them. The company also provides sports facilities such as basketball, baseball, track and field, tennis, and fencing, for its employees.

If he is looking for a wife, he is often assisted in the effort by one or another of his superiors. At the wedding of a *sarari man*, the chief of his department is likely to be asked to take a place of honor. Often the chief sits as *nakodo* or (matchmaker) in the ceremony, whether he in fact was instrumental in bringing the couple together or not. After the wedding the *sarari man* and his bride can have an inexpensive honeymoon in one of the company-owned resort facilities.

Americans are familiar with office Christmas parties, but Japanese office sociability goes much farther. They have one-day office picnics and week-end office excursions. Employees of a department in a bank, government office, or hospital, sometimes numbering thirty or more, will go by train or in chartered buses to spend the week-end in a resort or hot springs hotel. As we noted in Chapter 1, in such excursions the Japanese will go with his office superiors and subordinates, leaving his wife behind.

Two conclusions can be drawn from these facts. On the one hand, the Japanese employee's life with his family is very much segregated from his life with his co-workers. His spouse has little or nothing to do with his work-connected activities (Vogel 1967:102-103). On the other hand, the Japanese factory hand or office worker maintains close personal ties with co-workers, superiors and subordinates in his work unit far beyond his work requirements. Participation in and maintenance of work-connected social ties is voluntary, not compulsory. But non-participation is regarded as abnormal and as a sign of dissatisfaction.

In both respects, the Japanese worker differs significantly from his American counterpart. The American's personal affairs and recreational activities are his own. They are unconnected with his employment. And the American's spouse has much to do with his business-connected travel and entertainment.

Most Japanese corporations reinforce their employees' identification with the company through daily and periodical ceremonies. For example, before starting each day's work, workers and employees in every factory of Matsushita Company get together to sing the following song:

For the building of a new Japan
Let's put our strength and mind together,
Doing our best to promote production,
Sending our goods to the people of the world,
Endlessly and continuously,
Like water gushing from a fountain.
Grow, industry, grow, grow, grow!
Harmony and sincerity!
Matsushita Electricity!

This kind of song is not unique to a particular corporation called Matsushita. Compare it with the song sung by all the employees of a medium-sized bank in northern Japan to which Thomas Rohlen, the ethnographer, gave the fictitious name Uedagin:

A falcon pierces the clouds,
A bright dawn is now breaking.
The precious flower of our unity
Blossoms here.
Uedagin Uedagin
Our pride in her name ever grows.

Smiling in our hearts with glory,
For we carry the responsibility for tomorrow's
Independent Japan.
Our towns and villages prosper
Under our banner of idealism raised on high.
Uedagin Uedagin
Our hopes inspired by her name.

Marching forward to the new day
With strength unbounded,
We continue forward step by step.
Oh, the happiness of productive people.
Uedagin Uedagin
Brilliantly radiates her name.[3]

(Rohlen 1971:73)

Such employee devotion is not mere wishful thinking on the part of the company. The Japanese employees respond by acts which certainly help achieve the company's objectives. For example, most Japanese workers, and especially white collar employees, tend to work overtime without demanding compensation. The clock watching syndrome is generally absent. Many employees, especially new ones, but old ones as well, tend to work long after the normal office hours just to complete what they think should be finished before they leave the office or shop. It is not uncommon for a majority of the members of a given office to work until nine or ten in the evening three or four times a week.

The turnover among white collar workers is even lower than among blue collar workers. The seniority system assures a salaried man not only a permanent place in a company, but automatic promotion as well. A Japanese diplomat-author compares the position of a Japanese salaried man to one who has found himself on an escalator. All he has to do is to stand still and he will automatically get to the top (Kawasaki 1969:97-98). Consequently there is far less mobility from one company to another in Japan than in the United States. Japanese companies do not raid each other for talent, however desirable, no matter what the competition is. For the Japanese employee, leaving one company to join another is even more risky than trying to switch escalators in the middle of a ride. A man who changes from one company to join another is likely to be an object of some ostracism. He will not easily find a new place to go to. If he does, he is less likely to be trusted than before. One anthropologist rightly observes that termination of a job other than by retirement, or resignation because of marriage for women employees, carries an extreme sense of failure. It is an "embarrassing and unhappy affair similar in atmosphere to marital divorce" (Rohlen 1971:143).

I am aware that while these observations agree with those of Abegglen (1958), they differ somewhat from those of others. For example, Marsh and Mannari (1970:795-812) criticize Abegglen on two main grounds. First, the pattern of lifetime commitment, which Abegglen regards as the central aspect of Japanese factory social organization, is more characteristic of factories with over 1,000 employees. yet such factories employ only one-fifth of Japan's manufacturing labor force. Second, even those employees who exhibit lifetime commitment behavior by remaining in the same firms "often do so not on the basis of lifetime commitment values but for a variety of reasons extraneous to these values" (Marsh and Mannari 1970:810-811).

I think neither of these criticisms should deflect us from the reality that the Japanese employee is considerably less likely than his

American counterpart to leave his firm, a fact which Marsh and Mannari do not deny (Marsh and Mannari 1970:811). This point is confirmed by many other observers, including Whitehall and Takezawa (1968:151-153). In view of our extensive analysis of the importance of the *iemoto*-pattern in Japanese life, we have no reason to suppose that the more pronounced lifetime commitment behavior of the Japanese employees in large firms is an anomaly. To the contrary, we must regard the large Japanese firms as being more capable than their smaller counterparts in providing the conditions for the realization of behavior patterns central to the Japanese way of life. Furthermore, as the industrial process moves further ahead in Japan, is there any good reason to believe that the proportion of large firms will not increase? On the other hand, the verbal or outward justification of traditional behavior on the basis of reasons not in accordance with traditional values is a common phenomenon seen elsewhere. For example, the fear of loss of property values is a recurrent defense among white Americans who object to Blacks as neighbors. But only the most culturally naive will fail to see that kind of reason as covering up for the real cause of racial discrimination, namely, the traditional American value of white superiority over Blacks.

Intensifying the sense of identification with the place of employment are several other features. One of them is the fact that the white collar employees of each company, and especially of each department or section of the company, are sometimes products of the same colleges. For example, most officers of the Bank of Tokyo in Osaka are graduates of the prestigious Tokyo University, and a few other national universities. I know an officer who felt out of place there because he came from a missionary institution, Sophia University. The fact that this man's father was a vice-president of the bank and one of its directors did not make too much difference. Another friend of mine began his life as a *sarari man* in a major trading company in Osaka after graduation from Osaka Foreign Language University. Although he had only been with this large company of over a thousand employees for less than two months when we first discussed the subject of school ties, he was able to give me the following rather precise list of particulars:

1.   The President of the corporation graduated from Osaka University;

2. The Vice-President of the corporation graduated from Kyoto University;
3. A majority of the white collared employees in the corporation graduated from Keio University;
4. The next largest group of white collared employees in it graduated from Waseda University;
5. About five or six were graduates of Kobe University and Kansei Gakuen University;
6. A small number graduated from Tokyo University, but among them are three heads of departments;
7. A few graduated from Osaka Municipal University among whom was a director of the company;
8. A few are graduates of Konan University. (My informant commented: "The University is not good, but the parents of its students are 'good'—they are usually wealthy. Also a former President of the company was once a professor at Konan University"), and no one was from Doshisha University (a missionary institution).

My informant proudly mentioned that two department heads of the company were from his own alma mater, namely, Osaka Foreign Language University, though the total number of its graduates in this company was among the smallest.

However, a year after I left Japan this informant wrote to me in a state of great consternation and unhappiness. His trading company decided to merge with another to become truly a giant concern, but the few graduates from his alma mater were now like a "few grains of sand in a giant ocean." He actively considered resigning from the company, and for the next two years, this was a sentiment reflected in every one of his letters. He only decided to stay on after that because, I suspect, a change of employment, which would involve much social readjustment, was far less attractive than the prospect of keeping a position in which he already had some seniority.

This highly vertical organization and strong seniority system combined with closed origin ties would seem to be detrimental to the selection and use of talent. But here Japanese industries and business are helped by two factors.

On the one hand, there is the continuing devotion of the Japanese employee to his superiors and to his company, already pointed out, which makes him work harder and for longer hours than his Western counterpart.

On the other hand, there is the operation of the *ringi* system, unique to Japan. The *ringi* system typifies the group nature of Japanese management decision-making processes. It consists of five steps:

a. A proposal written up by middle management;
b. Cautious horizontal consideration of the proposal;
c. Cautious vertical consideration of the proposal;
d. Formal affixture of the necessary seals to the *ringisho* document, which contains the proposal;
e. Deliberate final ambiguity with respect to authority and responsibility for the proposal (Glazer 1969:88-90).

The Japanese thus reduce the chance of incompetent decision-making by the top executives who arrived at the top merely by way of the seniority route. The devoted young talents do the brain work. They are secure in the knowledge that they do not risk their own individual careers by wrong individual decisions and that they too will eventually be promoted through the seniority system. Executives on the highest level of prominence are also protected from risking their individual careers. This in part accounts for the fact that Japanese businesses are "run" by old men over 60 or even 70.

In a Tokyo office a *sarari man* let me witness a gesture of devotion to his office superior which I had never experienced in the Western world. We were at the end of an interview in his office which, being that of a lower-middle ranking officer, was small and sparsely furnished. But the size and nature of his office were never part of our conversation. As I was preparing to take my leave, he said, "Let me show you the office of my Section Chief." He took me to an office three times as big as his, very well furnished, pointed to the empty chair behind the big desk ornamented with lots of bric-a-brac and proudly said: "This is the desk of my Section Chief."

The pattern of permanent bond between inferiors and superiors even exists among corporations and between corporations and the government. The *zaibatsu* Mitsubishi illustrates this point well. By 1963 this extended corporation had 21 manufacturing companies with 103 factories, plants and mines all over Japan. Imported iron ore is processed in one of her iron and steel works in Tokyo. It is made into a cracking tower in her factory in Kawasaki, consumed in her petro-chemical plant at Yokkaichi. The latter uses the oil she imports to make synthetic fibers which are woven into cloth in Nagoya and exported by her trading company in her own ships made at one of her yards in Nagasaki, Yokohama, Kawasaki, Toyko, or Hiroshima.

Two other giants, Sumitomo and Mitsui do their business in much the same way. Sumitomo is Japan's largest producer of chemicals. She has 200,000 people in her employ. Mitsui was responsible for nearly ten percent of all of Japan's imports and eight percent of her exports in 1963. She deals with everything from bridges to buttons and cars to canned goods.

Various *zaibatsu* compete with each other. In view of the fact that each of them comprises so many enterprises in the same or similar lines of endeavor, some Japanese scholars have become alarmed by what they describe as excessive competition among the *zaibatsu*. One of these scholars, Professor Shuji Hayashi of Tokyo University even likened this competition with that between the Japanese Navy and Army during and before World War II. For example, the two military arms of the Japanese government each developed its own separate air force without coordination with each other and no exchanges of technical know-how. "The Navy developed the world famous Zero fighter and the Army, the Hayabusa fighter, quite independently" (Hayashi 1965).

Americans are likely to see monopolistic practices and price fixing in the Japanese *zaibatsu*, and may think some anti-trust laws are in order. In fact the Occupation under General McArthur ordered the *zaibutsu* disbanded. But one by one they were revived as American authority in Japan diminished. In the Japanese context, not only are the American fears of monopoly unnecessary, but the *zaibatsu* are unavoidable. For *zaibatsu* too are an expression of the *iemoto* pattern of doing business. The *zaibatsu* not only cooperate with each other in some instances (for example, in the new petro-chemical industry), but also with the Japanese government. The *zaibatsu* willingly put government plans into action. This cooperation between government and *zaibatsu* is not realized by force of law but through the close, subtle *iemoto*-like relationship linking the government, the central bank, and the *zaibatsu*.

Thus, at the core of the phenomenal Japanese economic development is the mutual and nearly permanent bond between vertically placed individuals (the master and his disciples, or the boss and the workers, etc.), a bond similar to that found in the *iemoto*. This is the bond on which the Japanese individual lavishes most affection and which is the central ingredient of his PSH. Hence, quitting a company is rare and, if and when it occurs, is an "embarrassing and unhappy affair similar in atmosphere to marital divorce."

The groups formed through this bond compete with each other (there is competition among departments, among factories, among *zaibatsu*, etc.), but there is no competition within each group. In this way, devotion to superior, to place of work, and to higher authority is generated and nurtured while danger to personal security is minimized and eliminated. These establishments or groups and their branches or divisions or offshoot companies (*kogaisha*) are not called *iemoto*. But they all partake of the *iemoto's* basic features. For each factory or division or unit of a company is like an *iemoto*, linked with the larger *iemoto*. In a similar manner, the different component companies of a *zaibatsu* relate to the *zaibatsu*, and the different *zaibatsu* relate to the government. Being accustomed to the hierarchical way of relating to one another, in which the business world and the personal one are not rigidly segregated, the Japanese are more free than Americans and other Westerners to work and cooperate with their equals and unequals without fearing charges of "authoritarianism" or "dictatorship" or the onus of "bootlicking" or "submissiveness."

Some Western students have said that the Japanese economy has succeeded so well because the Japanese government has played so large a hand in encouraging and subsidizing business and industry. The truth is that such government aid would have been deeply resented as "interference" in America. Americans, as members of corporations or as individuals, are not averse to obtaining fruits from the government preserve if they can get them on their own terms. They will milk the government in the same way that they will exploit the natural resources. But in doing so they do not want to appear subservient to the government. On the other hand, strong government planning, regulations and support in India and a host of other countries have not led those economies out of their apathetic states. There is an old proverb which says you can lead a horse to water but you can't make him drink it.

The secret of Japan's economic success is the human factor, not what goes on in the individual Japanese, but how the Japanese seek their satisfactory level of PSH through their particular way of relating to and working with each other.

Sino-Japanese Contrasts in Perspective

In Chapter 1, we noted how Bellah's explanation of Japan's rapid economic (and military) rise, in contrast to China on the basis of differing values, is inconsistent with the facts. China and Japan did not have fundamentally different values. Instead, it was the differing nature of the social groupings through which the same values expressed themselves that seems to have made the difference. Perhaps Bellah is not totally unaware of this fact when he observes: "The rationalism inherent in the Confucian ethic seems to need to be linked with a value system in which political values have primacy if it is to have an influence in the direction of modernization. This was the case in Japan and perhaps of present-day China" (Bellah 1957:192).

But seeing the need for such a link and demonstrating how such a link can become reality are different matters. Bellah fails to appreciate that political values, too, are powerless unless they find themselves in the fertile soil of human groupings. What we have done in the foregoing chapters is to detail how the dynamics of PSH requirements for the individual, institutional arrangement, and cultural orientation conjointly made that link possible in Japan but not in China.

Our starting point is kinship—that fundamental social structure and content in which all human life begins. Like that of the Chinese, the Japanese kinship system is father-son dominated; but unlike the Chinese, its structure is made more flexible and its content is considerably altered by unigeniture and the markedly hierarchical and sometimes binding relationship between the heir and his other brothers. Those Japanese who have to leave the kinship group of their origin must find the fulfillment of their PSH needs elsewhere. In doing so they do not free themselves entirely from kinship. They are merely propelled by a more flexible kinship structure and are strongly conditioned in the particular composition of their kinship content. That is why they devote themselves and are bound to their secondary groupings such as *dōzoku* and especially *iemoto* based on the kin-tract principle, the essence of which is found in religion as in occupation, in government as in the military, in intellectual pursuits as in artistic endeavors. Japanese kinship content, in contrast to its Chinese counterpart, enables the Japanese to expand his kinship-like *iemoto* almost indefinitely.

When the Japanese individual is freed from the structural restrictions of the *iemoto*, as, for instance, when he is born and raised in the United States, the content of the *iemoto* remains operative. What Caudill and DeVos say about the Japanese Americans' success in the American business and industrial world bears on this:

> A simile is useful in pointing up the similarities and difference between Japanese American and white middle-class *achievement orientations;* the ultimate destinations or goals of individuals in the two groups tend to be very similar. But Japanese Americans go toward these destinations along *straight narrow streets lined with crowds of people who observe their every step,* while (white) middle class persons go toward the same destinations along wider streets having more room for maneuvering, and lined only with small groups of people who, while watching them, do not observe their every movement. In psychoanalytic terminology, this means that the *Japanese Americans have an ego structure that is very sensitive and vulnerable to stimuli coming from the outer world,* and a *superego structure that depends greatly upon external sanction.* This tends to be true of middle class Americans as well, but not nearly to such an extent. For example, individuals in both groups are interested in acquiring money in amounts sufficient to be translated into the achievement of social class prestige; however, every move of a Japanese American toward amassing money is carefully watched, and the way he does it, *and the ultimate use he makes of it in benefitting the community are equal in importance to the financial success itself.* This is less true of the American middle class, where an individual can make his money in a great variety of ways and, so long as these are not down-right dishonest, the ways are sanctioned because of the end product—the financial success (Caudill and DeVos 1956:1117; italics mine).

The notion of achievement motivation is rooted in the American individual-centered way of life. It may be useful in gauging how well minority groups in the United States perform according to white American standards but this has no true intersocietal validity. What is more important here, is the way the Japanese Americans, according to Caudill and DeVos, perceive themselves and relate to others. They work toward their destinations "along narrow streets lined with crowds of people who observe their every step," they have "an ego structure that is very sensitive and vulnerable to stimuli coming from the outer world," and the "ultimate use" the successful Japanese Americans make of the wealth they have acquired "in benefitting the community are equal in importance to the financial success itself." These are all intrinsic expressions of the content of the *iemoto*, even though the social atmosphere among the Japanese American is not organized on the *iemoto* model (e.g. with the *iemoto*'s generational seniority and rigidity of personal affiliation) and is not called "iemoto." But it is among Japanese Americans that we find such clear distinctions between *issei, nisei,* and *sansei* (respectively first, second and third generation Japanese Americans), just as in Japanese corporations we find such clear distinctions between *sempai* and *kōhai* (respectively upper and lower generations of employees).

The age old content of the *iemoto* has given the Japanese a goal orientation and a pattern of obedience to authority that fit extremely well with American corporation needs. If present trends continue, I expect many American employers to prefer Japanese employees to Americans. In fact many American employers in Hawaii already do so.

Chinese Confucianism and Indian Buddhism did not give rise to the Japanese type of blind obedience to authority and religious commitment which link the family with the nation. Japan received Confucianism and Buddhism from China but made use of them through Japanese kinship structure and transformed them in accordance with Japanese *iemoto* content. It was the Japanese who changed the meaning of the Chinese word for scholar (*shih*) into *samurai*, thereby transforming the four ranked classes of Japanese society into *samurai,* farmers, artisans and merchants. (In China, the scholar, not the warrior, headed the social order.) It was the Japanese who placed devotion to Buddha (or master) higher than that to parents. It was the Japanese who merged the ancestral souls with Buddha and worshipped the same ancestor as the ruling imperial house.

Therefore, while we do not disagree with Bellah that "a great deal of Chinese society can be seen as the symbolic extension and generalization of kinship ties" (Bellah 1957:189), we must note that this is not what basically differentiates the Chinese from the Japanese. Our analysis reveals that most of Japanese society, too, can be seen as "the symbolic extension and generalization of kinship ties." The most significant difference between China and Japan lies in the fact that most of Chinese society is a symbolic extension of the father-son dominated kinship system while Japanese society is a symbolic extension of a similar kinship system complicated by unigeniture and an intensified hierarchy. The latter propel a majority of Japanese males into much wider circles of relationships than the Chinese, but these wider relationships are kinship-like in structure and especially in content, as we see clearly in the *iemoto* system.

The Japanese did not develop universalism any more than the Chinese, in Parsons' terms, in these wider circles of human affiliation symbolized by the *iemoto* system. On the contrary, "particularism remained unchallenged. Japanese nationalism remained peculiarly particularistic due to its focus on the imperial family . . . the main family of which all Japanese families are branch families" (Bellah 1957:181), and the Japanese *iemoto* system remained peculiarly particularistic due to its focus on the person of the founder or the big master, who was the fountainhead of all wisdom and discipline for all members of each system. But while the Chinese kinship system provided for no more extension than the clan (the size of which is always limited because it is founded firmly on the principles of birth and marriage), the Japanese kinship system provided for affiliation of men into much larger groupings across kinship lines, each founded primarily on the principle of kin-tract and undergirded by the attributes of a father-son dominated kinship content, but modified or intensified by attributes originating from unigeniture and a markedly hierarchical and binding relationship between *honke* and *bunke*.

Having already been loosened from the primary kinship bonds, the Japanese were, more easily than the Chinese, drawn into larger enterprises (economic, political, religious, military) whose objectives were not those of the narrowly defined kinship ones. Furthermore, the Japanese were more readily drawn into modern enterprises than the Chinese. Long before intensive contact with the West, they already had established among themselves a system, as Marion Levy put it, of "tight control over the vast majority of . . . individuals" (Levy 1953:195). In the light of our analysis so far, Levy's use of the words "tight control" is not appropriate. What really occurred was that, through the *iemoto*, a vast majority of Japanese found themselves affectively linked in relatively larger arenas, and that those links more easily adapted themselves than the traditional Chinese human links to certain requirements of modern industrialization and nationalism.

Compared with the Chinese *tsu*, based on the kinship principle, the *iemoto*, based on the kin-tract principle, has two outstanding advantages in the modernization process. First, with the attribute of volition it allows the introduction of new blood whenever necessary. This fact has two consequences. On the one hand, the size of the establishment, once it is freed from the restriction of agriculture, may be expanded indefinitely. And the sizes of many Japanese *iemoto* are enormous, unmatched by any comparable grouping in China. Being centrally based on the kinship principle, wider Chinese affiliation was always strictly dependent upon the biological facts of birth and death within the narrow limits set by that principle.

On the other hand, the selection of unrelated individuals for inclusion more readily fits in with the criterion of performance, and this nurtures goal orientation of the achievement motive to an extent that cannot be matched by groupings primarily based on the kinship principle, as among the Chinese. The achievement motive is not absent among the Chinese, but the kinship principle was so strong that the sons and grandsons of wealthy or prominent fathers, being assured from birth of their wealth or position, usually turned out badly. As a result, the prominence of a Chinese family name and the integrity of its wealth or business never lasted beyond two or three generations (Hsu 1949:256-278). The sons of prominent or wealthy Japanese fathers have not been subject to the Chinese type of unfavorable educational influences. The custom of unigeniture and the hierarchical relationship among siblings reduced the unfavorable influences of parental wealth and power on the younger sons. The resulting pattern of stress on performance cannot but have affected sons fortunate enough to be heirs. The long histories of prominence of most Japanese *iemoto* and business establishments stand in sharp contrast to Chinese non-kinship and even kinship groupings.

The other Japanese advantage in the modernization process is that the *iemoto*, like its rural counterpart, is a corporation consisting of many branch corporations in which the individual enjoys permanent membership and to which he has made permanent commitment. This is the arena that provides him with his basic source of PSH.

The head *iemoto* commands extreme obedience from the branch *iemoto*, but the former does not interfere with the internal affairs of the latter. In particular, the former cannot replace the latter or any one of the latter's disciples. Since performance is a main criterion for one's place in the hierarchy, and since each branch corporation has autonomy, the whims and personal predilections of the superior have much less chance of affecting the organizational regularity of the whole. The individual on a lower rung of the hierarchy cannot rise above his senior, but his own rank cannot arbitrarily be lowered or taken away, nor can the conduct of his duties be significantly altered by order of the "big boss."

The importance of the *iemoto* for the PSH of the Japanese and the extension of the content of the *iemoto* into Japanese government is what, in my view, has prevented widespread corruption in Japanese government in sharp contrast to what occurred in the pre-1949 governments in China. Since kinship and locality ties were the objects of individual affect for the Chinese, giving them their basic sources of PSH, bureaucratic considerations stood generally outside their PSH needs. The common Chinese expressions to describe a man just appointed to a post are *shang t'ai la* (gone up the stage) and a bureaucrat just resigned or who has been dismissed from his post, *hsia t'ai la* (gone off the stage). The Chinese truly regard government work as mere role performance. Consequently, the Chinese in the bureaucracy had neither fixed places in it nor any permanent committment to its hierarchical organization or goals. Any Chinese could move up or down, due to either his own actions, or to the arbitrary actions of his superiors or his superior's superiors. It was well known that competitive bribery (not fixed dues as in the Japanese *iemoto*) was an indispensable means for maintaining a position in Chinese officialdom or for promotion in it.

These factors were responsible for the spectacular and speedy Japanese advancements after contact with the West, just as their absence in China was responsible for Chinese stagnation and chaos during an entire century of Western domination. The Japanese advantages had their roots in the *ie* and in the *dōzoku*, just as their extension literally enables us to regard, at least figuratively, the entire Japanese nation as one huge *iemoto*.

However, the Japanese have reached modernization and industrialization via a very different psycho-social route than that found in the West. Japanese non-heirs were not, as were their Western counterparts, encouraged to seek, or bent on seeking, their own fame and fortune on their own terms. Their kinship system encouraged them to look for mutual dependence instead of independence. Therefore, instead of individualism and freedom, the Japanese proceeded from their *iemoto* system based on the kin-tract principle. They developed newer and larger groups with non-traditional objectives, without feeling a need for significant changes in their traditional pattern of human relationships. That pattern is based on the attributes of the father-son relationship modified by unigeniture and a hierarchical relationship between the heir and his brothers. The structure, but especially the content, of the *iemoto* system has provided modern Japanese enterprises with their most important sources of organizational loyalty and strength. The widespread *oyabun-kobun* or *oyabun-kobun*-like relationships in modern Japanese industries and commerce is only the most formal expression of this fact.

In the *oyabun-kobun* relationship we find the emphasis on vertical affiliation with an establishment or interest group *(batsu)* and seniority (continuity), yet a disregard for actual kinship (discontinuity and volition); the overwhelming importance of being a product of a certain school (exclusiveness) but the relative lack of discrimination among individuals on the basis of talent (inclusiveness); and finally, the intensification of the most explicit pattern of superordination and subordination (authority).

For the Chinese the transition from the traditional to the modern was more difficult. Levy puts his finger on a crucial element in this contrast when he says:

> The new forces in Japan undercut many of the old patterns just as they had in China, but they did not simultaneously undercut the sole or the major sources of control over individuals as they did in China (Levy 1953:194).

Again we must object to Levy's use of the term "control." What the Chinese traditional social organization lacked was provision for strong non-kinship and non-local secondary groupings in which individuals could find sources for PSH.[4] Consequently, when new objectives (development of nationalism and industrialization along Western lines) arose under Western impact, the traditional Chinese human framework was unresponsive to its new organizational requirements. Instead, most Chinese floundered about and were unable to unite in strength in the wider arena once they had left their kinship or local moorings. They retained their basic kinship attributes, some of which could have been utilized to good advantage in the new situation as they were in Japan. But there was no traditional structure to which to harness them for the new ends.

A useful analogy may help us to understand this better. Bravery is an admirable virtue in many societies. Bravery is also a necessary attribute for winning a war. However, poor leadership and inefficient organization, not to speak of inadequate and inefficient equipment, can render this quality fruitless. The deciding factor is not the existence or non-existence of the attribute of bravery, but the organizational channels by means of which the potentials of this quality can be realized.[5] The Chinese may have been brave, to pursue this analogy, but they did not have the structure through which they could make use of this attribute of bravery. The Japanese, as we have shown, had both the attribute and the structure which enabled its realization.

Social Organization, Cultural Ideal and The Individual: The Dynamics of Mutual Escalation

Our basic hypothesis which runs through this book is that, if the individual cannot, because of the nature of the kinship system in conjunction with a particular type of cultural orientation that shapes the direction of his ideal life, find the fulfillment of his PSH in the basic kinship group, he must join or form other groups for this purpose. In doing so, the patterns of his search for a group and of his conduct in that group are very much governed by the kind of content his initial kinship group has imparted to him. Diagram 13 is a sketch of the dynamics of the interrelationships linking the cultural orientation, the individual PSH needs, and the social grouping in the Japanese situation.[6]

The Japanese have the same starting point as the Chinese: mutual dependence. Between the parents and heir (often the eldest son) there is complete community of interests and automatic sharing of honors and responsibilities. However, while his interpersonal relationships may also be described by the term situational determinism as in the Chinese case (a pattern Ruth Benedict describes as the ability to turn suddenly about face without embarrassment), but in effect is the tendency to be more sensitive to the requirements of one's place in a network of interpersonal relations than to one's own personal predilections. His cultural ideal is loyalty to the lord and emperor which, when the occasion demands it, overrides harmony among men and everything else.

Kin-tract relationship supplements and replaces kinship ties

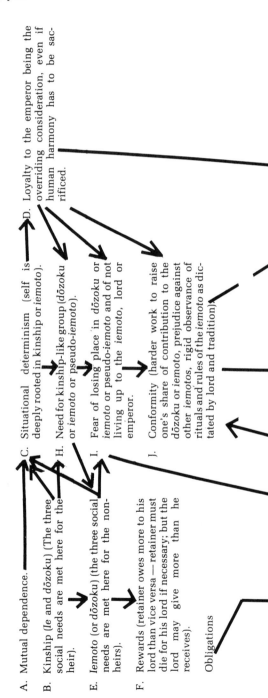

A. Mutual dependence.

B. Kinship (*Ie* and *dōzoku*) (The three social needs are met here for the heir).

C. Situational determinism (self is deeply rooted in kinship or *iemoto*).

D. Loyalty to the emperor being the overriding consideration, even if human harmony has to be sacrificed.

E. *Iemoto* (or *dōzoku*) (the three social needs are met here for the non-heirs).

F. Rewards (retainer owes more to his lord than vice versa — retainer must die for his lord if necessary; but the lord may give more than he receives).

H. Need for kinship-like group (*dōzoku* or *iemoto* or pseudo-*iemoto*).

I. Fear of losing place in *dōzoku* or *iemoto* or pseudo-*iemoto* and of not living up to the *iemoto*, lord or emperor.

J. Conformity (harder work to raise one's share of contribution to the *dōzoku* or *iemoto*, prejudice against other *iemotos*, rigid observance of rituals and rules of the *iemoto* as dictated by lord and tradition).

Obligations

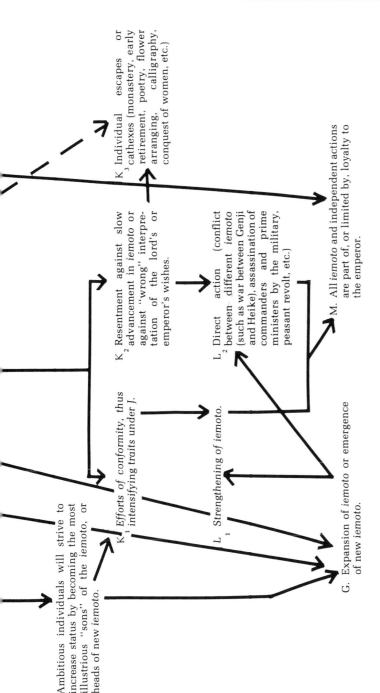

K₃ Individual escapes or cathexes (monastery, early retirement, poetry, flower arranging, calligraphy, conquest of women, etc.)

K₂ Resentment against slow advancement in iemoto or against "wrong" interpretation of the lord's or emperor's wishes.

L₂ Direct action (conflict between different iemoto (such as war between Genji and Heike), assassination of commanders and prime ministers by the military, peasant revolt, etc.)

M. All iemoto and independent actions are part of, or limited by, loyalty to the emperor.

Ambitious individuals will strive to increase status by becoming the most illustrious "sons" of the iemoto, or heads of new iemoto.

K₁ *Efforts of conformity, thus intensifying traits under J.*

L₁ *Strengthening of iemoto.*

G. Expansion of iemoto or emergence of new iemoto.

DIAGRAM 13: Japanese Orientation

Since the kinship group is the basic source of the Chinese individual's PSH he can ignore the world outside. Hence the Chinese ideal of harmony among men as described by Confucius and as depicted in Chinese literature is one of live-and-let-live rather than one of positive action to maintain or change anything in the name of it except within the kinship sphere. He would disturb the ideal of harmony among men only if his kinship group was threatened or violated by another kinship group. For example, if his father was murdered by someone, he must avenge it at all cost. Or if his mother desired something difficult to obtain, he would be justified in going to all lengths to secure it. The kinship group is the beginning and ending of his immutable world.

The Japanese cannot rely on his basic kinship group to satisfy his PSH requirements. Instead, he has to leave it and secure them in a larger, yet kinship-like, group which we term *iemoto* (E in Diagram 13). Since the boundary of the *iemoto* is not limited by kinship, it is more flexible than the Chinese *tsu* and it allows far more room for large scale expansion. In its widest extension the imperial house is something of the *honke* heading a giant *iemoto* comprising all Japan.[7] This gave Japan but not China the basis for patriotism and nationalism under Western pressure in modern times. The resources for development in the Japanese human situation are easily mobilized for various objectives: political, artistic, military or industrial.

The reward-obligation ratio (F in Diagram 13) is unequal, but unlike the Hindu situation, individuals situated on the lower rungs of the hierarchy owe the superior lords more obligations than vice versa (they must die for their lords but the lords need not die for them). On the other hand, the lord may also voluntarily give to his subordinates more than what he receives in return, although this never works automatically (the lord's honors do not automatically go to his subordinates), in contrast to the relationship between the Chinese father and his son.

However, every way of life has a tendency of escalating itself. That is, though sharing the same culture with others, some individuals are more ambitious or active than others. If the culture says adventure is a desirable goal, some members want to travel farther and make more difficult journeys than others. If the culture says there should be taboo against eating pork, some members want to surpass others by avoiding even the mention of the word pork in their conversation. If the culture says filial piety is a good thing, some members want to honor their parents in ways calculated to outshine all other filial sons in the past.

Ambitious individuals will not stop at merely doing the right thing according to the accepted rules. They want to do more according to those rules. How far such ambitious individuals can and will go is dependent upon the limitations set by the size of the arena within which he has been conditioned by his culture to derive the resources for his PSH. Since the Chinese PSH is confined to the kinship group, the ambitious Chinese is most likely still to define his ambitious acts within that group. He will give bigger weddings for his children than his neighbors, stage more colossal funerals for his deceased parents to outshine others, and reach for higher places in officialdom or perform more spectacular acts to glorify his ancestors or ensure the welfare of his descendants yet unborn. He may even lavish a good deal of money to improve his home town by repairing roads, building bridges and giving donations to schools. But the effects of how far his ambition carries him are limited in extent as far as the entire Chinese society is concerned.

Not so in Japan. The ambitious Japanese will try to become the most illustrious "sons" of the *iemoto*. But as they have escalated their individual contributions to the cultural ideal, their exalted statuses will necessarily provide a stamp of approval so that the generations which follow them are bound to find in their acts sources of inspiration and models for imitation. The results of following such patterns of ambition cannot but have a major or minor impact on the social organization in part or on the whole. Thus the individual, social organization and the cultural ideal escalate each other.

How do ambitious individuals in Japan help in this mutual escalation process? If they are already *Iemoto*, they will try to obtain more disciples or retainers, or to be masters who have more secret formulae that are the envy of other masters. If they are only members of *iemoto*, they may try to achieve eminence in their *iemoto* or become the most illustrious branch *iemoto* under the grand *Iemoto*. If they are not affiliated to some master already they may start new and bigger *iemoto*. We use the word "new" here not to denote anything drastically different in design or aim, but in the sense of a freshly begun *bunke*-like establishment, with a more ambitious representation and the same aim as the *honke* establishment, with the same old social design and the same old social aims. Here is where the ambitious Japanese and their Chinese counterparts will differ. They differ in the extent to which their ambitious acts affect society as a whole.

For one thing, whether their ambitions may drive them to expand their existing *iemoto* or to start new *iemoto* (G in Diagram 13), the number of Japanese involved is likely to be large, much larger than what their Chinese brethren can do since the kinship principle severely curtails the latter's efforts for recruitment. Even more important is the almost unlimited variety of objectives of the Japanese *iemoto* in contrast to the extremely limited objectives of the Chinese *tsu*. Consequently, the ambitious Japanese not only can affect more of his countrymen but can steer them into a larger variety of goals not previously embodied in the traditional Japanese culture and society. The Japanese who follow them are swayed not so much because they are convinced of the importance of the new goals but because their relationship with the leaders of their *iemoto* or pseudo-*iemoto* is necessary for their PSH.

The forces for conformity in the Japanese situation combine with those operating in Hindu India and in China. On the one hand, there is the fear of not living up to the ideal of devotion to the *Iemoto*, lord or emperor (corresponding to the fear the Chinese have of not living up to ancestral names, etc.). On the other hand, there is the fear of losing place in the *iemoto* or pseudo-*iemoto* (corresponding to the Hindu fear of losing caste; I in diagram 13). The answer to such fears in the Japanese interpersonal context of situational determinism (C in Diagram 13) is the Japanese way of conformity (J in Diagram 13). In this case conformity means harder work to raise one's share of contribution to the *iemoto*, prejudice against other groups or *iemoto*, rigid observance of rituals and rules of the *iemoto* as dictated by lord and tradition.

But the more flexible nature of the kin-tract principle does not only enable the ambitious Japanese individual to expand the old *iemoto* and begin new *iemoto*. He can also intensify conformity (K_1 in Diagram 13), or resent slow advancement in his *iemoto* (K_2 in Diagram 13). The two courses of action will of course strengthen the hold of the existing *iemoto* on the individual (L_1 in Diagram 13). But the resentment against slow advancement under the circumstances is conducive to direct action (L_2 in Diagram 13). Japanese history provides numerous examples of direct action: not only conflicts between different *iemoto* such as the war between the Genji and the Heike, peasant revolts, but also assassination of military commanders and government ministers, in the name of the divine will of the emperor. Superficially, the latter type of Japanese examples of direct action appears to be similar to that also found in Chinese history, but that is not the case. Chinese rebels mostly aimed at replacing the dynastic ruler (no matter what they publicly proclaimed); but Japanese rebels, as a rule, acted on behalf of the emperor, with or without his consent or even knowledge, since no new imperial dynasty ever emerged (M in Diagram 13). For although *iemoto* is capable of enormous expansion, its greatest expansion is via the pseudo-kinship ties which proceed from the great shrine at Ise to the emperor's ancestors, to the Japanese nation as a whole, as all Japanese have a common ancestress, Amaterasu. Therefore, although the immutable world of the Japanese is his *iemoto*, that secondary group is capable of linking the individual with Japan as a whole, in contrast to the Chinese secondary group *tsu* which provides no comparable foundation.

As we noted before, neither the Chinese nor the Japanese developed universalistic approaches to ethics or religion or any other major social and cultural activity or objective. Both Chinese and Japanese were particularistic when compared with Westerners. The real Chinese-Japanese difference is that the particularistic approach of the Chinese was narrower in application than its Japanese counterpart. In the Chinese scene, the particularistic approach is confined by the kinship principle, but in the Japanese scene it enjoys a wider scope of opportunities because of the more flexible kin-tract principle. Through the *dōzoku* system the Japanese individual has already been lifted out of his immediate kinship roots which would have put a low ceiling on his wider involvements. At the same time, the attribute of continuity from the father-son relationship prevents him from going too far afield; he incorporates himself in a kinship-like *iemoto*, with the imperial house as his ultimate limit.

Compared with Westerners, the Japanese have never been truly universalistic in their thinking. The ultimate confirmation of this observation is found not only in the non-acceptance of non-Japanese in Japan, a fact we noted before, but in the Japanese scheme for the world at the height of their power and conquest before and during World War II. Their Greater Asia Co-prosperity Sphere was not a model for present or future universal egalitarianism, even at the conceptual level. What they wanted was a world hegemony in which all would live in harmony if they would accept their proper (inferior) places below the Japanese in a graded hierarchy of races and peoples—a sort of world establishment in the *iemoto* model.

Our analysis so far leaves no doubt that the Japanese way of life is considerably different from that of the Chinese and both are very different from that of the Americans. The question is, is it quite similar to that of Hindu India? My answer is no. The reason is that the role of the mother-son relationship is the dominant one in India, but its importance in Japan is greatly overshadowed by the father-son relationship, unigeniture, and markedly hierarchical and binding ties between the heir and his brothers.[8]

The attributes of diffuseness, dependence and libidinality originating from the mother-son relationship are at most points held in check by, or greatly subordinated to, those originating from the father-son relationship. Though sharing the Hindu view of the impermanence of life and the all-embracing nature of the universal God, or Buddha, the Japanese confine themselves to specific creeds originating from particular ancestral father figures, buttressed by their pseudo-kinship relationship to the emperor through the Shinto shrines. Though dependent upon the master or the imperial super-master, blind devotion for the Japanese demands not *passive* following, as in Hindu India, but *active* carrying out of the will (actual or supposed) of the father figure of his *iemoto* (or of the super-*iemoto*, the national state). It is a relationship in which diffused dependence takes a secondary place to more specific actions commensurate with the attributes of continuity and authority.

In *Clan, Caste and Club* (Hsu 1963) I concluded, from my analyses of the interrelationship between social organization, cultural ideal and the individual in the Chinese, Hindu and American ways of life that the Chinese way was the least dynamic and generated the least amount of internal impetus to change; the American way is most dynamic and generates the most internal impetus to change; while the Hindu way leads to a society remarkably dynamic in appearance which in the long run undergoes little real change. Now we must observe that the Japanese way, though it is basically Chinese, has led to more dynamic results because it always had a wider human field in which to play.

The Japanese scholar Hayashi, whom we quoted before, wants

the Japanese to develop a new concept of work. According to him, instead of their present unshaken faith in the group (corporation, university, government department, etc.), Japanese about to begin working careers should "select their specialty carefully" as American students do; and instead of devoting their time and energy in analyzing "the financial conditions of the nation's leading enterprises" in the hope of entering one of them for life regardless of what jobs they will be obliged by the company to accept, they must aim at becoming professionals who take pride in their chosen professions as individuals. Otherwise, in Hayashi's opinion, ". . . there is a long way to go for Japanese society to be democratized" since it is composed of human clusters, not individuals equal to each other as in the West, where social status differences have "nothing to do with the value of those engaged in certain professions because of the Christian idea of 'anyone is equal before God'"(Hayashi 1965).

In view of our analysis, Hayashi's exhortation to Japan that "clusters must go" and that his countrymen "must do away with their faith in their group" is simply unrealistic. It is as unrealistic as if he were to ask Americans to forget their individualism. In both cases the visible values sprang from deep historical and psycho-cultural roots, and they cannot be altered for the asking. On the other hand, Hayashi needs to examine more closely the Christian West, especially the differences between what it does and what it professes. Had he done so, especially in the light of our PSH formulation, he might also have realized that not only have Christian ideals failed to eliminate social inequality based on work in the West but that the very individualism which he wants his fellow Japanese to develop has much to do with the genesis and maintenance, by force if need be, of that very inequality in the Christian West and in the attitude of the Christian West toward the rest of mankind. As long as the Western way of life continues to make the PSH resources scarce for the individual, the strife for superiority (either by advancing or by keeping and pushing others to a lower place) will be intensified rather than otherwise. Furthermore, is Professor Hayashi not aware of the fact that all the totalitarian ideologies no less than those of democracy and individual freedom were creatures of the West (see Hsu 1970:422-440)? In fact, American scholars like Edward T. Hall favor the Japanese culture over its American counterpart "in any race to solve both environmental problems and human problems" (Hall 1970:234).

Most recently another Japanese scholar, Professor Shōzaburo Kimura, of Tokyo University, expresses concern in a somewhat similar vein. He acknowledges that Japan has indeed gone far in the contemporary world and he agrees with our conclusion that the iemoto-pattern with its kin-tract principle of human organization is principally responsible for it. However, he feels that the same characteristics in human relations which propelled Japan to such great success today are truly stumbling blocks to Japan's future participation in a cosmopolitan and rationalized world and that they will forever prevent Japan from becoming a true member of a United Europe or of a United World. According to Kimura, in that larger world, America included, the trend is from national enterprises towards multiple-national enterprises, even towards international enterprises unhampered by narrow, national interests (Kimura 1972:35).

I think Professor Kimura, too, has misread the future of a world still dominated by the West. Those who are impressed by the recent European Common Market developments need to remember the West's numerous efforts for an universal Christendom. The fact is that, not only the Christian West as a whole but within each individual Western nation, Christian unity is nowhere in sight. Instead, what we witness is numerous ecumenical calls combined with perpetual divisiveness among the professed Western believers of Christ. To go back to our PSH formulation again, as long as the resources for PSH are scarce most human beings will suffer from insecurity which cannot lead them to cooperate with each other except temporarily in face of some real or imagined common crisis. The scarcer the resources for PSH, the higher the interpersonal tension within the society, the lower the level of its rationality and the harder it will be for such societies to unite with each other for any length of time. I am by no means a pessimist, but the objective evidence points to more intense separatism and nationalism rather than greater world unity, at least in the foreseeable future.

The Japanese are fortunate in that they have in their traditional iemoto pattern of human relationship no lack of PSH resources, and at the same time it also provides them with the psycho-cultural wherewithal for military or economic capabilities to defend themselves against genuine threats from without.

Under the stimulus of Western expansionism during a

shamelessly colonial era, the Japanese imitated the expansionist and colonial minded West and lost. Should the Japanese not consider a different destiny in which they can make the best of all possible worlds?

[1] Here and again below the term *Oyaji* ("father") refers to the supervisor who is generally considerably older than the men he supervises.

[2] As I write these passages I notice an article in the current issue of *Life* magazine (Sept. 1, 1972, pp. 30-38) entitled "Boredom on the Assembly Line," which deals with job dissatisfaction among Detroit auto workers. The author claims this to be a new industrial revolution with which the factory will have to contend. Typically, some American auto makers have thought of what they call "Job Enrichment," which would enable workers to exercise their creativity. But no real, economically feasible solution for this American problem is in sight.

[3] These songs are sung by all employees together, male and female. However, Japanese society and culture is, of course, male-centered. Nearly all the important positions are occupied by males. Consequently, all the exuberance and enthusiasm towards the corporation described here is primarily relevant to male employees. As early as the 1920's some female factory workers voiced dissatisfaction with their conditions of life to which the following song of *Joko* (female worker) bears witness:

Joko's Song

The life in a dormitory is more trying than the bird's
    life in a cage and the prison living.
The factory is a hell; the supervisor, a demon;
    and the machine, a fire wheel.
How I wish I had wings to get out of here and fly
    over to the other side of the water.
Senior Residents behave so arrogantly,
    but they too used to be the same *jokos.*
Working a factory is just like serving in a prison;
    only difference is that we do not have metal chains.

I am a *joko,* a vain bird.
I cannot fly in spite of my wings.
I cannot fly in spite of the open sky.
(Because) I am in a cage even though I can see the sky.
I am a small bird, but with the wings broken.

As my parents were unsuccessful,
no, they were not unsuccessful, but as I was shiftless,
I was deceived by a tail-less fox,
and brought to this place.

Rather than working in this dreadful mill,

I would run away to the end of the Manchuria border.
I would rather experience hardship in the strange land.
(Even the work at Manchuria must not be as dreadful
    as it is here.)

Please listen to me ——(name) san.
Because of my wish to be loyal to my parents,
I am going through such a hardship, hundreds of miles
    away from home.

Filling up the pockets with gravel,
I prepared myself to be drowned.
— But if I die, it would be a disgrace to the company.
— But if I return home, it would be a disgrace to
    my parents.
Only bitter tears come out when I think of my situation.

Really this is a terrible world for jokos.
What kind of people their parents are,
if they brought them to this world
knowing their fate to be *jokos*.

How I wish to treat my parents to a cup of *sake*,
with joyful tears in my eyes.
When I imagine their saying
"When is our daughter coming home (it can be very soon)?"
my mind is flooded with tears of agony.

I wish I would be a wall board in the company office
so that I could read the letters from my home.

How can we spin well when we eat nothing but vegetables
    for the three meals.

(Collected by Hosoi 1922)

It is important to note that the song writer, instead of rebelling against the exploitation, laments her own fate. In fact, even under such distress she is concerned with the company's reputation and her parents' face.

With economic prosperity and American influence, especially after World War II, more women have entered into the business and industrial world (*Rō Dō Shō* 1967:78-84), the lot of female workers has improved and more females have been admitted to white collar ranks. But the female employee's position remains inferior to that of her male counterpart in wages and as a matter of hierarchy. For example, in 1966, in the non-agriculture and non-forestry trades, female temporary employees hired on a daily basis still outnumbered female regular employees hired on a permanent basis, while the picture was totally reversed among the males. Far more males were hired on a permanent than on a daily basis (*Rō Dō Shō* 1967:85). As another example, female clerks in the same office as a rule serve tea to their male office mates, but not vice versa. In recent years faint noises of female rebellion are occasionally heard and the posted demands of one such female rebellious effort I knew as early as 1965 stated: "no more pouring tea for male colleagues." But these rumblings of female dissatisfaction have not yet made serious inroads into male dominance.

[4] The provincial and occupational "guilds," which have been noted by many students of China, were no exception to this statement. (See Hsu 1968.)

⁵ Exactly the same thing holds true for natural resources, the abundant presence of which in many regions of the earth never assures their effective utilization unless the requisite skills, tools, capital, and human organization are at hand.

⁶ This analysis follows that given in *Clan, Caste and Club* (Hsu 1963:162-191 and 204-224), where the Chinese, Hindu and American situations are compared and contrasted with each other.

⁷Of course, the great importance of the emperor was built up by the Meiji reformers. But if Japan did not have the *iemoto* type of human organization based on loyalty to *daimyō* etc., and the Japanese did not have their particular *iemoto* type of approach to religious affiliation, such reformers would have found it impossible to glorify the emperor by reviving State Shintoism for modernization purposes. The *iemoto* structure and content were the true foundation which made such developments possible. The Chinese reformers in the 19th century never put their thoughts in that direction, and even if they did, they would not have succeeded.

⁸ After the publication of *Hikaku Bunmei Shakai Ron* (Hsu 1971c) Dr. Tsurumi Kazuko wrote in a review:

The author argues that the Japanese family system is a synthesis (*nuiawase*) of Chinese and Indian (Hindu) types, whereas the *iemoto* combines Chinese and American types. Yet, if the author's postulate that the secondary grouping in a society is determined by its family system is correct, then the Japanese *iemoto* should be a mixture of Chinese and Indian (Hindu) type of secondary groupings instead ("Nihon kazoku no genri o saguru." *Shūkan Gen Ron*, Jan. 28, 1972).

I think Dr. Tsurumi has misunderstood our position and her misunderstanding comes from two sources: (a) the term kin-tract which we describe as the basic principle governing *iemoto* is derived from an abbreviated combination of the terms kinship (the basic secondary grouping in China and contrast the basic principle of secondary grouping in the United States), and (b) the notion that one system as a whole could simply be a cross between two other systems as wholes. No suggestion is made that the basic principle of Japanese *iemoto* organization combines that of the Chinese clan with that of the U.S. club. Instead, the term kin-tract denotes the fact that the criteria for recruitment to the *iemoto* is more flexible than to the kinship group but that once the relationship is entered into it becomes as binding as in kinship. However, no term can encompass all the reality it is designed to call attention to. This superficial difficulty is easily reduced by realizing that the important *guides* for our comparison and contrast are the attributes, not the systems as wholes. For example, authority (part of the principle of the hierarchy), is as prominent an attribute in the Japanese situation as it is uncharacteristic of the U.S. system. Except for the element of volition connected with entry into the *iemoto* or *iemoto*-like relationships, the latter has little else in common with the U.S. club or club-like organization. This conclusion is inevitable once our attention is focused on attributes. Our analysis should leave little doubt that in kinship system and in secondary grouping, the U.S., the Hindu and the Chinese stand apart, each from the others. However, to the extent that father-son dominance and mother-son dominance offer no attribute leading to rejection of kinship, the Chinese and Hindu systems are more similar to each other than either is to the U.S. system. The Japanese system, being primarily a variation of its Chinese counterpart, is therefore, closest to that of the Chinese, less close to that of the Hindu, and farthest apart from that of the U.S.

BIBLIOGRAPHY

Abe, Haruo
  1963 "The Accused and Society: Therapeutic and Preventive Aspects
        of Criminal Justice in Japan." In Arthur Taylor von Mehren (ed.),
        Law in Japan: The Legal Order in a Changing Society. Cambridge:
        Harvard University Press. Pp. 324-363.
Abegglen, James C.
  1958 The Japanese Factory. Glencoe, Illinois: The Free Press.
Anesaki, Masaharu
  1961 Religious Life of the Japanese People (revised by Hideo
        Kishimoto). Tokyo: Kokusai Bunka Shinkokai (The Society for
        International Cultural Relations).
Aoki, Kazuc
  1965 Nara no Miyako, Nippon no Rekishi (Japanese History, Capital of
        Nara) Vol. 3. Tokyo: Chuo-koron-sha.
Ariga, Kizaemon
  1939 Nambu Ninoe-gun, Ishigami-mura Ni Okeru Daikazoku Seido To
        Nago Seido (Large Family and Tenant System in Ishigami Vil-
        lage, Ninoe Country, Nambu District). Tokyo: Attic Museum Ihou
        No. 43.
Basabe, Fernando M.,
        (in collaboration with Anzai Shin and Federico Lanzaco)
  1968 Religious Attitudes of Japanese Men: A Sociological Study.
        Tokyo: Sophia University in cooperation with Charles E. Tuttle
        Co.
Basham, A. L.
  1954 The Wonder That Was India. New York: Grove Press.
Beardsley, Richard K., Hall, John W., and Ward, Robert E.
  1959 Village Japan. Chicago: University of Chicago Press.
Befu, Harumi
  1962 "Corporate Emphasis and Patterns of Descent in The Japanese
        Family." In R. Smith and R. Beardsley (eds.), Japanese Culture.
        Viking Fund of Publications in Anthropology, No. 34, Pp. 34-41.
  1963 "Patrilineal Descent and Personal Kindred in Japan," American
        Anthropologist, 65:6:1328-41.

Bellah, Robert N.
    1957   *Tokugawa Religion.* Glencoe, Illinois: The Free Press.
Ben-Dasan, Isaiah
    1970   *Nihonjin to Yudyajin* (Japanese and Jews). Tokyo: Yamamoto
            Shoten.
Bennett, John and Ishino, Iwao
    1963   *Paternalism in Japanese Economy.* Minneapolis: University of
            Minnesota Press.
Berreman, Gerald D.
    1960   "Caste in India and the United States," *American Journal of
            Sociology,* 66:2:125.
    1966   "Structure and Function of Caste System." In George DeVos and
            Hiroshi Wagatsuma (eds.), *Japan's Invisible Race: Caste in Cul-
            ture and Personality.* Berkeley: University of California Press.
Blauner, Robert
    1964   *Alienation and Freedom.* Chicago: University of Chicago Press.
Brannan, Nash S.
    1968   *Sōka Gakkai, Builders of the Third Civilization.* Seattle: Univer-
            sity of Washington Press.
Brown, Keith
    1966   "*Dōzoku* and the Ideology of Descent in Rural Japan," *American
            Anthropologist,* 68:5:1129-51, 1146-1147.
Buck, Pearl S. (trans.)
    1933   *All Men Are Brothers* (*Shui Hu Chuan* by Shih Non-an). New
    & 1937 York: John Day.
Caudill, William and DeVos, George
    1956   "Achievement, Culture and Personality: The Case of the Japanese
            Americans," *American Anthropologist,* 58:1117.
Caudill, William and Plath, David
    1966   "Who Sleeps by Whom? Parent-Child Involvement in Urban
            Japanese Families," *Psychiatry,* 29:4:344-366.
Chu, Chieh-fan
    1967   "The Analyses of the Legend of 'Chasing of Liu Hsiu by Wang
            Mang,' "*Bulletin of the Institute of Ethnology, Academia Sinica,*
            23:37-104.
Cox, Oliver
    1945   "Race and Caste: A Distinction," *American Journal of Sociology,*
            50:360-368.
DeVos, George and Wagatsuma, Hiroshi
    1961   "Value Attitudes Toward Role Behavior of Women in Two
            Japanese Villages," *American Anthropologist,* 63:1204-30.

DeVos, George and Wagatsuma, Hiroshi (eds.)
1966   *Japan's Invisible Race: Caste in Culture and Personality.*
Berkeley: University of California Press.
Doi, Takeo
1956   "Japanese Language as an Expression of Japanese Psychology,"
Western Speech, 20:90-96.
Dore, Ronald P.
1958   *City Life in Japan.* Berkeley: University of California Press.
Embree, John F.
1939   *Suye Mura.* Chicago: University of Chicago Press.
1945   *The Japanese Nation: A Social Survey.* New York: Farrar and
Rinehart.
Gamō, Masao
1958   "Shinzoku." In section on *Shakai to Minzoku* (Society and Folk-
lore) in *Nihon Minzoku Gaku Tai Kei* (Outline of Japanese Folk-
lore), Vol. 3. Tokyo: Hei Bon Sha. Pp. 233-258.
Glazer, Herbert
1969   "The Japanese Executive." In Robert J. Ballon (ed.), *The Japanese
Employee.* Tokyo: Sophia University, and Rutland, Vermont:
Charles E. Tuttle Co. Pp. 77-97.
Goldthorpe, John H. et al
1968   *The Affluent Worker: Industrial Attitudes and Behavior.*
Cambridge: Cambridge University Press.
Hall, Edward T.
1971   "The Paradox of Culture." In Bernard Landis and Edward S.
Tauber (eds.), *In the Name of Life.* New York: Holt, Rinehart and
Winston.
Hamaguchi, Esyun
1970   "Behavioral Foundations of Japanese *Iemoto* Organizations."
Paper delivered at Seminar on Psychological Anthropology, Uni-
versity of Hawaii.
1971a "Nihon Shakai no Kazoku teki Kōso Saikō" (A Re-examination of
the Pseudo-familial Structure of Japanese Society). In *Kazoku to
Shakai,* a volume in memory of Professor Tsutomu Himeoka.
(Vol. XVII, Nos. 1 and 2 of *Soshioroji.* Kyoto: Shakai Gaku Kenk-
yukai. Pp. 1-17).
1971b "Dochaku Shiso" (Indigenous Ideology), in *Bessatsu Keizei
Hyōron* (Special Issue, Economic Forum), No. 7, Pp. 118-127.
Hamaguchi, Esyun and Keichi Sakuda
1971   "Keisetsu" (Interpretation). In Francis L. K. Hsu, *Hikaku Bunmei
Shakai Ron* (Sociology of Comparative Cultures).

Haring, Douglas G.
    1956   "Japanese National Character: Cultural Anthropology,
            Psychoanalysis, and History." In Douglas G. Haring (ed.),
            Personal Character and Cultural Milieu. 3rd ed. Syracuse, New
            York: Syracuse University Press.
Hayashi, Shuji
    1965   "The New Japanese Concept of Profession." *Chuo Koron* (Central
            Forum), Tokyo, May issue. As reported by Takeo Nakao, in
            Mainichi Daily News, Tokyo, May 14, 1965, P. 7.
Hirano, Ryuichi
    1963   "The Accused and Society: Some Aspects of Japanese Law." In
            Arthur Taylor von Mehren (ed.), *Law in Japan: The Legal Order in
            a Changing Society.* Cambridge: Harvard University Press. Pp.
            274-296.
Ho, Ping-ti
    1968   "Salient Aspects of China's Heritage." In Ping-ti Ho and Tang
            Tsou (eds.), *China in Crisis*, Vol. 1, *China's Heritage and the
            Communist Political System.* Chicago: University of Chicago
            Press. Pp. 1-92.
Hosoi, Wakizo
    1922   *Tragic History of Jokos* (female workers). Tokyo: Kaizosha.
Hsu, Francis L. K.
    1943   "The Myth of Chinese Family Size," *American Journal of Sociol-
            ogy*, XLVIII:555-562.
    1949   *Under the Ancestors' Shadow: Chinese Culture and Personality.*
            New York: Columbia University Press. Enlarged and revised edi-
            tion, 1971. Stanford: Stanford University Press.
    1961   "Kinship and Ways of Life: An Exploration." In Francis L. K. Hsu
            (ed.), *Psychological Anthropology: Approaches to Culture and
            Personality.* Homewood, Illinois: Dorsey Press. 2nd edition,
            Cambridge, Mass.: Schenkman Publishing Co.
    1963   *Clan, Caste and Club.* Princeton, New Jersey: Van Nostrand.
    1965   "The Effect of Dominant Kinship Relationships on Kin and
            Non-Kin Behavior: A Hypothesis," *American Anthropologist*,
            67:638-661.
    1968   "Chinese Kinship and Chinese Behavior." In Ping-ti Ho and
            Tang Tsou (eds.), *China In Crisis*, Vol. 1, *China's Heritage and
            the Communist Political System.* Chicago: University of Chicago
            Press.
    1969   *The Study of Literate Civilizations.* New York: Holt, Rinehart and
            Winston.

1970   *Americans and Chinese: Purpose and Fulfillment in Great Civilizations.* New York: Doubleday, Natural History Press.

1971a   "Psychosocial Homeostasis and Jen: Conceptual Tools for Advancing Psychological Anthropology," *American Anthropologist,* 73:1:23-44.

1971b   *Kinship and Culture.* (F.L.K. Hsu, ed.) Chicago: Aldine Publishing Co.

1971c   *Hikaku Bunmei Shakai Ron* (The Sociology of Comparative Cultures). Consisting of the Japanese translation of *Clan, Caste and Club* and "Japanese Kinship and *Iemoto,*" three new chapters specially written for the Japanese version of the book. (Translated by Keichi Sakuda and Esyun Hamaguchi.) Tokyo: Baifukan.

Hu, Shih
1940   "The Modernization of China and Japan: A Comparative Study in Culture Conflict and a Consideration of Freedom." In Ruth Nanda Anshen (ed.), *Freedom, Its Meaning.* New York: Harcourt Brace and Co. Pp. 114-122.

Inkeles, Alex
1960   "Industrial Man: The Relation of Status to Experience, Perception and Value," *American Journal of Sociology,* 66:1-31.

Inoguchi, Shoji
1965   *Nippon no Soshiki* (Japanese Funeral Ceremony). Tokyo: Hayakawa Shobo.

Ito, Teiji
1968   *Iemoto Shido O Kangaeru* (A Study of the Iemoto System). A series of 20 articles published in the Asahi Shimbun, Tokyo, April 22 to May 27, 1969.

Kato, Masaaki
1959   *Noiroze: Shinkeishō Towa Nanika* (Neurosis: What is It?). Tokyo: Sogensha.

Kato, Tetsujiro
1966   *QC to Ningen Kanke* (Quality Control and Human Relations). Vol. 4 of a series entitled *Genba QC Tokuhon* (The Workshop Quality Reader). Tokyo: Nikkagiren.

Kawasaki, Ichiro
1969   *Japan Unmasked.* Rutland, Vermont and Tokyo: Charles E. Tuttle Co.

Kawashima, Takeyoshi
1957   *Ideorogi Toshite no Kazoku Seido* (The Family System as an Ideology). Tokyo: Iwa Nami Shoten.

Kimura, Shōzaburo
    1972   *"San Shi Shū Dan to Ie no Ko Shū Dan"* (Warrior Grouping and Iemoto Grouping). *Bun Gei Shun Ju* (Literary Spring and Autumn) March, Pp. 22-35.
Kojima, Toshio
    1948   *Kinsei Nihon Nōgyō no Kōzō* (Structure of Japanese Agriculture in Recent Times). Tokyo: Tokyo Daigaku Shuppan Kai.
Kondo, Heijō
    1877   *Zoku Nihon Sei Ki* (Second Part of History of Japanese Political Affairs). Vol. 5:5. Tokyo: Sakagami.
Legge, James
    1960   *Chinese Classics,* Vol. 1. Hong Kong: Hong Kong University Press.
Levy, Marion J., Jr.
    1953   "Contrasting Factors in the Modernization of China and Japan," *Economic Development and Cultural Change,* II:161-197.
Maeda, Takashi
    1965   *Sosen Suhai no Kenkyu* (A Study of Ancestor Worship). Tokyo: Aoyama-Shoin.
Mannari, Hiroshi
    1965   *Bizinesu Erito* (Business Elite). Tokyo: Chuokoron Sha.
Marsh, Robert and Hiroshi Mannari
    1970   "Lifetime Commitment in Japan: Roles, Norms and Values," *American Journal of Sociology,* 76: 795-812.
Morioka, Kiyomi
    1965   "Chūsemakki Honganji Kyōdan ni Okeru Ikkeshu" (The Relatives of the Abbot of Honganji Order at the Close of Medieval Age). *Syakaigaku Hyoron* (The Journal of Japanese Sociology), No. 9, Pp. 41-51.
Murata, Kiyoaki
    1969   *Japan's New Buddhism: An Objective Account of Soka Gakkai.* New York & Tokyo: Walker Weatherhill.
Myrdal, Gunnar
    1944   *An American Dilemma.* New York: Harper and Bros.
Nagai, Michio
    1953   *Dōzoku: A Preliminary Study of the Japanese "Extended Family" Group and Its Social and Economic Functions* (based on the researches of K. Ariga). Ohio State University Research Foundation Interim Report No. 7.

Naito, Kanji and Yoshida, Teigo
  1965 "Ritō Sonraku no Shakaijinruigakuteki Ken Kyū" (A Social Anthropological Study of an Island Village, Komuta Community on Koshiki Island). *Minzoku Gaku Ken Kyū* (Japanese Journal of Ethnology), 30:3:209-227.
Nakamura, Hajime
  1960 *The Ways of Thinking of Eastern Peoples*. (Translated from the Japanese by Japanese National Commission for UNESCO: Tokyo.) Japanese version: *Tōyōjin no Shii Hōhō*. Four vols.: 1961, 1961, 1962, 1962. (Another translation, Philip R. Wiener (ed.), 1964, entitled *Ways of Thinking of Eastern Peoples: India, China, Tibet, Japan*. Honolulu: East-West Center Press.)
Nakane, Chie
  1967a *Kinship and Economic Organization in Rural Japan*. London: Athlone Press.
  1967b *Tate Shakai no Ningen Kankei* (Human Relations in a Hierarchical Society). Tokyo: Kodansha.
Newell, William H.
  1967 "Some Problems of Integrating Minorities into Japanese Society," *Journal of Asian and African Studies*, II: 3-4: 212-229.
Nishiyama, Matsu-no-suke
  1962 *Gendai no Iemoto* (Iemoto Today). Tokyo: Kobun-do.
Norbeck, Edward
  1966 "Little-Known Minority Groups of Japan." In George DeVos and Hiroshi Wagatsuma (eds.), *Japan's Invisible Race: Caste in Culture and Personality*. Berkeley: University of California. Pp. 184-199.
  1970 *Religion and Society in Modern Japan—Continuity and Change*. Houston, Texas: Tourmaline Press.
Ōmachi, Tokuzō
  "Kazoku." In section on *Shakai to Minzoku* (Society and Folklore) in *Nihon Minzoku Gaku Tai Kei* (Outline of Japanese Folklore), Vol. 3. Tokyo: Hei Bon Sha. Pp. 203-232.
Osako, Masako M.
  1972 *Employee Responses to Technology and Organizational Structure*. Ph.D. dissertation, Dept. of Sociology, Northwestern University.
Parsons, Talcott
  1955 "Family Structure and the Socialization of the Child." In Talcott Parsons and Robert F. Bales (eds.), *Family, Socialization, and Interaction Process*. Glencoe, Illinois: The Free Press.

Price, John
  1966   "A History of the Outcaste: Untouchability in Japan." In George
          DeVos and Hiroshi Wagatsuma (eds.), *Japan's Invisible Race:
          Caste in Culture and Personality*. Berkeley: University of
          California Press.
Rō Dō Shō
  1967   *Rō Dō Haku Sho* (Labor White Paper). Tokyo: Okura Sho Insatsu
          Kyoku.
Rohlen, Thomas P.
  1971   *The Organization and Ideology of a Japanese Bank: An Ethno-
          graphic Study of A Modern Organization*. PH.D. dissertation,
          Department of Anthropology, University of Pennsylvania.
Sakuda, Keichi
  1967   *Haji no Bunka Saikō* ("Shame" Culture Re-examined). Tokyo:
          Chiku Ma Sho Bō.
Sato, Shinichi
  1965   *Namboku-chō no Dōran* (Disturbances in the Mamboku Dynas-
          ties), *Nippon no Rekishi* (Japanese History). Vol. 9. Tokyo:
          Chuo-koron-sha.
Schneider, David M.
  1961   "Introduction: The Distinctive Features of Matrilineal Descent
          Groups." In David M. Schneider and Kathleen Gough (eds.),
          Matrilineal Kinship. Berkeley: University of California Press. Pp.
          1-32.
Schooler, Carmi and Caudill, William
  1964   "Symptomatology in Japanese and American Schizophrenia,"
          Ethnology, 3:172-178.
Sofue, Takao
  1962   "Heike Densetsu no Mura:Kōchi Ken Takaoka Gun Niyodo Mura
          Miyako Buraku Jittai Chōsa Hōkoku" (A Village Having a *Heike*
          Clan Legend: Research Report on Miyako-buraku in Kochi Pre-
          fecture), *Seikei Ronsō* of Meiji University, Vol. 31, No. 2, Pp.
          212-251.
  1964   "Tokyo no Daigakusei ni Okeru Tekio no Ichi Bunseki" (An
          Analysis of the Degree of Adjustment in Tokyo College Stu-
          dents). *Nenpō Shakai Shinri Gaku* (Japanese Annals of Social
          Psychology), 5:133-160.
  1965   "Regional Variations of Japanese Personality: An Analysis by the
          Aid of the Sentence Completion Test" (Preliminary Report).
          Sendai: Paper read at the Annual Joint Meeting of the An-
          thropological Society of Nippon and the Japanese Society of
          Ethnology.

Spiro, Melford E.
1951 "Culture and Personality: The Natural History of a False Dichotomy," *Psychiatry,* 14:34:19-46.
Suzuki, Daisetsu
1967 "An Interpretation of Zen Experience." In Charles A. Moore (ed.), *The Japanese Mind—Essentials of Japanese Philosophy and Culture.* Honolulu: East-West Center Press.
Takeda, Choshu
1957 *Sosen Suhai* (Ancestor Worship). Kyoto: Heirakuji-shoten.
The Institute of Statistical Mathematics
1961 *Nihonjin no Kokuminsei* (Japanese National Character). Tokyo: Shiseido.
1964 *Kokuminsei no Kenkyo: Daisanji Zenkoku Chōsa ni Tsuite* (A third study of Japanese National Character). Kasai-Shuppan.
Thomsen, Harry
1963 *The New Religions of Japan.* Tokyo: Charles E. Tuttle Co.
Vogel, Ezra
1963 *Japan's New Middle Class.* Berkeley: University of California Press.
Walker, Charles R. and Robert H. Guest
1952 *The Man on the Assembly Line.* Cambridge: Cambridge University Press.
Wang, C. C. (trans.)
1958 *The Dream of the Red Chamber.* New York: Twayne Publishers.
Whitehall, Arthur M., Jr. and Shin-ichi Takezawa
1968 *The Other Worker: A Comparative Study of Industrial Relations in the United States and Japan.* Honolulu: East-West Center Press.
Yang, C. K.
Religion in Chinese Society: A Study of Contemporary Social Functions of Religion and Some of Their Historical Factors. Berkeley: University of California Press.
Yoshida, Teigo
1963 "Cultural Integration and Change in Japanese Villages," *American Anthropologist,* 65:102-116.
1967 "Belief in Mystical Retribution, Spirit Possession, and Social Structure in a Japanese Village," *Ethnology,* 6:237-262.

AUTHOR INDEX

SUBJECT INDEX